Between
Ballots
and
Bullets

WILLIAM B. QUANDT

Between Ballots and Bullets

Algeria's Transition from Authoritarianism

BROOKINGS INSTITUTION PRESS
Washington, D.C.

Copyright © 1998 by
THE BROOKINGS INSTITUTION
1775 Massachusetts Avenue, N.W., Washington, D.C. 20036

Library of Congress Cataloging-in-Publication data:

Quandt, William B.
    Between ballots and bullets : Algeria's transition from
authoritarianism / by William B. Quandt.
        p.   cm.
    Includes bibliographical references and index.
    ISBN 0-8157-7302-1 (cloth : alk. paper)
    ISBN 0-8157-7301-3 (pbk. : alk. paper)
    1. Algeria—Politics and government—1962-   2.
Authoritarianism—Algeria.   3. Democracy—Algeria.   I.   Title.
    JQ3231 Q36 1998
    320.965'09'049—ddc21   98-19668
                                                            CIP

9 8 7 6 5 4 3 2 1

The paper used in this publication meets the minimum requirements of the American
Standard for Informational Science—Permanence of Paper for Printed Library Materials,
ANSI Z39.48-1984.

Typeset in Palatino

Composition by Harlowe Typography
Cottage City, Maryland

Printed by R. R. Donnelley and Sons Co.
Harrisonburg, Virginia

Foreword

ALGERIA in the 1990s is, for many observers, what Lebanon was in the 1980s, a country wracked by violence of the most horrific sort. Today Lebanon has returned to a fragile peace, while Algerians are still struggling to bring an end to their trauma. This study of Algeria's past decade seeks to provide a political account of the erosion of the authoritarian regime, the turn toward democracy early in the 1990s, and the outbreak of violence in recent years. Contrary to many accounts, *Between Ballots and Bullets* does not foresee the victory of the radical Islamists; nor does it anticipate a return to the old order. Instead, William B. Quandt expects a prolonged struggle that will eventually produce a more democratic outcome than most observers have imagined possible. As in Lebanon and elsewhere, however, the path to democracy is unlikely to be straight, short, or peaceful.

Quandt brings to his study of Algeria the experience of thirty years of observation. His first book on Algeria was published in 1969, and he has traveled to Algeria dozens of times since then, including twice in the past two years as part of this project. His study is not, however, just about the specific Algerian case. In fact, he goes to considerable length to show that the problems confronting Algeria are typical of those encountered by countries emerging from authoritarian rule, although often they are seen in Algeria in an extreme form.

While acknowledging the weight of history and culture, and the importance of socioeconomic conditions as background to the Algerian crisis, Quandt concentrates on political institutions and the choices made by political leaders at key moments to understand how Algeria's initial experiment with democracy went wrong. He maintains this political focus as he analyzes the weakness of the Islamist opposition in its challenge to the regime, as well as when he assesses the current efforts to create new institutions of governance.

The author, currently the Harry F. Byrd, Jr. Professor of Government and Foreign Affairs at the University of Virginia, and a nonresident senior fellow in the Foreign Policy Studies program at Brookings, received travel and research support during 1996–98 from Brookings to carry out this project. He is particularly grateful to John Steinbruner and Richard Haass of the Foreign Policy program for their encouragement.

Quandt also wishes to thank several Algerian friends of long standing, especially Redha and Rafida Malek and M'Hammed Yazid, who over the years have helped him to understand their country. More recently, he has been grateful for the help of Algerian political leaders, including Belaid Abdesselam, Hocine Ait Ahmed, Ahmed Attaf, Noureddine Boukrouh, Lakhdar Brahimi, Ahmed Djaballah, Mouloud Hamrouche, Khalida Messadia, Hadj Nacer, Mahfoud Nahnah, Said Saadi, and Mohammed Touati, all of whom agreed to be interviewed. Algerian academics, and in particular Rachid Tlemcani, Boutheina Cheriet, and Daho Djerbal were generous with their time and cooperation. Christopher Ross, Mary Anne Casey, Ronald Neumann, and Cameron Hume are fine diplomats who have served in Algiers and who shared their knowledge and provided hospitality.

In France, Quandt spent the summer of 1996 at the *Institut de Recherches et d'Etudes sur le Monde Arabe et Musulman* (IREMAM), whose director and staff were most helpful. François Burgat, Gerard Chaliand, Bruno Etienne, Jose Garçon, Arun Kapil, Séverine Labat, Rémy Leveau, and especially Ghassan Salamé shared their ideas and knowledge of Algeria and the Arab world. In Algiers, two courageous journalists, Omar Belhouchet and Salima Ghezali, were particularly helpful. Les Campbell and Arsala Deene of the National Democratic Institute invited Quandt to join them for a visit to Algiers in March 1998, during which they held extensive meetings with Algeria's new parliamentarians. Finally, the author wishes to thank Amine Khene for his friendship and advice throughout this project.

Robert Mortimer, Yahya Zoubir, and Saad Benmiloud reviewed the manuscript and made very useful comments. Research assistance was provided by Negar Akhavi, Abdelmajid Arrif, Katherine Carroll, and Agnieszka Paczynska. Farid Senzai verified the manuscript; Kerry V. Kern edited it; and Max Franke compiled the index. As always, Helena

Cobban provided moral and intellectual support throughout the project.

The views expressed in this book are solely those of the author and should not be ascribed to the trustees, officers, or other staff members of the Brookings Institution.

Michael H. Armacost
President

May 1998
Washington, D.C.

To Tarek and Leila

Contents

Between Ballots and Bullets

1

Introduction

E ACH AUTHORITARIAN regime, Tolstoy might have said, is authoritarian in much the same way—but what comes after is another matter altogether. As dictatorships in the developing countries and in Eastern Europe have stumbled and sometimes fallen, they have been challenged or superseded by a remarkable array of political experiments and experiences. We can find impressive examples of young democracies, appalling instances of civil war and bloodshed, and much else in between. A great challenge for many peoples around the world is to find a style of governance that steers between the apparent order without freedom of the authoritarian systems, on the one hand, and the freer but sometimes chaotic and violent alternatives. In coming decades most of the world's people will probably live somewhere in this realm of limited liberalization, and partial, imperfect democracy.

The purpose of this study is to understand the impulses that force authoritarian regimes to reform, how liberalization can give rise to political conflict, how violence can threaten to undermine democratization, and how institutions make a difference in the way people pursue their goals. The case to be examined in detail is Algeria, in part because it shows in extreme form the flaws in the authoritarian model, the possibilities and dangers of reform, and the extreme difficulty of containing politically motivated violence once it takes hold.

Algeria has typically been treated as a deviant case, unlike any other. I do not accept that view. Algeria, like any country, has its distinctive features, but many of the problems that it faces are familiar from other settings. What differ are the specific choices that politicians have made in the Algerian context. While analyzing these choices, Algeria will be shown in comparative context, keeping an eye on anal-

1

ogous developments elsewhere in the Middle East as well as in other parts of what used to be called the second and third worlds.

The past two decades have seen a remarkable consensus emerge in many parts of the world that the old authoritarian order, often propped up by the imperatives of the cold war, has exhausted its hold on people. The ideological claims of dictators ring hollow; charismatic leaders are in short supply; populations have grown more demanding and more skeptical; foreign conspiracies cannot easily be invoked to explain away domestic problems; and economic payoffs are rarely enough to buy reliable political acquiescence. Rapid economic growth can buy time, but is difficult to achieve and sustain, and sets in motion a whole new array of demands that will eventually have to be met. In the absence of economic prosperity, regimes are left with force and repression as their mainstays, and reliance on sheer force proves to be an extremely ineffective way to govern in the long run. So the unraveling of the authoritarian model is not much of a surprise.[1] The difficulty for politicians and analysts is to figure out what comes next.

Optimists of the "end of history" school have argued that liberal democracy is the wave of the future.[2] It may indeed be true that the end of the cold war has left liberal democracy without a convincing ideological adversary comparable to communism, socialism, or fascism. But this is not to say that liberal democracy in practice will everywhere prevail. There are still many variants of nationalism and dictatorship that may endure in large parts of the world, even if such beliefs have little ideological appeal beyond those borders—and perhaps not much within as well.

Those of a more gloomy disposition have seen a different model for the future, a period of growing anarchy as governments fail to cope with the many problems of their societies, with people retreating to primordial identities that they are prepared to defend with violence. Ethnic and religious conflict, in this scenario, will become more prevalent. Over the horizon is a "clash of civilizations," as modernity increases potential for conflict among different cultures, rather than producing a uniform westernization.[3] Reflecting on Bosnia, Lebanon, Somalia, Congo, and Cambodia, among many other similar cases, one might well conclude that the old authoritarian system had, at least, the virtue of maintaining order, and indeed there has been some tendency of voters to return to the "reformed" communist and nationalist parties in the hope that they can at least prevent crime, corruption, and conflict. But it is not easy to go back. The old order failed precisely because it was good only at maintaining order—if that—and most people want order, and prosperity, and freedom, and justice. It was the inability of the authoritarian orders to meet these latter demands that was their undoing.

Much of the world, including most countries of the Middle East, is caught somewhere between these optimistic and pessimistic visions. They have not managed to achieve democratic stability, but they have avoided full-scale breakdown and civil war. In the Middle East/North African context, Sudan stands as perhaps the most desperate case of a failed state, torn by civil war. Turkey, by contrast, despite endemic violence in the southeastern Kurdish areas, has clung to the basics of democratic politics for most of the past fifteen years and has seen modest economic growth. Algeria, sometimes seen as another failed state because of the high incidence of political violence in recent years, is far from the Sudan model; it is probably closer to that of Turkey, but with less experience with multiparty politics.

All these cases involve efforts by regime politicians and their opponents to find balances between conflicting values—order and freedom, state control and private initiative, communal and individual rights and interests, growth and equity, personal gain and national aspiration, religious values and secular practices. Sometimes a blend of these seemingly competing values is possible, but more often choices must be made to favor one or another. It is here that political calculus and judgment come into play, but not in a pure, unfettered way. Choice is always contextual, historically and situationally rooted, but that does not mean that individual leaders are simply playing out a predetermined script. The margin for choice may be narrow, but it is still there, and this is what makes politics such an important part of a nation's development. Politics, in much of the world, trumps economics as the key determinant of change. Lenin understood this, even if Marx seemed to think otherwise.

It is through political action that tradeoffs among competing values are made in societies. And it is through political institutions that the rules for acquiring and using power are established. Political development may involve debate and persuasion; it may involve elections and mass organization; and it may involve force and intimidation. Whatever the method of political contestation, the main protagonists have their eye on gaining power over the apparatus of the state. One of the legacies of the authoritarian era that is not so easily shaken is the belief that control of the state is the main prize in politics. Democrats may be found in the postauthoritarian era, but not many of the Jeffersonian type. More commonly politicians of whatever background continue to believe that the state is the means by which the ills of society can best be fixed. The answer to the question, Who governs? is still seen as a life and death matter in many parts of the world. Not surprisingly, political competition in such circumstances is often intense. That certainly has been the case in Algeria.

Why Algeria?

Cases that surprise us are often the most rewarding to study. Algeria, for those who have followed its modern history, has been a source of continuing surprises. For an earlier generation of French colonists, officials, and intellectuals, the surprise was that Algerians, who seemed to have only a fragile sense of national identity, were prepared to fight a long and costly war for their independence.[4] Algeria, in the 1930s, was widely viewed as the most assimilated of colonies, hardly a candidate for revolution.

Also shown to be wrong were the leftist intellectuals who thought that independent revolutionary Algeria would become a model of development with social justice.[5] Within a few years of independence, it was clear that such romantic notions were far from reality. The *pieds rouges*—European leftists who flocked to Algiers after independence—were just as wrong about Algeria's path as the *pieds noirs*—the European settlers in Algeria—had been.

The next to be surprised were those who believed in Algeria as a benign model of authoritarianism, a kind of third-world Robin Hood calling for a new economic order. For a while, Algeria seemed to have achieved a modicum of stability, economic growth, and international recognition.[6] Some saw it as one of the most promising examples of development in the Arab world.[7] Its revolution provided a degree of legitimacy for the regime; oil revenues eased the strains of modernization; and Algeria's educated, secular elite seemed well prepared to lead the drive for industrialization and a new north-south relationship. But those hopes also turned sour in the 1980s.

To the astonishment of many, for a brief moment Algeria seemed to be embarked on an experiment in democratization.[8] In the late 1980s

Algeria was suddenly the most free, most pluralistic, and most enthusiastic defender of democracy in the Arab world. Or so it seemed. But
the democratic spring ended suddenly when the Islamist party, the
Islamic Salvation Front (*Front Islamique du Salut*, FIS)—seemingly
emerging from nowhere to become the dominant political movement
in the country—was on the verge of electoral victory.

The military stepped in and cracked down on the Islamists, some
of whom took up arms, and soon analysts were predicting that Algeria
would be the next Iran—that is, a relatively modern country in which
an Islamic revolution would sweep away the westernized elite by force
and impose Islamic law.[9] That belief also has fallen on hard times. No
consensus exists today about where Algeria is heading. In short, Algeria has been a puzzle for analysts, for its own politicians, and for
the Algerian people.

The Algerian case, because it has challenged so much conventional
wisdom, deserves careful attention. It contains in extreme form some
of the elements that are often used to explain developments elsewhere,
and can therefore prove to be a valuable test for theories of political,
social, and economic change. We may be able to assess the impact of
colonial rule because that period of history looms so large, and was
so long and intrusive. Similarly, a link may be seen between the means
by which independence was won—violent revolution in the Algerian
case, compared to gentler cases elsewhere—and the postindependence
practice of politics. Since Algeria has been exposed to both intense
"Frenchification" and "Arabization," the role of language and culture
in influencing Algeria's political trajectory should be visible. Addition-
ally, Algeria has experienced all the rapid social change found elsewhere in the third world—population explosion, migration to the cities, mass education—and that too must be taken into account in any
political analysis. Finally, Algeria has been dominated by a "rentier"
economy, one in which the state is the recipient of vast "rents" for the
country's oil and gas, which it then distributes in ways that provide
opportunities for widespread corruption and discourage efficient investment in productive sectors. This economic reality has had a major
impact on Algerian political life. The task for the observer is first to
untangle, at least conceptually, these varying strands of Algerian history and then to assess why Algerian politicians have made their
choices.

In examining the Algerian case, a number of other Middle East examples (Egypt, Turkey, and Iran) as well as Latin American cases (Brazil, Mexico, Chile, Argentina, and Peru) come to mind. Each represents a certain type of post- or late-authoritarian politics. None is a fully institutionalized liberal democracy, and none is a Stalinist-style dictatorship. Each has a degree of political openness, side by side with residues of the authoritarian state. The military plays a central role in most of these countries, but in some cases so do political parties. Elections are held, some more meaningful than others, and a postauthoritarian political discourse can be found that values pluralism, competition, free markets, initiative, and human rights. Of course, many of the old themes of order, hierarchy, respect for tradition, and community can also be found.

Looking at Algeria from this comparative perspective, we must change lenses several times to see which one gives the sharpest focus. First the arguments that attribute great importance to history and culture must be weighed. Indeed, this is perhaps the dominant approach to explaining Algerian events. Many in the Middle East, for example, are quick to explain Algeria's bloody struggles by referring to the temperament of its people, shaped by its particular history and culture, some would even say by its climate and geography. Algerians themselves will often give similar explanations for the clannishness and distrust that pervades political life. Such explanations cannot be readily discounted, but they should be treated with great caution.

An alternative approach is to start this inquiry with an examination of Algerian society—its class structure, demographic shape, solidarity groupings—and then assess political change in terms of these social categories. Marxists take naturally to this approach, but so does any political sociologist, including the great fourteenth-century North African, Ibn Khaldun. Few would deny that the fit between state and society is an important issue to investigate, but it is less clear how much will be explained once this analysis is complete.

Given the role of oil and gas revenues in independent Algeria, it is tempting to look seriously at economics as the heart of the matter. The regime, after all, regardless of its makeup, is the recipient of a vast inflow of capital. Control of the state means control of billions of dollars, without even having to reach into the pockets of the citizenry. Many believe that rentier states of this type have special features, are less susceptible to mass political movements, are able to buy acquiescence, and spawn an avaricious, predatory elite that clings to power as the sole path to well-being. Iran's problems during the Shah's era, some would argue, were compounded by this economic model. When the price of oil stagnates or collapses, these regimes are incapable of adjusting. Much about the Algerian case fits the broad outlines of this model.

Political scientists are increasingly prone to look at institutions— agreed upon rules of the political game, often forged in the heat of intense political battles—as the key to political development. This perspective would privilege the one-party system as the key to Algeria's crisis. This system, consisting of the National Liberation Front (*Front de Libération Nationale*, FLN), the military, and the bureaucracy, was challenged in the mid-1980s by a proliferation of political organizations and parties, the most important of which was the Islamic Salvation Front. An institutionalist's view emphasizes the effect of specific electoral systems on political outcomes, and it seems true that in Algeria a different voting system in 1991 might have produced a fundamentally different—and more manageable—outcome.

All these approaches help to bring parts of the Algerian story into focus. But they all fall short in certain respects, since they leave out of the equation the choices made by individual actors at crucial moments in the country's history.[10] Without accepting the notion that individual volition is everything, one still needs to be wary of overdetermined explanations of politics that ignore human choice. History, culture, society, and political institutions may well constrain choice, but they do not erase it altogether. And even if we cannot get into the minds of key decisionmakers, we can try to reconstruct the probable political calculus they confronted at various moments. This does not mean that a purely rational model of choice will suffice, as the economists are wont to posit.

Politics has a different logic from economics, one measured in less tangible units, but not devoid of calculus. Indeed, the art of politics— and of good political analysis—is to try to figure out the political strategy that key players, in power and in opposition, are following at any given moment. In doing so, one must remember that they operate under conditions of great uncertainty, that they face many constraints on their choices, that history and culture and society and economics do matter—but in the end many of their choices will have a somewhat experimental quality to them.

Politicians must act without knowing the consequences of their actions, or the strategies of their adversaries. They are constantly having to judge the effects of their decisions, and successful politicians will adjust to suit changing circumstances. But to a large degree, they will be guided by beliefs that they have acquired in the course of their political socialization. They will rely on so-called lessons of history. They will act in the present to prevent the mistakes of yesterday, without knowing what the real problems of tomorrow will be. We must try to see those moments of choice as they do. In analyzing critical turning points in history—and Algeria has had many in recent years—this approach will help us to ask the right questions, even if it cannot guarantee the correct answers.

My emphasis on decisions made by leaders—in power and in opposition—at critical moments stems from a belief that political change is not continuous. Rather, it proceeds in fits and starts, with moments of considerable innovation and creativity followed by long periods of inertia as politicians try to figure out the consequences of their previous actions. No single political actor has more than a limited repertoire of ideas and strategies. Some may work better than others, but at some point even the most skillful politician will be forced to reassess and reconsider his actions. During these moments, new possibilities may emerge, either as a result of change in policy or change in leaders.

By looking at critical moments—sometimes of deep crisis, sometimes when new leaders emerge on the scene—both the potential for change and the limits on flexibility that stem from the particular form of governance that Algeria has experienced can be seen. More than many political systems, Algeria has had a hard time forging reform-minded coalitions; factionalism within the elite has often meant immobilism; and opposition movements have also tended to fragment. Why this has been the case, and what it might take to produce a more responsive system, will be concerns throughout this study.

This account of Algeria's recent past will proceed as follows. First we will sketch the authoritarian system when it seemed to be working reasonably well, under the leadership of Houari Boumediene, from the late 1960s to his death in 1978. Then the unraveling of the Boumediene legacy in the 1980s, culminating with the mass uprisings of October 1988, will be examined. By any standard, this was a turning point in recent Algerian history.

Next we will reflect on the remarkable response to those uprisings— a liberal opening of unprecedented magnitude. Why did the regime rush forward with a democratic agenda, when little in the past had prepared the country for this taste of freedom? Was this a case of "democracy without democrats," merely a game of maneuver rather than a commitment to new rules of the game? Or did genuine reformers have a moment when they could steer events as they chose? And where did the FIS come from? Almost overnight, it seemed, an Islamist opposition movement ruled the streets in the heretofore nationalist and somewhat secular state of Algeria. Was this religious resurgence, or societal discontent spilling over into militant politics?

The military intervened to stop the second round of parliamentary elections in January 1992, another turning point of great importance. This moment has become a symbol for many. Passionate arguments can be heard in Algeria and abroad about whether it would have been wiser to let the elections continue, even if the Islamists were poised to win, or whether the military saved democracy by preventing a fascist-like movement from using elections to put an end to democracy.

However one comes out on that debate—and it is not an easy question to resolve—few would deny that the years since have been an unparalleled disaster for independent Algeria. Political violence—and just plain violence—has become endemic, and the human and economic costs of the political crisis that has hit the country are incalculable. Several attempts to bring the crisis to an end—through political accommodation, technocratic planning, institutional reform, elections, and repression—will be assessed. Each of the chapters that follow will be organized around a central set of decisions that put the country on a particular course at that time. Inherent in this approach is a conviction that other choices might have been made.

Building from the basic political narrative provided in Part I, Part II looks at the contending interpretations—cultural, social, economic, institutional, and political choice—to see what each reveals about our four main concerns: the collapse of the authoritarian model, the abortive turn to democracy, the descent into political violence, and the effect of the creation of new political institutions.

The study of the Algerian case provides insights into several broad issues of concern to students of political change in developing countries. First, the difficult relationship between the military—the backbone of the old system—and the forces for change in the postauthoritarian era will be shown in detail. No problem has been more troublesome for democratizing countries than to find a legitimate role for the military, without sacrificing freedom or risking a coup d'état. Especially in systems like Algeria, Egypt, and Turkey where the military see themselves as the guardians of the national project, it is not easy for civilian politicians to move them to the sidelines.

Second, the Algerian case illuminates issues of civil society and democratization. It is often believed that the key to democracy is the existence of intermediate groupings—beyond the family and tribe, but short of the state itself—where people with common interests can come together to pursue their goals. These voluntary associations, it is argued, create trust, educate in the ways of coalition building, and provide a laboratory for nurturing values conducive to democratic governance.[11] But where can such associations come from when authoritarian regimes have suppressed them? Algeria shows that they can emerge quickly, but they do not necessarily immediately play the hoped-for moderating role, nor are they necessarily strong, even when they seem to have a wide following. Still, one of the lessons of postauthoritarian politics is that civil associations develop once restraints are lifted and can play an important role in shaping a new order. The existence of a relatively free press in Algeria is one of the most impressive examples of how these new groups can forge a strong sense of their own identity.

Third, Algeria provides a look at the hotly debated issue of Islam and democracy. During Algeria's democratic spring, the FIS nearly succeeded in coming to power by free elections. To many democrats, this would have been a nightmare scenario, comparable to Hitler's electoral victory in the 1930s. Once in power, some believed, the Islamists would close the door to any future political contestation. In short, there would be "one person, one vote, one time." But others believe that an elected Islamist movement would have been obliged to moderate its goals and share power with the military; it either would have been transformed into a legitimate party in a pluralistic system or ousted in subsequent elections. We will not be able to answer these questions with any certainty, but the behavior of the FIS and other Islamist parties at different moments will be examined in depth.

This analysis will conclude with an assessment of the prospects for democratization in Algeria, drawing general lessons where possible. Somewhat surprisingly, the prospects may not be dim, despite Algeria's troubled past and problematic present. If, as some have argued, democracy is always preceded by a hot family feud that neither side can win, leading to a codification of rules of the game for sharing power, then Algeria may be setting the stage in its unhappy present for a more hopeful future.

PART ONE
Political History

2

The Legacy of
Colonialism and Revolution

W HEN ALGERIANS say that their country is unique, they
usually have two things in mind: unlike any other Arab
country, Algeria was under an intense form of colonial control for 132
years; and unlike any other country in the Middle East, it fought a
long and bloody war of independence, lasting more than seven years
and costing hundreds of thousands of lives, perhaps as many as one
million. Even a generation after independence was won, this dual
legacy of colonialism and revolution weighs heavily on the politics of
Algeria. Yet today, a shrinking percentage of the population has any
live memory of either period. A generation gap of immense propor-
tions exists between those who were fundamentally shaped by the
experience of French domination and the struggle to win freedom, and
those who take independence for granted and feel no special debt to
the early generation of nationalists.

French colonial rule began in Algeria in 1830 without any grand
design, but with the expansionist and self-confident *mission civilisatrice*
that characterized all such encounters between Europe and the countries of Africa and the Middle East in the era of "colonialism with a
clear conscience." Several points need to be underscored concerning
French rule in Algeria. First, Algeria came to be a "settlement colony."
That is to say, large numbers of Europeans were encouraged to move
to Algeria and to become farmers, shopkeepers, and administrators.
By the twentieth century, a fully articulated European society had
taken root with an identity of its own. These were the *pieds noirs*,
whose influence was such in Paris that Algeria was considered to be
an integral part of metropolitan France.[1] Algeria was far different,
then, from India, where the British ruled with a thin layer of their own

15

top administrators, coopting allies from amongst the "natives," while leaving much of Indian society untouched.

The intrusiveness of French colonial rule in Algeria had several consequences. First, it produced a prolonged and violent resistance from 1830 to 1847, when the Emir Abd al-Qadir was finally defeated and sent into exile. Along with this remarkable leader went thousands of the traditional elite of the day, a truly stunning blow to Algerian society.[2] A few more uprisings were attempted, but by the end of the nineteenth century Algerian society had been reduced to "human dust," in the words of one French administrator.[3] Its traditional leaders had been driven away or had been defeated and humiliated. Replacing them at virtually all levels of power were Europeans. In addition, Algerians had been pushed off the best land, which was then placed under European control.

Algerian nationalism, as a result of this form of colonial encounter, did not grow out of the traditional elite's demand for rights, as was often the case elsewhere. Indeed, until the 1940s many believed that there was no such thing as Algerian nationalism, so fragmented, repressed, and passive was the indigenous population.

The first real sparks of national consciousness can be seen among Algerian workers in France around the time of World War I. There they encountered modern society, including labor unions, and soon they were organizing to demand their rights. The most remarkable of the early leaders of Algerian nationalism was Messali Hadj, who combined a working-class oriented nationalism with Islamic overtones. From the beginning, Algerian nationalism had a populist bent, blending national symbols with themes from the Middle East, such as Arab revival and Islamic reform. Algerian nationalism in its origin borrowed from both East and West. But it took some time before it struck roots in Algeria itself—an odd beginning for what soon became such a powerful force.

If Messali represented a working-class type of populist agitation against French rule, several other strands of thought could be found by the 1930s. One consisted of a few religious scholars who called for the reform of Islam as a defense against French policies of assimilation. The Association of Ulama, led by Abd al-Hamid Ben Badis, played an important part in trying to keep Algeria's Arab and Muslim identity intact in the face of determined efforts to undermine it. Less a political movement than a social and intellectual one, it still played a part in the formation of the nationalist movement.

Another trend, rather typical of other colonial experiments, could be found within the newly educated Algerian elite. This group's members were often proud of their accomplishments at French schools, fluent in French, trained in professional schools, and resentful that they were not accorded the full rights of Frenchmen. Typical of this current was Ferhat Abbas. Educated to be a pharmacist, and outspoken in his demand for equal rights, in the 1930s he turned to France seeking the right of French citizenship for Muslims, arguing that there was no Algerian nation. (Ben Badis was the one who refuted him.) Twenty years later, Abbas was a prominent member of the nationalist movement and eventually became the first president of the Provisional Government of Algeria. But these liberals never had much of a chance. They were too moderate and too few. There would be no Algerian equivalent of the Indian Congress Party, a movement filled with lawyers who had absorbed much of the colonizer's political tradition. Algeria's nationalism was a rougher variety, forged in violent upheaval.

The other small political current in Algeria was the Communist party, secular in its thinking, preaching class struggle. It had little mass appeal but attracted some intellectuals. It suffered from its hesitancy in calling for a clear break with France. For communists, the issue was imperialism, not colonialism. Although the party was small, it provided one of the few places where Muslims and non-Muslims worked together for political ends.

If Algeria miraculously had achieved its independence without violence in the 1930s, there might have been a reasonable chance for some sort of democratic practice to take root. There were already several distinct political currents organized in the country. The most important of these, the Algerian People's Party of Messali Hadj, was about to split along generational lines. Messali still stood for a populist nationalism tinged with Islam; the younger generation was more modern and secular in its nationalism. Other political currents, including Abbas, Ben Badis, and the communists, would all have had some following as well. The Berber-speaking minority, especially in the region of Kabylia, most likely would also have formed a party of some sort.

The great mass of Algerians in the 1930s were illiterate peasants. If independence had been won at that time, politics would most likely have been conducted among the politicized elite, with each group coming to the realization that they needed to build a mass base to win elections. No single group could have hoped to dominate political life on its own. Coalitions would have been needed. It might have worked, but it did not happen.[4] The reason was simple. The Europeans were not about to cede control of Algeria without a fight. They could not contemplate living as a minority in a new Algerian state, as whites in South Africa eventually did. There was, quite simply, no prospect for compromise between the *colons* and the nationalists. So legal Algerian parties, wedded to the idea that rights could be won by peaceful means, were soon discredited in the eyes of the post-World War II generation, which was quickly convinced that France would only listen to force, not to petitions and pleading.[5]

Not only Messali and Abbas, but also those in Messali's party who were willing to challenge his leadership, were viewed by their younger, more radical contemporaries as interested only in their own organizational interests. They would never be capable of shaking off the colonial yoke. None of the political instruments in their hands—elections, mass organization, labor unions, propaganda—seemed worth much. In the minds of those who eventually launched the revolution, politics had failed, elections were a sham, the parties were a disgrace, and the colonial regime would never give Algerians their rights. Algerian politicians of whatever stripe were hardly better than the *Beni Oui Ouis*, the native "yes men" recruited by the French for minor jobs.

In this view only direct action—the use of force—would stand a chance of breaking the French hold on the country. So, the revolution that was launched November 1, 1954, was not only against the French, but also against the existing political institutions that Algerians had forged over the previous generation. In its origins, the Algerian revolution was antipolitics and antiparty. Like populists everywhere, these self-appointed fighters for their country's freedom saw themselves in heroic light, sacrificing all for the people. Those who represented parties were seen as self-interested and divisive; they weakened the common will, playing into the hands of the French, who were skilled at divide-and-rule politics. The revolution, they hoped, would unify the masses and lead to a break with the past. To a large extent, it did. But it also sacrificed the incipient democratic tendencies in Algerian political life for a kind of radical populism that eventually came to be seen as responsible for many of Algeria's problems.[6]

The Algerian revolution—or war for independence—lasted from November 1954 until independence in July 1962. At the outset, the struggle was launched by a handful of men calling themselves the *Front de Libération Nationale* (FLN). Most were from modest backgrounds. There was no immediate response to their call for independence. But with time, most of the existing currents of Algerian political life rallied to the FLN. The one glaring exception was Messali himself. He would not join with the young men who had challenged his authority, and they would not make way for him and his autocratic methods. Thus the most famous figure of modern Algerian nationalism at the time of the revolution was shunted aside, treated as a traitor, and his followers were systematically eliminated. The French tried unsuccessfully to play on this split and the FLN won out in this internecine struggle, but many of Messali's followers never forgave the FLN. No one knows for sure how many Algerians died in this rarely discussed internecine war, but some claim the number was very large. The consequences of this bloodletting in a culture where revenge is considered a matter of family honor have been devastating. Some of those who rallied to the banner of the Islamists to challenge the FLN in the 1980s were descendants of Messalists who had been destroyed by the victorious nationalist wing. Generational revenge has played a part in Algerian politics, including the appalling massacres of civilians in 1996–98.

The FLN, distrustful of Messali and his "cult of personality," was never led by a single individual. There was no Nelson Mandela, Mao Tse-Tung, or Lenin in the Algerian revolution. Instead, there were committees, cliques, and clans. Collective leadership was the motto, which often masked a reality of intense rivalry. To keep the FLN together as a broad front, the leaders kept the focus on the one thing they agreed upon—Algeria's independence within an Arab/Islamic framework. But it was nationalism rather than any other ideology that inspired the movement. In the ranks of the FLN were socialists and Islamists, Berbers and Arabs, peasants and intellectuals. Only Algerian nationalism bound them in common cause. Out of this matrix came the FLN's obsession with the unity of the people, its hostility to old-style political parties, and its distrust of a single strong leader.

The Transition to Independence

As the struggle for independence came to a close, several distinct centers of power existed within the FLN. First there were the guerrilla *mujahideen* of the interior, the leaders of the military regions (called *willayas*) and their followers. Algeria had been divided into six zones, or willayas, each with its own command. These came to resemble fiefdoms, whose leaders were jealous of their autonomy and resentful of the external leadership for having done too little to help them in the face of enormous French military pressure. They saw themselves as the real freedom fighters, and therefore entitled to prominent places in the postindependence scheme of things.

The other military component was the *Armée de Libération Nationale* (ALN), which had been formed on the borders of Algeria in Morocco and Tunisia. It had received professional training and had modern armaments, but had done little real fighting. Its commander was an austere colonel known as Houari Boumediene (his *nom de guerre*). Unlike most FLN leaders, Boumediene had received a fairly good education in Arabic, studying in Tunisia and Cairo. He had little patience for the quarrels of the politicians.

Then there was the Provisional Government (*Le Government Provisoire de la République Algérienne*, or GPRA), the recognized voice of the FLN during the negotiations with France.[7] Many of the old-guard politicians such as Abbas found positions in the GPRA, as did some intellectuals and a number of the earliest leaders of the revolution.

Finally, there were a number of prominent personalities who had spent most of the revolution in French jails. They were well known because of the press attention that had followed their capture in 1956. Each had a high opinion of his contribution to the cause and seemed to expect a top position upon his release. While they were hardly on speaking terms with each other and without followers, they did retain considerable symbolic prestige that could help tip the faction fights one way or the other.

This was the FLN on the eve of independence—hardly a disciplined movement, but one that enjoyed immense prestige among ordinary Algerians for its role in winning independence. For a brief moment in mid-1962, it was probably true that most Algerians saw the FLN as the embodiment of their hopes. That moment was not to last long, as the various factions plunged the country into near civil war.[8]

Without a single individual to symbolize the Algerian struggle, or at least no consensus on who that should be, the FLN made the revolution itself the icon to be worshipped. The revolution had charisma, even if no individual leader did. Glory was accorded to the "one million martyrs," and streets were named for the most famous of them. Algeria's first president, former prisoner Ahmed Ben Bella, made the mistake of trying to forge a personal following and was soon ousted by the faceless men of the army.

This myth of unity, this elevation of the martyrs, and the anonymity of those who held power created a distorting lens for the understanding of Algeria's past and present. The emphasis on unity, and the fear of division, masked the real complexity and diversity of Algerian society. The regime would talk about "the people," as if the people spoke with a single voice. Anyone who did not agree with the regime's interpretation of the popular will was a potential traitor. And the regime could not be questioned since it was acting on behalf of the people. Such an ideological mold left little room for politics in the sense of legitimate competing claims by recognized social groups, with political institutions to mediate and resolve conflicts according to agreed rules. Despite the common bond of nationalism, Algeria on the eve of independence was far from being an undifferentiated, homogeneous country. There was a small, French-educated elite, mostly in the cities and larger towns; there was also a sector of small shopkeepers and minor functionaries. The majority of Algerians lived in the countryside as peasants; there were few large landowners. The Berber-speaking Kabyles, from the mountainous area east of Algiers, were the most assertive concerning their distinctive identity of the regional minorities, but in general there was a strong sense of regionalism. And there were political overlays on these social distinctions, many of which had been exacerbated by seven years of costly struggle against the French. This pluralistic and divided society, which badly needed a legitimate political order to help forge a sense of shared purposes now that independence had been achieved, was instead treated by its self-appointed leaders as a unitary body.

In the Russian and Chinese revolutions there had been a class basis for the revolution. There were victors and vanquished, and the rules of the game were fairly clear. But in Algeria the entire people were the victors, except for traitors—the notorious *harkis*, who had actually fought on the French side, with many ending up in exile in France.

Everyone else was entitled to expect that they would benefit from the revolution, without distinction. This placed an enormous burden on the new regime.

The myth of unity and the cult of martyrs led to some odd public displays. Unwilling to reveal how deeply divided the FLN had been during the revolution, the new regime elevated a number of martyrs to iconic status, naming major thoroughfares in downtown Algiers after them. Few knew that Abane Ramdane, for whom one street is named, had actually been killed by his colleagues, not by the French. In present day Algiers, one finds the name of one of his principal adversaries, Belkacem Krim—who was himself assassinated by the Boumediene regime—adorning another street not far away. This falsification of history is still too touchy a subject to treat openly, but it has created a kind of cynicism about the past that eventually robbed the FLN of much of the legitimacy that it tried to claim. The official history also glossed over the real tragedy of the Algerian revolution, namely that many Algerians were responsible for the deaths of other Algerians during the struggle for independence.

Thus the revolution, instead of unifying the people after independence was achieved, became the source of intense conflict within the elite.[9] Most Algerians were appalled to see their self-appointed leaders fighting amongst themselves the moment French forces had left the country. Many ordinary Algerians poured into the streets crying "Seven years, enough!"

The scramble for power produced a fragile coalition of those who were opposed to the provisional government, which had just succeeded in negotiating independence. Ahmed Ben Bella became the president, with backing from the regular army and some of the willaya commands. Soon after his rise to power, he turned on many of his corevolutionaries, alienated the willaya commanders, and was soon left face-to-face with Boumediene, who kept control of the regular armed forces. On June 19, 1965, Boumediene ousted Ben Bella, and a new era began.[10]

The Boumediene Era

Algeria's first president, Ahmed Ben Bella, laid the groundwork for Algeria's experiment in authoritarian rule, but his successor, Colonel Houari Boumediene, perfected the system. Ben Bella lacked an institutional base of support when he became president and spent much of his three years in office pitting one faction against another in order to stay in power. The initial election of a National Assembly that gave genuine voice to various currents within society showed promise, but this experiment with limited pluralism was brought to an end after only one year. Ben Bella then established a single-party system and proclaimed a populist/socialist ideology. All the while the military and security services became the real powers behind the president.

Ben Bella's demise did not lead to great popular upheaval. By then many Algerians were already disappointed that political maneuvering had replaced the high-minded idealism of the first days of independence. Many were ready for the quiet and stability that the new, faceless regime of Boumediene seemed to promise.

Although hardly known to the public at large, Houari Boumediene was a formidable leader who had worked his way up from modest origins to the position of commanding the Algerian armed forces. He had learned the art of clandestine politics at the knee of the master, Abdelhafid Boussouf, the godfather of Algeria's secret services.[11] Boumediene had gone on to eclipse Boussouf and outmaneuver any number of rivals by the time independence was achieved. He had a reputation as an ascetic, a strong nationalist, with more of an Arabist education than most of his contemporaries.

Boumediene lacked charisma of the conventional kind—he was hardly a crowd pleaser. He preferred to work in obscurity, with a small coterie of confidants. On the day Boumediene ousted Ben Bella, he read the proclamation of the "rectification," but the TV announcement showed only a microphone. Boumediene initially eschewed any hint of a cult of personality. Those who knew him respected him for his intelligence, apparent integrity, and toughness, but the public at large only gradually became aware of who their new rulers were.

Boumediene first set about consolidating his own power, as any new ruler must. He shunted aside many of Ben Bella's cronies, brought in his own clan—the so-called Oujda group, named for the town on the Moroccan border where Boumediene and several of his close allies forged their initial ties. The FLN was downgraded in importance; Boumediene kept the presidency and ministry of defense for himself; the Military Security organization—the much feared secret police—was strengthened and became the centerpiece of the system's control over political life.

The first serious challenge to Boumediene came from the remnants of the guerrilla leaders who were being pushed aside by the more professional army officers, some French trained, who were entirely dependent on Boumediene. In late 1967 Colonel Tahar Zbiri attempted a feeble move against the regime, but it was easily put down when Boumediene ordered the air force, the most modern branch of the military, to intervene. From 1968 onward, Boumediene faced little internal opposition. This was the high tide of Algeria's authoritarian experiment.

In addition to using the security institutions to check dissent, Boumediene adopted social and economic policies that were designed to win acquiescence, if not support, from ordinary citizens and possible challengers alike. Algeria had inherited a fairly developed infrastructure from France. The state took charge of empty apartments and houses, allowing Algerians to live in them at virtually no cost. These *biens vacants* became an enormous source of patronage and part of the social contract with the masses. In time, this policy also produced a terrible housing crisis, since no one had an incentive to invest in new housing if people thought that housing was a free good. Instead, more and more people crowded into the existing housing stock, making Algiers one of the most densely populated cities anywhere in terms of inhabitants per room. Still, shelter was cheap, even if people sometimes ended up sleeping in shifts.

The state also undertook to provide free education and medical care to everyone. Here the regime faced an enormous challenge. At the time of independence, only fifteen percent of the adult population was literate, probably more in French than in Arabic. A small fraction of school-age children was actually in schools. During the war for independence, university students had gone on strike, so few university graduates were available to help build the new state. Education therefore became a top national priority, regularly taking the largest percentage of the state budget. Health care was probably the next highest priority. There, too, the state was overwhelmed, but it made a serious effort to reduce infant mortality and provide the rudiments of a nationwide medical system.

The effect of offering education and health care to the masses was to accelerate the flood of people to the cities, where cheap housing, schools, doctors, and perhaps a job in the new government could be found. Algeria at independence was predominately a rural society. Before long, a majority of its citizens lived in cities.

Ben Bella had experimented with volunteerism, with worker self-management, and with the collectivization of agriculture. Boumediene was much less convinced that the spontaneity of the masses could be counted on. Instead, he wanted the state to control the economy from the top down, relying on the state's monopoly of oil rents to provide capital for new industries. Boumediene, like other leaders of this era, bought into the notion of state planning as the most efficient means of running an economy. By controlling investments from the center, scarce funds could be directed to sectors of highest value. The allocation of foreign exchange would presumably be rationalized, insuring funds for important industrial projects, while avoiding superfluous spending on imported luxuries. The state would ensure high levels of investment; excessive private wealth would be prevented; an egalitarian ethos would be maintained; and the country would become self-sufficient by producing what it had formerly imported. This model of "import-substituting industrialization"—or ISI—had many fans in the 1960s and 1970s.[12] The fact that it produced distortions and inefficiencies of its own, opened the way for corruption, and reduced incentives to innovate and to work, was less obvious then than it became later. This, after all, was a period when the Soviet Union was still seen as something of a successful model of industrialization, and the "Asian tigers" such as South Korea and Taiwan had not yet really shown themselves to be impressive alternatives.

The agriculture sector was managed with careless disregard for the interests of Algeria's peasants. Somewhat surprisingly, since many of Algeria's leaders had peasant roots, no one made much of a case for leaving peasants to do what they did best—work hard to grow crops that would fetch decent prices. Instead, the lands abandoned by the French, and those of a few large Algerian landholders, were turned into collectives where peasants were told what to plant and were paid controlled, low prices for their output. Not surprisingly, this accelerated the rural exodus, and agricultural production plummeted. Soon Algeria would be importing a large percentage of its food needs. Throughout the 1970s, one of the main complaints of ordinary Algerians was the scarcity of food. While available supplies were inexpensive, thanks to government subsidies, shortages of certain commodities were a constant problem into the 1980s.

Here we have the outlines of the familiar authoritarian regime. Its legitimacy lies in its adherence to revolutionary, nationalist, and populist values; its control comes from monopoly over the instruments of violence, especially the army, police, and Military Security; and its implicit bargain with the masses in whose name it governs is that it will provide services, and a modicum of social justice and stability, in return for political passivity. Like Egypt, but unlike Syria, the regime favored the city dwellers, reflecting a common "urban bias."[13] For a while, the system seemed to work.

The 1970s were good for the Boumediene regime. He personally was gaining some self-confidence and respect from the population. He was a dictator, but not of the gratuitously bloody-minded sort. He was more like Syria's Hafiz al-Asad than Iraq's Saddam Hussein. As the price of oil from 1973 onward skyrocketed, the regime was given the chance to pursue its ambitious policy of "industrializing industries"—a notion that big industries would create a market for light industry. (Who would buy the products of all these factories was something of a mystery.) But there was money to go around, social progress could be measured in tangible ways, schools were sprouting up everywhere, and life was getting a bit easier for ordinary people. With oil and gas revenues to spend, the regime did not have to resort to heavy direct taxation. The other side of the "no taxation" coin, of course, was "no representation."[14] Only slowly did Boumediene turn his attention to building political institutions.

From the moment of his accession to power on June 19, 1965, Boumediene annulled the 1963 constitution and put in place a Council of the Revolution that would exercise supreme authority until new institutions were established. In practice, Boumediene himself was the supreme figure in the new structure of power. He methodically set out to modify the nature of the political system without a new legitimacy formula. It was as if he was determined to put new structures in place, then give them legal standing.

Boumediene's distrust of politics can be seen in his decision to begin with changes at the communal and provincial levels. Consistent with his populist bias, these were the institutions closest to the people, so he would begin the process of change at that level. Limited competition for positions in elected assemblies was introduced, giving some semblance of pluralism within the single party. But power flowed from the top down, making these local institutions little more than cogs in the administrative machine. They could serve the purpose of providing patronage, but did little for representation.

Further expanding the regime's scope of authority, Boumediene moved to extend the state's control over industry and agriculture. Nationalizations in the early 1970s placed most of the economy under state ownership, setting the stage for a form of "state capitalism." With the bureaucracy, local administration, and economy in his grip, Boumediene set about regularizing his rule.

On the tenth anniversary of seizing power, Boumediene announced that a new national charter would be established, to be followed by a new constitution. He invited the public, through its various associations, to debate the draft charter. Although this was once again a "top down" initiative, there was some genuine argument about key elements in the charter. Over ensuing months, one of the main issues was whether socialism should be declared to be the primary ideological matrix of Algerian politics, or whether greater emphasis should be given to Islam. By the time the charter was finally adopted and submitted to popular referendum, the socialist option had won out.

This is not to say that Islam was marginalized by Boumediene. It remained the religion of the state, but it did not thereby become the source of all legislation. The state might be Arab and Islamic in its basic cultural orientation, but it would be much more like a secular socialist country in practice. Algerian socialism was not like socialism in the communist world. Algeria still did not buy into the entire logic of class struggle. The regime still represented the people as a whole, not the revolutionary working class.

In fact, Boumediene's socialism turned out to have a fairly strong technocratic side to it. Its goals were rapid development, the creation of a strong industrial base, and the maintenance of a viable safety net to keep ordinary people satisfied while the state laid the foundation for a modern society. There was little effort to mobilize the masses, create labor intensive industries, or transform the countryside. Instead, the masses were almost treated as observers who would passively await the payoffs from this technocratically managed social and economic experiment being carried out in their names.

Soon after the adoption by referendum of the national charter, a

new constitution was presented and submitted to referendum in November 1976. The constitution enshrined the principle of the single
party, the FLN, which would select the candidate for president, who
would have virtually all power in his hands. Although there would be
an elected legislature—the National Assembly had been suspended
in 1965—it would not have great powers. Instead, the president could
propose legislation and could rule by decree. Although long on words,
the constitution did little more than enshrine the system as Boumediene had developed it. Socialism was defined as the state's basic
orientation and Islam was declared the state religion. There were few
surprises in the document. In 1977 elections for the Popular National
Assembly were held, with some limited competition within the party
for seats. Mostly, it was a rubber stamp parliament. The president
formed the cabinet and retained the all-powerful position of defense
minister.

Despite the concentration of power in Boumediene's hands, as institutionalized by the new constitution, he faced some opposition from
ideological extremes at opposite ends of the spectrum. On the one
hand were the culturalists, who saw in his "socialism" a threat to
Algeria's Islamic character. Some were simply cultural conservatives
who rejected westernization; others were large landowners who clung
to Islam as a way of protecting private property rights against state
confiscation.

Boumediene countered the Islamist challenge by repression—Islamist groups were not allowed to operate independently—and by
sponsoring part of the Islamist agenda as his own. For example, Boumediene pushed for rapid Arabization of education, a typical demand
of the Islamists. By the late 1970s most of the educational system had
been Arabized, with the exception of those faculties at the university
where French was still used as the language of instruction, such as
medicine and engineering.

Boumediene also tried to counter the Islamists by creating a kind of
state-controlled Islam. For example, the state sponsored the building
of many mosques and undertook the training of many new Imams for
those mosques.[15]

On the left, Boumediene was criticized by "scientific socialists" for
keeping too much power in the hands of the military, ignoring the
need for an elite party of militants, allowing a "new class" to emerge,
and providing too much space for religion in politics. Boumediene,

like many other leaders of his era in the Middle East, was prone to play Islamists and leftists against one another, sometimes favoring one, sometimes the other. By the end of his rule, he was relying more on the left than on the Islamists.

The other constituency that was uneasy with the Boumediene regime was the small but articulate emerging middle class. Algeria had its share of lawyers, doctors, writers, small businessmen, and others who were beginning to enjoy some measure of economic well-being but were uncomfortable with the many restrictions on freedom, the unwieldy bureaucracy, the abuses of the hated Military Security, and the frequent shortages of consumer items. By the late 1970s it was frequently said that Algerians had money but nothing to buy, whereas Moroccans had less money but the markets were full. Belt tightening may have seemed patriotic in the early years of independence, but as Algeria began to approach its fifteenth year of independence, such privations were a source of frequent complaint.

At the height of his power, and at a time when some pressures for change were beginning to be felt, Boumediene disappeared from public view in September 1978. He was struck with a mysterious disease—poison was suspected—and was rushed to Moscow for treatment. He was returned home where a series of Algerian and foreign doctors tried to figure out what was wrong. He was finally diagnosed as having a rare form of cancer and died in December of that year. He had never been a popular figure, but he had been respected. Crowds lined the street on the day of his funeral and one could sense a mood of apprehension about the future. Boumediene, at least, had brought stability to a country that had known far too much political violence.

During the several months of his illness, the inner circle around Boumediene had worked to ensure a smooth succession. The main contenders were Abd al-Aziz Bouteflika, Boumediene's foreign minister and close friend, and Mohammed Yahyaoui, the left-leaning head of the FLN. Key members of the military and security services, however, preferred a figurehead from within their own ranks and turned to Chadli Benjedid, a senior military officer who headed the Oran military region.[16] Compared to Bouteflika and Yahyaoui, Chadli (as he was almost always called) was weak and less politically experienced. For this reason, those who controlled the succession opted for Chadli. In 1979 the Chadli era began with strong indications of continuity. Before long, however, it was clear that things were changing in Algeria.

3

Pressures for Change

A UTHORITARIAN REGIMES, even when they seem most stable and well entrenched, are vulnerable to pressures for substantial change. This is due to the particular manner in which authoritarian rulers maintain their grip on power. In broad outline, authoritarian regimes rely on a mixture of four ingredients to survive: ideology, repression, payoffs, and elite solidarity. The mixture of these ingredients may change, but each is present to some degree and each is vulnerable to change.

Reliance on ideology to enhance legitimacy is, of course, not a unique feature of authoritarian regimes, and some authoritarian leaders, content with apathy rather than displays of manufactured enthusiasm, make little effort to indoctrinate their populations. When they do invoke ideology, however, little differentiation is made between the leader, the state, and the nation. Authoritarians try to justify their rule by citing the goals pursued by the state. Populist dictatorships represent themselves as pursuing a common good—national independence, social justice, glory, religion, future prosperity, traditional values—and charismatic leaders may indeed be able to rally support to their causes, at least for a time. This type of support—loyalty of a self-sacrificing kind—is an enormous benefit to any ruler. It may reduce the need to depend too heavily on other techniques of rule. But there are limits on the value of ideology and loyalty. And once these beliefs are shaken, they are hard to restore.[1]

Precisely because loyalty and ideological commitment may focus on an individual leader, they are unreliable over the long term. Max Weber noted this when he spoke of the "routinization of charisma" as a problem for patriarchal regimes.[2] How can one transfer support for a popular leader to support for institutions that he has created?

Ideology and personal loyalty are especially hard to transmit across a generational divide. Those Egyptians who came of political age with Gamal Abd al-Nasser and Arab nationalism may remain committed to some aspects of Nasserism throughout their lives, but their children are unlikely to respond to the same symbols. In the Algerian case, those who made the revolution are likely to have a special feeling of responsibility for the state—they fought for it and have the duty to defend it. But these claims ring hollow for the younger generation, which feels let down or marginalized by the postindependence regimes.

Sometimes it is possible to maintain a sense of ideological commitment, of patriotism, by playing on a fear of external threat. But if that fear is not present, and as new generations enter politics, claims of loyalty based on shared ideology are likely to land on deaf ears. In fact, the risk to the regime is that it will be held accountable by the ideological criteria it has upheld and will be found wanting. Then a charge of hypocrisy or incompetence will be heard, and the stage may be set for another ideological movement to challenge the incumbents.[3] The advantage of an ideological movement in opposition is that it will not be judged at the outset by its performance. It will have the luxury of pointing to all the shortcomings of the incumbent regime, while leaving its own program for governing shielded in generalities. "Islam is the Solution" may be an effective campaign slogan for an opposition movement, but it will not suffice for long as a platform for actual governance.

The second prop of authoritarian regimes is repression. All states use coercion and violence to some degree to maintain their authority.[4] But the distinctive characteristic of authoritarian regimes is the totally unaccountable manner in which violence can be used. The ruler, or the regime, is not subject to institutionalized checks and balances in its use of force. There is no recourse for groups or individuals that run afoul of the regime. They may try to use the judicial machinery of government, but it is simply an extension of the regime and will not provide redress except, perhaps, against minor officials. The simple fact is that the authoritarian regime can use its power in the most arbitrary of ways. Thus there is always some danger, some element of fear, on the part of the population—and, indeed, among those who hold power. No one is secure; no one is protected by the law.

Some authoritarian regimes depend heavily on repression across

the board. Saddam Hussein's Iraq is a case in point.[5] When fear becomes such a key element of a regime's control, one can rightly speak
of a totalitarian regime. But in most parts of the Middle East, fear is
not pervasive, and violence is not the everyday currency of discourse
between rulers and ruled. Sometimes violence is targeted against specific groups—Kurds in Turkey, Islamists in Syria—but even then most
of the population does not live in fear of the regime on a daily basis.
Still, those who live in authoritarian regimes know that there are limits
on what one can do and say. Those who stay within the bounds are
usually left alone, but repression can come swiftly. In the case of
Algeria, Military Security forces developed a reputation for dealing
harshly with opponents of the regime, and a number of leaders in
exile were assassinated over the years. In the Boumediene era, few
overt challenges to the regime took place after the Zbiri coup attempt
of 1967. But force and repression remained the ultimate defense of
the regime, and under the ostensibly more liberal regime of Chadli
Benjedid, political violence actually became more pronounced.

The third building block of authoritarian regimes is a system of
payoffs. All regimes rely on rewards to maintain support, but the
authoritarian state has typically seized control of most of the economy
and thus has enormous resources for dispensing forms of patronage.
Some of these payoffs are available to all in society—free education
and health care, subsidized food and housing, low rates of taxation.
Others are targeted to special groups and individuals. Jobs in the
bureaucracy may be available to loyalists and relatives of those in
power; fortunes can be made as the regime allows a share of the
"rents" to go into the pockets of supporters and collaborators.[6] There
are many ways of circulating money to those whose help is needed.
Rich businessmen can count on government contracts—no competitive
bidding required—and kickbacks to regime officials make for mutually
beneficial relations.

Some degree of subsidy, payoff, patronage, and corruption is present in all political systems, but the special feature of the authoritarian
regime is that there are no checks on this practice. There is no accountability, no transparency. The public has no voice in these matters
and no way of really knowing what is being done in its name. Ordinary
people may keep their mouths shut as long as they are getting some
benefits, but if those are withdrawn, they will deeply resent the lavish
lifestyles that some enjoy from their close association with power.

Corruption then becomes a political issue, one easily exaggerated—anyone with wealth must be dishonest—and readily used by opposition movements to rally popular support.[7]

Finally, authoritarian regimes, even when they have available the instruments of ideology, repression, and payoffs to deal with popular pressures for change, need some means of keeping the inner circle of power holders intact. Even the strictest of authoritarian regimes must rely on more than a single person to govern effectively. There must be a group, an elite, that works together, has some degree of trust, and realizes that it will share a common fate if the regime fails. The bases of solidarity may vary. Ethnicity, region, or tribe may count; shared experience in politics may be the source of enduring bonds; family ties, by blood or marriage, often carry weight. Military officers frequently have a sense of corporate loyalty, perhaps reinforced by the typical hierarchical command system of the military. Whatever the bonds, a ruler will spend great efforts to keep the inner circle loyal, fearful, or sufficiently corrupted so that exit is hardly an option.

It is striking how many regimes in the Middle East, such as those of Hafiz al-Asad and Saddam Hussein, have toyed with a dynastic succession principle, despite their ostensible republican bases. This suggests that family ties, when all else fails, may be the most reliable cement for an authoritarian regime. But even these can be sundered, and one of the most critical moments for an authoritarian regime is when arguments over succession threaten to bring down the entire structure.[8] This is a crucial vulnerability of authoritarian regimes, a challenge that differs from dealing with the broader populace.

The politics of keeping the elite intact is often opaque to outsiders, but rumors abound concerning *le pouvoir* or the *nomenklatura*, as the Algerians have labeled their rulers. It is well understood that this is the realm where authoritarian regimes succeed or fail, all other things being equal. Politics of the *serail*, the inner chamber, may be informal and Byzantine in its complexity, but it is the politics that counts, not the staged elections and fake institutional arrangements. Governance is easier than politics for authoritarian regimes. And when politics at the core becomes a problem for a ruler, he may be tempted to open up the system as one stratagem for outmaneuvering political rivals.

Authoritarian regimes rarely come to the realization all at once that something needs to be changed. A series of challenges often precedes any serious attempt at reform. The impetus for reform, when it finally comes, is likely to be to preserve the system—although not all of its components—not to change it. But change is inevitable, and this is where authoritarian regimes are usually found wanting. They do not adapt well to altered circumstances; they are poor at managing succession crises and are vulnerable to economic downturns. They all suffer from the law of declining legitimacy.[9] All these problems came to plague the post-Boumediene rulers of Algeria, but it took years before the magnitude of the damage was recognized.

Initial Challenges

When Chadli Benjedid became president in 1979, he was little known outside the army. He had headed the Oran military region and had reached the senior level of the military, but he was not known for any particular achievement during the revolution or after independence. His record was honorable but undistinguished. Few thought that he would exercise the kind of authority that Boumediene had held.

Even if Boumediene had survived, there would have been pressures for change. Algerian society was being transformed, in large measure due to the state's policies of education and health care, as well as to massive bureaucratization and rapid urbanization. A middle class of sorts was emerging, and with it some expectations of an easing of the strictures on political life. Also, the new generation, educated entirely since independence, and increasingly in Arabic, no longer showed automatic deference to the nationalists and revolutionaries who had won the country's freedom.

Chadli and his colleagues in the military moved initially to ease aside those who were closest to Boumediene. This consolidation of power is quite common in any political system in moments of transition, and especially in authoritarian regimes where personal relations within the inner circle count for so much.[10]

Chadli managed to take over the party apparatus and get himself elected president without much difficulty. He then set out to liberalize some aspects of the Boumediene system in the hope of winning support from the new middle class. Import restrictions were lifted, more consumer goods were in the market, exit visas were easier to come by, and the whole society seemed to breathe a bit more easily.

The new regime had the great advantage from the outset of presiding over the second oil "price shock." Triggered by the Iranian revolution in early 1979, the shock sent the price of oil soaring, from around $13 a barrel to over $30 a barrel. For Algeria, this was a splendid windfall that allowed the regime to spend lavishly on industrialization and welfare, while putting plenty of spare change in the pockets of the new middle class at the same time. The boom was not to last long, however, and export revenues began to decline slowly after 1982. To keep up spending, Algeria began to borrow heavily. This gave the regime a bit more time to indulge its belief that it could win legitimacy, and thus maintain its hold on power without too much challenge, with an open pocketbook and some measures of liberalization.

The more tolerant and liberal environment of the early Chadli years led to long-suppressed demands for change. One of the first indications of change came with the "Berber spring" of 1980. Algerian society is remarkably uniform in terms of religion—virtually all Algerians are Muslim—but it does have a minority of Berber speakers.

Berber—or Tamazight—was the language spoken throughout North Africa prior to the arrival of the Arabs in the seventh century. Most Berbers eventually adopted Arabic as their language, but in the mountainous areas of Morocco and Algeria, and in the far south, significant numbers of people continued to speak one of several Berber dialects. Although Berber can be written and has an alphabet of its own, it is essentially an oral language, and many Berber speakers are also fluent in colloquial Arabic—and often in French as well. In contemporary Algeria, about twenty percent of the population speaks Berber.

Of the Berber-speaking populations, the most significant politically have been the Kabyles, originating in the mountainous area east of Algiers. Many Kabyles have worked in France and many have moved to Algiers. They have always been strongly represented in the ranks of Algerian nationalism and many highly placed political and military figures are from Kabylia.

Most inhabitants of the Aures mountains in the east—the Chaouia, as they are called—are also Berber speakers, but this area has been more Arabized than Kabylia and there has only been limited cooperation between Kabyles and Chaouia on behalf of their common linguistic heritage.[11] The term *Chaouia*, in fact, is often used by Algerians to refer to somewhat rude mannered, country boys from the eastern part of Algeria. Many in the ranks of the military are believed to be

Arabized Chaouia. Finally, the Tuareg nomads of the south speak a Berber dialect, as do the Mzabites, followers of the Ibadi rite of Islam, who are concentrated in a few villages in the south. These latter two communities are quite small.

Insofar as there has been a "Berberist" phenomenon in Algeria—that is, a conscious demand for recognition of Tamazight as a national language that should be supported by the state and for Berber cultural rights—it has been the Kabyles who have been at the head of the movement. In the late 1940s there was a crisis over Berberism within the nationalist ranks, and many Algerians have ever since looked at Berber demands as divisive, potentially opening the way for foreign intervention.[12] The Berbers are often seen as the most French-oriented in their ways, since many have worked in France, have become literate in French, and are reluctant to be forced to learn classical Arabic, which has been the goal of state educational policy since the 1970s. Although there are strong nationalists and Islamists among the Kabyles, they tend to support the idea of a secular political order in which their distinctive cultural rights can be protected. During the Boumediene era, efforts were made to discourage the use of the Berber language.

The first sign of Berber political agitation in independent Algeria came in April 1980, shortly after Boumediene's death. A well-known Kabyle writer was prevented from giving a lecture on Berber culture, and in response the university students in the town of Tizi Ouzou, in the heart of Kabylia, went on strike and protested the authoritarian nature of the regime. This led to a harsh crackdown and subsequent politicization of many Berbers. By the mid-1980s the Chadli regime's repression had succeeded in laying the groundwork for an outspoken Berber cultural movement with the potential of rallying support from some 10 to 20 percent of the society. Among its demands were greater democracy.[13]

As if to offset the demands of the Berber minority, an Islamist movement began to make itself heard in the early 1980s. The revolution in Iran had heightened everyone's awareness of the political potency of radical Islam, and within a short period Islamic activists were asserting themselves in Egypt, Syria, Tunisia, and Algeria, all relatively secular nationalistic Arab states. In Algeria, Islam had always been a component of nationalism, in fact the primary unifying element of the Algerian identity in the face of French colonialism. No one was overtly anti-Islamic, and the state went to great lengths to show that it was upholding religion. Mosques were built with state funds, the teaching of Arabic—often by religiously trained instructors from the Middle East—was promoted, and the constitution established Islam as the state religion. But those who turned to Islam as a form of protest against the regime saw nothing in the regime's promotion of official Islam that merited support.[14]

Ben Bella and Boumediene had faced demands from Muslim religious groups to be allowed to organize in the 1960s, and these had been rejected in the name of populist unity. Only official Islam would be sanctioned, just as only one party would be tolerated. But in 1982 a more militant form of Islamic protest arose. The first sign of Islamic activism came on university campuses, where Berberists, Communists, and Islamists fought bitter battles for control of student politics. At times these disputes turned violent, and the regime was just as willing to crack down on the Islamists as on the Berberists.

In 1982 the Algerian Islamic Movement, led by a young activist named Mustafa Bouyali, whose brother had been killed by the police, took up arms in the countryside.[15] For several years, an Islamist armed group, or *maquis* continued to operate, inflicting some modest damage, until its leader was killed in 1987. The seeds of armed Islamic dissent were sown.

Faced with these challenges—none of which seemed to have deep mass roots or extensive organization—Chadli sought to revive the almost dormant political party, the National Liberation Front (*Front de Libération Nationale* FLN), to make it a more effective link between the population and the regime. This revival of the party also gave Chadli the chance to try to form a political base of his own, outside the strict control of the clans within the military that had brought him to power.

Aware, perhaps, of the need for a group of trustworthy advisers loyal to him, Chadli also brought into his circle a group of young intellectuals who were interested in trying to reform the economy to make it more efficient and productive. They went about their work without much fanfare, proposing modest reforms but not exercising much clout at the outset.[16]

Meanwhile, the social mobilization that had been reflected in the Berberist and Islamist movements gained momentum in the mid-1980s. In response to a very conservative "Family Code" voted by the FLN-controlled parliament in 1984, which gave great authority to husbands and fathers, many educated and modern Algerian women took to the streets.[17] Women activists had played a part in the revolution, but after independence had been shoved to the background of public life.[18] Now they—especially the educated and Westernized among them—wanted to be heard on an issue that directly affected them and their daughters. Women's movements, led by impressive and outspoken secular women, took form rapidly, but were not able to prevent the adoption of the Family Code. The regime seemed to view the restrictive Family Code as a sop to the conservative Islamists who worried about too much Western cultural penetration, a sign of which were the demands by women for a greater role in public life.[19]

Finally, during this period one also saw in Algeria the emergence of human rights activists, who argued that individuals should be safe from arbitrary treatment by the regime. Since one of the strongest causes of irritation on the part of ordinary Algerians was the regime's *hogra*—its arbitrary, and usually arrogant, use of power—many Algerians became strong supporters of the idea of making the regime accountable for its behavior.

As long as the regime was able to make good on the welfare bargain that linked it to most Algerians, the voices of protest were muted. Too many people had a stake of some sort in the existing order, and the sources of discontent did not converge. The regime could pit Berberists, Communists, women, and human rights activists against Islamists of both the conservative and radical variety. But in 1986 the bottom fell out of the oil market. The price per barrel of oil fell from its high of more than $30 in 1982 to a low of around $10. Almost overnight Algeria had to adjust its economic strategy, cut spending, borrow more, and hope for better days. But the price of oil did not rebound much, and by 1988 the regime was no longer able to count on buying off or manipulating protesters.[20]

The oil-price drop set the stage for the "retreat of the state," a typical moment of crisis for authoritarian regimes. Both in reality and in popular perception, the state was no longer able to fulfill its part of the bargain with a passive citizenry. This caused resentment and also made the state seem weak and vulnerable. Shaken it may have been, but the regime was still able to defend itself, provided it did not split at the core. Chadli's challenge in the October 1988 crisis was not only to deal with an angry populace, but also to manage a covert challenge to his leadership from within the regime itself.

October 1988

All Algerians who lived through the events of October 1988 have a theory of what happened. Where the precise truth lies is impossible to say, but the mass protests of October 1988 proved to be one of those turning points that define a country's political trajectory for years to come. Those events become a reference point, a source of bitter debates by those who defend the actions of the protesters, and those who feel they were dupes being manipulated by occult forces within the regime. How to ensure this never happens again, or how to ensure that it happens peacefully next time, are the dividing lines between the partisans of order and the partisans of democratic politics. There is little middle ground.

Why were the events of October 1988 so important? First, they represented a nationwide youth revolt, comparable in some ways to the Palestinian *intifada*, or uprising. Throughout the country, young men took to the streets in angry protest against the regime. Somehow, as the protests grew, Islamist activists appeared on the scene and seemed to take charge. Pictures from the time show crowds of young Algerians dressed in jeans and T-shirts, with a sprinkling of older men wearing Islamic garb, including the fashionable "Afghan" outfit made popular by those Algerians who had returned from fighting with the Islamist revolutionaries against the Russians in Afghanistan.

If the marchers had staged their protest peacefully and then gone home, little would now be said about the events of October 1988. But instead, the military was called in to keep order, shots were fired—by whom?—and when the dust had settled hundreds of young Algerians had been killed by their own brothers and cousins in the armed forces. For the first time in independent Algeria, the "popular" army had fired on unarmed civilians. No one had doubted beforehand that the regime would use force if threatened by force, but many were shocked at the indiscriminate way in which the military imposed order. Many in the military were appalled as well, saying that they would never act this way again to prop up an unpopular regime.

It is still hard to pinpoint the spark that led to the protests. There was nothing quite so dramatic as the bread price increases that had provoked rioting in Cairo in January 1977, and in numerous other Middle East capitals in later years.[21] But there was a social and economic undercurrent to the protests.[22] Many of the young men were the products of the mass education system that had left them, as was often said, "illiterate in two languages," Arabic and French. They were unable to find jobs, while the children of the establishment, who went to private schools where they learned both French and Arabic—but especially French—were doing quite well. At a time when some Algerians were visibly enjoying unprecedented wealth, they were stuck in overcrowded slums ringing the big cities, often sleeping six or more to a room. These were the young men called *hittistes*, or those who hold up the walls, from their habit of lounging around with nothing to do, nowhere to go, no money to spend, no entertainment, no sociability. They simply stood on the streets, leaning against the walls.

There was a generational aspect to the protest as well. It was now twenty-six years since independence, and the same generation that had fought the revolution was in charge. The faces had changed, a bit, but there was still no sense that the system was open to the new generation born since the revolution. The old guard had won the state in 1962 and was treating it as their personal property.

These are all understandable background factors, but why did the protests break out when they did? No one doubts that there was plenty of raw material for discontent, but it takes something to produce a nationwide protest lasting several days.

Probably the most widespread belief among politically sophisticated Algerians is that conservative elements within the Chadli regime— particularly within the FLN and the security services—were somehow responsible for setting off the riots of October 1988. Proof is hard to come by, but the story goes as follows. Chadli had been maneuvering to build a base of support of his own. He had tried to revive the party, but found that it was discredited—too bureaucratic and unresponsive. He had allowed Communists to operate within the party in an attempt to give the party more energy, but this had simply alienated the party hacks. One of Chadli's errors, in many accounts, was to have publicly blasted the party bureaucrats in a speech on September 19, 1988. This seemed to imply that a purge was in the offing. The usually mild-mannered Chadli seemed to be declaring war—and in public—on the old guard.[23]

On the security front, Chadli had tried to put his own men in charge of the key positions in the Military Security, had reorganized the service, and had, no doubt, made some powerful enemies. In the process, some believe, he weakened its ability to know what was going on in society.[24]

In these circumstances, it is argued, elements within the party—the old guard—perhaps aided by elements in Military Security, saw a chance to move against Chadli by promoting popular protests that would call for the president's removal. In the minds of those who believe this version, this accounts for the fact that the protests took place all over the country, that the slogans shouted were all similar—"Chadli assassin," and that Chadli himself was the primary target of the protests. Some eyewitnesses claim to have seen party activists encouraging the crowds in the first days. The appearance of the Islamists on the scene was perhaps not part of the original plan, but the old guard had no problem with Islamist participation as long as the target was Chadli. He could be moved aside, order could be restored, the Islamists could be bought off or repressed, and the old system of privilege and patronage could be preserved.[25]

But Chadli was not pushed aside. Instead, he played his trump card—his control over the army—which crushed the uprising, but at enormous cost to Chadli's and its own reputation and legitimacy. The immediate crisis was past, but an even more serious one lay ahead. This is when Algerian politics took an unexpected turn—not back to the old authoritarian past, but into the unknown terrain of democratic contestation. Or so it seemed, for a brief, heady period.

4

The Politics of Liberalization

T HAT THE October 1988 demonstrations took place at all, much less on the scale that they did, was an indication that the "classic" authoritarian style rule of the Boumediene period was over. During the 1980s, there had been some opening up of both the economy and the political system, although the formal structures had not been much changed. The Algerian population was showing signs of both fatigue and unrest, the regime was criticized from many quarters, and corruption was becoming an issue as some Algerians became quite wealthy, while others were mired in poverty. Rapid social change, intense exposure to France (often through French television, which could easily be seen in Algiers) and the emergence of Islamist opposition groups were creating a volatile mix. Then came the economic downturn of 1986 and it did not take much to set a spark to the tinder.

But it did take something. The demonstrations of October 1988 almost certainly were a mixture of spontaneous protest and some degree of orchestrated political action aimed at undermining an unpopular regime. Rapid social mobilization of disparate alienated groups, coupled with splits within the regime, were at the heart of the outburst of political contestation and violence.

In moments of rapid change, strange alliances of convenience seem to form. After the events of October 1988, Islamists, who had quickly taken charge of the demonstrations, and the old guard in the party were both intent on advancing their political interests at the expense of Chadli Benjedid. Chadli, in turn, had been trying to divert blame onto the National Liberation Front (*Front de Libération Nationale*, FLN), from which he was beginning to distance himself. Much of what followed the October protests has to be understood as a competition among several centers of power—the president and his circle of reformers, the military, the Islamists and other opposition parties, the FLN establishment, and a generally dissatisfied and angry populace. Further, each of these "actors" proved to be internally divided, so one must also examine factions within groups maneuvering for power. This is not to say that there were no real issues of substance at stake— there were—but the political game revealed that each player at some point tried to manipulate some of the others, to disarm them, to out-maneuver them, to co-opt them. Surprisingly, this gave rise to a brief period of what seemed to be a democratic opening.

If the rules of the Boumediene era had been in play—or for that matter if the regime had been like that of Syria, Iraq, or even Tunisia or Egypt—the demonstrations, had they occurred in the first place, would almost certainly have been at least as severely repressed as in Algeria, and then the regime would have gone to considerable lengths to make sure that no further challenges of that sort took place. Chadli may have been tempted to return to an iron-fist policy, but then he would have remained reliant on the military and the party. And if the demonstrations showed anything, it was that the regime and its props were profoundly unpopular.

Perhaps Chadli consciously considered the "Gorbachev gambit"— a political opening, *glasnost*—which would weaken the party but might give the leader a lease on life as a reformer. (In 1988, of course, Gor-bachev's inglorious end could not be foretold.) Anyone following events in the Soviet Union and Central Europe must have been won-dering whether it was really possible to scrap the old one-party system without committing suicide, as Gorbachev seemed to believe. In any event, Chadli surprised many Algerians by plunging ahead with an audacious reform program.

The peculiar angle of Algeria's rush toward democratization is that it took place so rapidly and with so few indications of any committed democrats playing the game.[1] But the early stages of democratization or liberalization are often little more than defensive maneuvers by people who want to cling to power. The impetus for change does not come from a conversion to democratic ideals. Rather, it stems from conflict within the political system, especially among warring factions in the regime, who see a chance to improve their position by striking new alliances with emerging social forces, while cutting themselves loose from the dead wood of the old, unpopular order.[2] This is, roughly speaking, how democratization began in Turkey after World

War II.[3] With time and experience, the practice of democratic politics may indeed produce a commitment to the rules of the democratic game. But at the outset, the gamble looks much less idealistic and much more manipulative.[4]

Still, for Algerian society, the changes that took place between early 1989 and 1991 were breathtaking, whatever the intentions of those who set them in motion. And once the system was opened up, no one could be sure how things would work out. A great deal of improvising took place, decisions were made that proved to be amazingly short-sighted, and the whole experience ended quite differently from the way in which any of the participants could have expected or desired.[5] In short, political judgments were made that had unintended, and often disastrous consequences, but at the time the decisions were plausible, even understandable, once one takes into account the intense factional struggles that were occurring. Had there been a unified leadership within the regime and a coherent opposition, the game might have been conducted much differently. But instead there were at least half a dozen major players, each trying to figure out how best to maintain or seize power. Not surprisingly, some monumental errors were made.

The first experience of political reform in Algeria is important in its own right. It reminds us of how difficult it is to change old habits, forge new rules, and open up a political system without jeopardizing order and security. It shows the problem for an authoritarian regime of dealing with a challenge from an equally authoritarian opposition. Both sides tend to want all power and are often mirror images of one another, once adjustments are made for ideology and personalities.[6] Power sharing is not the name of the game. It is often more a matter of revenge and recrimination.

Opening up a political system is also an invitation to all sorts of demagoguery. Those who have exercised, and often abused, power are likely to be accused of terrible crimes; they can expect to be put on trial and possibly executed if the opposition comes to power. The military is rarely an enthusiastic onlooker when democratization begins. The opposition may try to win the military over, but if that fails, they are likely to call for its complete removal from the political arena—an alarming signal to the top brass that their lives and fortunes will be at risk if the opposition comes to power.

Political liberalization also has its positive and exciting side. Hope replaces the drab gloominess of everyday life, at least at the outset. People who have long been afraid to speak their minds suddenly find their voices. Freedom creates a heady mood, as long-suppressed currents come to light. Intellectual and cultural life blossoms. Civil society emerges, with an explosion of organizations, some tackling the most taboo of topics, such as those who speak out against torture and call for respect for human rights. These organizations may lack staying power, but their creation reveals much about public sentiment. Just months earlier one would have been jailed for the kinds of actions that quickly became routine.

There is much to be learned about the role of the military in the process of political change from the Algerian case. Everywhere that authoritarian regimes have opened up, defining an appropriate role for the military has been a crucial issue. It is extremely hard to find a way to move the military to the sidelines, as the Turkish and Chilean cases demonstrate. But it can be done more skillfully, and certainly more successfully, than in Algeria.

The Algerian reform period is also important because it is now consciously evoked as a model to be avoided by leaders in Algeria and elsewhere. When Egyptians and Tunisians crack down on Islamist parties, they mutter that they are preventing another Algeria from happening. When the Turkish military makes vague threats to Islamist leaders in the name of upholding secularism, Algeria is much on their minds. And more to the point, the Algerian leaders who took over in the 1990s have had something of an obsession with the first period of reform. Whatever else they might do, they have been determined not to make the same mistakes. This begs the question, of course, of what those mistakes really were.

Was it inevitable that this first effort at reform would end in such violence? Does it have something to do with Algeria's bloody history, the nature of its people, with Islam, or was it the result of a particular conjunction of political forces that might have come to a different outcome with different leaders and different choices at crucial moments? Was the failure of reform inevitable, in some deterministic sense, or was it the result of specific decisions made by quite normal, but fallible, politicians? These questions will be addressed more explicitly in the second part of this book, but they are inevitably linked to this review of the remarkable period of Algeria's first, brief experience with democracy.

Political Reforms

Following the military crackdown on the October demonstrations, which left hundreds dead and injured, Chadli found scapegoats in the leaders of Military Security and the FLN party, both of whom were summarily removed from their positions.[7] Soon thereafter, Kasdi Merbah, who had previously been head of Military Security in the early 1980s, and presumably knew a great deal about the various political and social movements opposed to the regime, was named prime minister. This seemed an odd choice, since Merbah was associated with the hated Military Security and was hardly a popular figure, but he was no doubt instrumental in keeping the security forces behind the embattled president.

Chadli was also reaching the end of his elected term as president. To help prepare for his reelection, Chadli pushed through several constitutional amendments in early November that suggested a willingness to reform and grant citizens more freedoms. A congress of the FLN was held in November and Chadli was chosen as the sole candidate for president. But at the congress, he raised the prospect of ending the monopoly of the party over the country's political life. The president stopped short of calling for a multiparty system, and the congress adopted a resolution warning that "in present circumstances" multipartism would represent "a danger for the people, for the nation and especially for national unity."[8] Observers expected some reform of the party, but not much more. In late December, Chadli was elected for another five-year term. He received about 80 percent of the vote.

In his role as reelected president and in his attempt to rise above party politics, Chadli pushed through a new constitution drafted primarily by his reform-minded allies. On February 23, 1989, it was adopted in a referendum by 73 percent of the voters.[9] By any standard, the new constitution—Algeria's third—was a major step in the direction of liberalization.

It is easy to dismiss the importance of a constitutional document in a country that has seen a new constitution in each decade and for each president. But this constitution can be read as a plan for changing some of the basic options of the state, and within a short time the words on paper were being translated into new practices. Most striking in the new constitution was the end of the identification of the state and the single party, the FLN. Nowhere in the body of the text was the FLN mentioned. Nor was socialism, once a major part of the constitutional order, ever mentioned. Instead, the constitution insisted that a state of law would be established in which there would be three distinct powers—executive, legislative, and judicial. In addition, significant guarantees of individual liberties were promised, including "freedom of expression, of association and of assembly" (Article 39) and the freedom "to form associations of a political nature" (Article 40). This latter provision was just short of being an endorsement of freedom to form political parties, and it soon was interpreted as such. The door was also opened to a free press, and within a brief period Algeria was flooded with a variety of new, and often quite interesting, newspapers and magazines.

Like its predecessors, the 1989 constitution gave a great deal of power to the president, including the right to declare emergencies when he could rule by decree. But there was some movement away from the all-powerful presidency. For example, while the president still selected the prime minister and the cabinet, the parliament could refuse approval. It could also refuse to adopt the government's program by voting a no confidence measure. In both cases, the president would have to present a new government. If the assembly were to refuse to approve the government a second time, then the assembly would be dissolved and there would be new elections.

The new constitution, like its predecessors, made Islam the religion of the state, and it also created a High Islamic Council to advise the president. The role of the council was left quite vague, but its mere existence was a sign of the times. Socialism was now out; Islam was in.

While the constitution seemed to open the way toward political liberalization and pluralism, much would depend on how it was carried out in practice. Liberalization was no guarantee that democratization would follow. One of the first tests would come with a new law governing the creation of political parties.

In March 1989 Chadli informed the Central Committee of the FLN that the time had come to let other parties express themselves. Perhaps more important, those members of the Central Committee who were officers in the military forces were obliged to leave the party. From then on, the army was to be above politics.[10] Furthermore, Chadli began to talk of renewing the party from the base up. To many of the "barons" of the party, this must have sounded like a threat.

By summer 1989 a number of "political associations" were lobbying the government to be recognized as political parties. In early July a new law on political parties was issued, and the minister of the interior said clearly that he was for democracy and that democracy inevitably involved multipartism.[11] Soon thereafter, the first parties—still called associations—were formally recognized by the government.

According to the law on parties, no political movement could be based "exclusively" on religion, language, or regionalism. This provision could have been used to prohibit parties claiming to be based on Islam or which demanded Berber cultural rights. But instead of such a restrictive interpretation, the government of Kasdi Merbah, widely viewed as lukewarm toward reforms, went ahead and recognized both the Rally for Culture and Democracy (*Rassemblement pour la Culture et la Démocratie*, RCD) of Said Saadi and the Islamic Salvation Front (*Front Islamique du Salut*, FIS).[12] It is hard to know what Chadli, who seems to have made the decision, had in mind in authorizing the FIS to enter the political arena, but it is possible that the FIS looked like an ally against some of the old-guard tendencies in the FLN.[13]

Within days of this decision, however, Chadli announced the removal of Merbah as prime minister and his replacement by Mouloud Hamrouche, a reformer who had been secretary general of the president's office under Chadli, but also came from a military background.[14] In a test of constitutional prerogative, Merbah claimed that Chadli did not have the right to dismiss him, since the parliament had voted confidence in his government. But the constitution was actually quite clear that the president had the right both to name and dismiss the government, so Merbah was obliged to make way for Hamrouche. But he did not do so with good grace and continued to play an active role behind the scenes, most likely using some of his old contacts in the security services.

The Hamrouche government took over at a time when the economy was in deep trouble. Reforms were needed, but they would not necessarily provide early relief. In fact, some reforms might make things worse in the short term.[15] Hamrouche had to deal with these day-to-day problems, as well as with the constant sniping from the conservatives in the FLN, who still controlled the parliament, and increasingly from the opposition parties, most important of which was the FIS. While the FIS supported economic reforms, it challenged the government on other issues.[16]

The Rise of the FIS

Islam had long been an integral part of the Algerian national identity, but by the 1980s it was also serving as a vehicle for protest against an increasingly disliked regime.[17] The politicized form of Islam, quite similar to other such movements in the Middle East, covered a range of currents. The FIS included cultural conservatives who held to traditional values, promoted the teaching of Arabic, and worried about corrupting western influences. It also welcomed educated, radicalized Islamic militants who wanted to seize state power to carry out a real revolution that would bring justice and self-respect to demoralized Algerians.[18] Some Islamists had already taken up arms; others had organized at the local level and were proceeding to try to build an Islamic state from the ground up.[19]

Before the October 1988 uprisings, it would have been hard to find anyone in Algeria who thought the Islamists were the wave of the future. And no one claimed that Islamists were behind these demonstrations at the outset. But there was already some structure to the Islamist movement, because it reacted quickly and saw the chance to identify itself with the protest movement that was sweeping the country. Chadli Benjedid obviously recognized the power of the Islamists, and on October 10, the day of much of the bloodshed, he met with three Islamist leaders to seek their help in quelling the uprising. Ironically, one of those he met was the young firebrand, Ali Ben Hadj, who was later held responsible by other Islamist leaders for having instigated some of the violence on that day.[20] By meeting with these leaders, Chadli was clearly indicating that he needed their help in restoring order. It was not long before they formed a potent political movement of their own.

Shortly before the referendum on the new constitution in early 1989, the *Front Islamique du Salut* was formed. In Arabic, the name was *Al-Jabha al-Islamiyya lil-Inqadh*. By August, it had applied for formal recognition as a party,[21] and that was granted by Merbah's government a few days before he was ousted from the prime ministership in early September.

The fifteen founding members of the FIS were a diverse lot.[22] They represented young and old, as well as each section of the country. Two names soon were recognized as the most prominent of the FIS leaders: Ali Ben Hadj, a young, militant, and charismatic man with a remarkable gift for words, and the older, more sedate, but very ambitious Abbassi Madani. In ensuing months, many of the founding members of the FIS ended up quarreling with one another and some left the movement altogether. But Ben Hadj and Madani stuck together, seeming to recognize that they needed one another.

Other Islamists were brushed aside by the FIS. This was the fate of Mahfoud Nahnah, who expected a major role in any Islamist front and went on to form a party of his own, Hamas (*Harakat al-Mujtamaa al-Islamiyya*—the Movement for Islamic Society). Nahnah was close to the Egyptian-based Muslim Brethren and concentrated on building grass-root organizations throughout the country. He did not have a large popular following, but he did have an organization.

In addition, Abdallah Djaballah, who had played an important role in organizing Islamic students in the Constantine area, ended up founding a party of his own, *An-Nahda*. A few other political figures with Islamist leanings also entered the arena, but none could compete with the amazingly popular FIS.

Who were the FIS stalwarts? Many were young men, unemployed, living in the sprawling slums around the major cities, especially Algiers.[23] They would flock to the mosques on Friday to hear Ben Hadj and Madani preach. The mosques became a gathering point, a place of sociability, a place for politics. Try as they might to impose official Islam in the mosques, the regime could not keep control. If Ben Hadj and Madani were denied access to the state mosques, they would simply go to one of the popular mosques that were cropping up.[24]

On the margins of the FIS, sometimes in and sometimes out, were the armed groups, some of whose militants had been trained in Afghanistan. The FIS began to act as if it were more than a political party.[25] It publicly acknowledged that its security forces had apprehended a young man and were holding him in detention. In short, the FIS was bragging that it had a militia and was beginning to function like a state within a state.[26] By 1990 a number of small-scale armed clashes were occurring between Islamist militants and the regime.

The reformers in the Hamrouche government, most of whom were secularists, looked on the FIS with ambivalence. They had little use for the rhetoric and extremism of some of the FIS leaders, especially Ben Hadj, but they also recognized the value of a political movement that could channel the discontent of the young and keep it from spilling over into violence. As a legal party, the FIS could also be held accountable, whereas if it were banned, it might become an underground movement. Chadli may also have felt that he could use the FIS to settle scores with some of his rivals. In any case, during this period the regime had regular meetings with the Islamist leaders. They were part of the new order. Even some in the military met with them.[27]

Tests of Strength

Once democratization begins, there is bound to be a test of strength at the ballot box. Elections, after all, are the centerpiece of democratic politics, although there is much else besides.[28] Where to begin? The regime, naturally cautious, proposed local elections first, starting at the commune and province level. Some in the opposition wanted presidential elections instead, or at least parliamentary ones. But Chadli was still in control and he set the date for local elections in mid-1990.

Toward the end of November 1989, the FLN held an extraordinary congress to prepare itself for the new political situation in a multiparty Algeria. Various factions were outspoken, most notably those who were skeptical of Chadli's liberalization and looked fondly back to the Boumediene era. On the opposite side of the debates were those who argued for change, for renewal, and who blamed the old guard for many of the country's problems. This was hardly a unified party, and the Congress did little to cover over the differences. But Chadli got his way: the secretary general remained Abdelhamid Mehri (his brother-in-law), and those he proposed for the political bureau were elected. Chadli had not yet cut himself off from the FLN.[29]

Meanwhile, other political forces were entering the arena. The leader of the Socialist Forces Front (*Front des Forces Socialistes*, FFS), Hocine Ait Ahmed, returned from Switzerland to join the fray. Then in his late sixties, he still had a following, especially among the Kabyles. In early December, his party, along with a dozen others, were all recognized as legal by the regime.

The electoral law chosen for the communal and provincial elections in June 1990 seemed designed to favor the largest party, presumably the FLN. Parties were to put forward lists in each electoral district (communal and provincial). If one party received a majority of the votes cast, the seats would be distributed on a proportional basis to all parties receiving more than 7 percent of the vote. If there was no party that received an absolute majority, then the largest party would receive half the seats, plus one, the rest to be distributed proportionately among all parties with more than 7 percent of the vote. This method of voting put the many small parties at a disadvantage and probably discouraged their supporters from voting at all.[30]

The electoral code also allowed a man to vote for his wife simply by showing his family identity card, or *livret*. According to one source, a great majority of men voted this way.[31] In addition, any elector could vote by procuration—requiring written consent—for up to three other voters. These rules allowed for serious abuses of the ballot.

As the date of the local elections approached, the parties, especially the FIS, but also the FLN and FFS, organized mass rallies. In the end, the FFS decided not to participate and called for a boycott. This had some impact in Kabylia and perhaps in Algiers.

When the vote was counted, the results were a shock to many Algerians. The FIS had won a resounding victory. It had received 4.3 million votes, compared to 2.25 million for the FLN. About 63 percent of all eligible voters participated in the election. Nearly 34 percent of all registered voters cast their ballots for FIS candidates. Because of the electoral law, the FIS actually won the large majority of communal and provincial seats.[32] Only in rural areas did the FLN do reasonably well. It was comparatively strong in the east, the Batna-Tebessa-Souk Ahras area—the Chaouia region where many senior officers in the military came from. But in Algiers and the cities of the west, the FIS was victorious.

Toward Confrontation

The fallout from the FLN's first defeat at the polls was not long in coming. The Islamists were emboldened, the FLN was split, and the army sought to firm up its "above-politics" position as guardian of the constitution.[33]

In July the FLN chose a new Political Bureau, including some of those who succeeded in the recent elections. But the members of the government who had been on the Political Bureau, including the prime minister, stepped down. Henceforth, government and party would not be so closely identified.

The prime minister, struggling with economic reforms, announced a new government in July. The most significant change was the naming, for the first time, of a minister of defense, a post always held by the president in the past. Algeria's new minister of defense was Khalid Nezzar, a strong figure who quickly set about putting his own men in key positions. One of them, the head of ground forces, was Mohammed Lamari. These two men were to play key roles in coming years. Another powerful figure, Mohammed Betchine, the head of Military Security, stepped down in September, possibly in protest against the government's lenient treatment of the Islamists.[34] He also would be heard from again.

During the fall, major political figures asserted their independence of the FLN. Indicative of the end of the FLN's monopoly over government policy, the party decided not to take a stand on whether the long-imprisoned, and then exiled, former president, Ahmed Ben Bella, could return and be active in politics. In late September, Ben Bella returned to a less-than-enthusiastic response. He immediately set up a political party of his own.

Other political figures were soon leaving the FLN. The most senior of the original revolutionaries, Rabah Bitat, quit the party in October. He was followed by former prime minister (and former head of Military Security) Kasdi Merbah, who also founded a party of his own. Finally, another former prime minister, Abdelhamid Brahimi, quit the Central Committee of the FLN. He represented the Islamist wing within the FLN and made history by declaring publicly that the various FLN governments had robbed the country of $26 billion since independence, a figure that just happened to be the size of Algeria's foreign debt (and a figure that was almost certainly invented for maximum political impact). The effect of all these departures was to further weaken and demoralize the party activists. In December, when a new Political Bureau was elected, it received a bare majority of the votes, an unprecedented signal of splits within the FLN.

Meanwhile, the Islamists were active. In June they formed a labor union to compete with one of the props of the regime, the General Union of Algerian Workers (*Union Générale des Travailleurs Algériens*, UGTA). No longer could the party or government count on control over the labor force.[35]

The Islamists were deeply affected by the Gulf War that erupted when Saddam Hussein invaded Kuwait in August 1990. The FIS in particular had been receiving money from Saudi Arabia, and initially came out against Iraq's invasion and annexation of this oil-rich principality. But the young supporters of the FIS had no sympathy for rich

Gulf sheiks and saw in Saddam's macho posturing an appealing model. As soon as American and other western troops were on their way to Saudi Arabia, the activists succeeded in redefining the issue away from Kuwait and toward western aggression against Islam. The FIS leaders tried ineffectively to mediate between Iraq and Saudi Arabia, but then gave up and threw their support to Saddam once the American-led offensive began in January 1991. The whole affair had the effect of radicalizing Islamist opinion—and removing whatever restraining influence the Saudis might have been able to exert.[36] By early 1991 the FIS was leading demonstrations against western policy in the Gulf and was calling on the government to open training camps for Islamist volunteers to go fight alongside their Iraqi brothers. Nothing the government could do would satisfy their demands.

Now the FIS sensed its power in the street and decided to press for new elections, parliamentary and presidential, and if the government refused, they would threaten to bring it down by mass action. Hamrouche opposed the idea of early parliamentary elections, arguing that he needed more time to push through economic reforms, and only then could the government organize an election. But the FIS was impatient and Chadli finally agreed that parliamentary elections should be held in the first half of 1991.

It is hard to know what Chadli and Hamrouche had in mind at this point. They were showing considerable restraint in the face of a determined, even provocative, challenge from the FIS. The military had issued vague warnings that it would not tolerate lawlessness indefinitely. The FLN was in no shape to compete with the FIS effectively, and most of the other parties were even weaker. Some suspected that Hamrouche, a clever politician, was counting on the FIS to overplay its hand, to alarm too many ordinary Algerians by its verbal—and sometimes real—violence. Meanwhile, Hamrouche would do nothing to salvage the old-guard FLN. As the FLN fell apart, he would try to reassert control with a new group of reformers, leaving the choice in future elections between enlightened nationalist reformers and obscurantist Islamic radicals. He thought at least the FIS would not win a clear victory, and he set about forging electoral rules to make sure that would be the case.

During the early part of 1991 a real show of force took place. The FIS was intent on asserting its power, calling strikes, threatening violence. Ben Hadj was fiery and outspoken; Madani was a bit more restrained, but clearly eager to take Chadli's place as president. Meanwhile, Hamrouche was in charge of drawing up the election law and proved to be quite masterful at the art of gerrymandering. The FLN had done well in the south, so the south would be greatly overrepresented in the new assembly. The justification would be that these disadvantaged areas needed more representatives so they could catch up with the rest of the country's development.

The FIS saw through this ploy. They also probably realized that many of their constituents in the municipalities that they governed—sometimes dubbed Islamic communes—were getting fed up with their moralizing and intrusiveness.[37] Mixed classes in schools were suspended; women were told not to work and to wear the veil; non-FIS constituents could not get jobs and permits. In short, the FIS had become as corrupt and difficult as the old FLN, although in some communes the new leaders got good marks for civic mindedness and keeping the streets clean. Still, the FIS was not winning accolades for its management of local government. Some in the FIS thought that they had been trapped.[38] They now bore the brunt of the populace's dissatisfaction, but they did not actually control their own budget and could do little more than take symbolic positions on social issues. Real economic power was still concentrated in Algiers, where the oil revenues flowed. If the FIS was to enlarge its domain of influence, it needed to win power at the center, not at the local level.

By May the FIS was worried that Hamrouche was about to hold elections in June and that they might lose.[39] As a result, they mounted a massive campaign of strikes to discredit the Hamrouche government. If there was to be a test of power between the FIS and le pouvoir, they did not intend that it be settled by elections alone. This was probably the crucial moment in Algeria's brief experiment with democratization. A number of outcomes were still possible, including compromise, a new electoral law, a postponement of elections, or the banning of the FIS for advocating violence. But instead, confrontation occurred and the military intervened—not to ban the FIS, but to oust Hamrouche.

The May Strike and the Aborted Election

Part of the political game in spring 1991 involved competition to become spokesman for those Algerians with grievances against the regime. For those who had been in power, this would require some repositioning, to say the least. The reformers in the government would have to distance themselves from the party, the trade union would have to make a show of independence, and the army would have to remain "above politics." Meanwhile, the Islamists were actively recruiting and mobilizing.

In April the UGTA trade union called a very successful strike, something of a first for a union that was supposed to be the creature of the regime. Demands were made for better working conditions, and large numbers of workers went on strike in a show of solidarity. The FIS may have concluded that it too needed a strike, but with a difference.

The FIS had many grievances, including the election law that the assembly had passed for the June elections. A classical strike of workers would not necessarily do much for the FIS. Instead, the FIS decided to call a "general and unlimited strike" aimed at occupying the streets, not just closing down factories.[40] Taken literally, the slogan of an unlimited strike seemed to imply that nothing short of the regime's collapse would bring the strike to an end. In fact, some in the FIS had written about "civil disobedience" as a tactic to weaken the regime.[41] On May 25 the strike began.

The strike did not immediately rally a huge number of people in Algiers. In a city that had witnessed an explosion of political activity in the past year, the FIS strike was not particularly noteworthy. Toward the end of the day the union affiliated with the FIS called on workers to strike, promising to secure better wages and working conditions. But the union also stated that the strike was the means "to bring down the present regime."[42] Overnight about one thousand strikers occupied several public places. These were party faithful who had been brought in from other parts of the country and who would be the shock troops of the strike. And their numbers would grow.[43]

Strangely missing from this crisis as it unfolded was the president, Chadli Benjedid. Instead, it was his prime minister, Hamrouche, and the minister of defense, Nezzar, who spoke for the government, and they did not see eye to eye. Hamrouche adopted the stance that the FIS should be allowed to carry on with its strike as long as it refrained from violence and did not try to seize public buildings. As long as the FIS was prepared to limit its actions to marching, speaking, and occupying several key public squares (Place des Martyrs, Place du 1er Mai), he would not react. Nor would he make concessions. His gamble was that the public would tire of the spectacle and that the FIS would have to end its "unlimited" strike with little to show for it. Meanwhile, he would proceed with the parliamentary elections, with or without the FIS. At most, the police and security forces might harass the strikers, but there should be no bloodshed—no repeat of October 1988.

Nezzar, by contrast, saw the strike as a threat to the state. If the apparent vacuum of power was not filled by the state, the FIS would win the battle by default. He believed Hamrouche was soft-headed in allowing things to drift and Chadli was too weak to provide a counterweight. All three players—Hamrouche, the FIS, and Chadli—were presumably seen by Nezzar and his supporters in the military as a threat to order and to the state. One by one, each would be dealt with.

The FIS leadership was neither perceptive nor well organized as it launched its bid for power through mass action. Taken literally, it appeared to be calling for the overthrow of the regime, which was not a subtle message and was bound to alarm all of the non-Islamist forces. As the strike went on, some FIS spokesmen began to threaten *jihad* if their demands for annulling the electoral law and holding early presidential elections were not met. Madani, eager for power but also more of a politician than some of his colleagues, was in frequent touch with regime figures, including Hamrouche, and agreed not to resort to violence. In return, he was told that the FIS would not be dispersed by force as long as it limited its activity to peaceful protest and the occupation of four designated squares in the city.

On June 1 or 2, as the strike was about to enter its second week, the military apparently persuaded the president to declare a state of siege and dismiss Hamrouche. As soon as Hamrouche learned of the decision to declare the state of siege, he submitted his resignation. On the night of June 4–5, by which time the number of strikers was actually declining, the army moved in to clear the squares by force.[44] Dozens were killed in a small-scale version of the October 1988 events. But Madani was still eager to portray the strike as a victory, and initially declared that the state of siege was not directed at the FIS. In fact, he seemed pleased with Hamrouche's departure and the offer of early presidential elections. The new prime minister, Sid Ahmed Ghozali, promised to organize free and fair elections with a new electoral law, which was also something of a victory for the FIS.[45]

Some in the FIS seemed to disagree with Madani's leadership. Several members of the Consultative Council of the FIS had criticized the conduct of the strike and had even issued a communiqué that Madani had denounced. Some of Ben Hadj's rhetoric seemed considerably more extreme than Madani's.[46] So the crisis unfolded with a divided government on one side and a divided Islamist opposition on the other. Even if there had been a modicum of good will, and there really was not much evidence of it, such fissures would have made it difficult to find a compromise solution.[47]

The new prime minister persuaded the FIS to call off its strike by promising fair parliamentary elections by the end of the year. But the FIS was on notice from the military that it would have to show exemplary restraint if it was to survive as a party. In the weeks following the strike, the army and police moved to disarm paramilitary groups and to strictly control the activity of the FIS. Instead of preparing to share power with the FIS at the expense of the government, the military was making it difficult for the FIS to operate at all. On June 30 Madani and Ben Hadj, along with a number of other FIS leaders, were arrested. But Ghozali did not ban the FIS. Instead, he allowed it to be restructured under the effective leadership of Abdelkader Hachani and Mohammed Said, leaders of the so-called Algerianist wing of the FIS.[48]

Toward Elections

It was not clear what lessons anyone could legitimately draw from the May-June strike and its aftermath. The FIS had shown its strength, but also its divisions. It had brought down a government, with the help of the army, but not the regime that was its target. And its most authoritative leaders were in prison.

President Chadli had survived, but not by showing leadership. Instead, he had initially given his tacit support to Hamrouche, and then had ceded to the military. Clearly the army and the FIS were the most powerful forces in the country, and it was not apparent how the new prime minister, Ghozali, intended to navigate between the two.[49]

By fall the National Assembly was again debating the election law. This version was somewhat less unfair to the FIS, but it maintained the French-style two-round majority ballot, which tended to enhance the chances of the largest party and to discourage small ones. Yet those who voted for the law were mostly FLN stalwarts who could not plausibly be accused of wanting to see an Islamist victory. The prime minister had apparently favored proportional representation at one time, but he had ceded to the assembly's views. It was as if no one was thinking realistically about what would happen in the upcoming elections. And yet the elections were the focus of a great deal of activity by many political parties, including Ait Ahmed's FFS, which this time decided to participate.

The FIS withheld its decision on whether it would participate until the last moment. It had demanded freedom for its imprisoned leaders, but the regime was unresponsive. Meanwhile, Hachani and his colleagues were rebuilding the party and were doing so quite effectively.[50] The FIS was still the primary vehicle for channeling discontent and was not hesitant to show its armed strength on occasion. On the Tunisian border in early December, armed men associated with the FIS attacked a military outpost at Guemmar and killed a number of soldiers.

The prime minister, aware of how unpopular the FLN had become, tried to encourage a number of independent candidates to run, presumably hoping that they would form a bloc in any future parliament that would be loyal to him. Some in the regime apparently believed that the vote would divide three ways—one-third for the FIS, one-third for the FLN, and one-third for independents and others, such as the FFS.

Elections were held December 26, 1991.[51] The FIS participated, along with many other parties. Compared to the municipal elections, the turnout was lower, as was the vote for the FIS. Still, the FIS received 3.26 million votes, about twice the number cast for FLN candidates. Of all eligible voters, only one-fourth had voted for FIS candidates; but of actual voters, 47 percent had done so. With that vote, the FIS was far ahead at the end of round one, with 188 seats out of the 232 decided, and with a good chance to win many more in the next round. The FFS, with less than one-third the vote of the FLN, had actually won more seats, because its voters were concentrated in the Kabylia area. Only three independents were elected in the first round.[52]

Several points need to be stressed about the election. The electoral system chosen was blatantly unfair.[53] Had the FLN won instead of the FIS, no one would have viewed it as a fair election, since the system was designed to overrepresent the largest party. If proportional representation had been used, turnout would have probably been a bit higher and the FIS might have won some 30 percent of the seats, with the rest going to an array of other parties and independents. No one would have been able to govern without forming a coalition with other parties. The stage might have been set for an important stage in de-mocratization, one in which it might have become clear that there could not be a single winner and that compromise was inevitable for government to work. Not choosing a proportional representation system of voting was one of the worst decisions made by the government.[54]

There were other problems with the conduct of the elections. In many municipalities where the FIS was in control, non-FIS supporters had trouble getting their voting cards. There were nearly one million blank or spoiled ballots, about three times the number in 1990. Vote by procuration was still allowed, although on a more limited basis than in 1990, so that many men ended up voting for the women in their family, with or without their consent. Still, with all these flaws, the election showed that the FIS was the single strongest political movement in the country. That was the reality that both the regime and its opponents now had to deal with.

The Cancellation of the Elections

In June 1991 the military had used the FIS strike to remove Ham-rouche and to arrest the FIS leaders. The December elections had a similar result. This time the army stepped in to persuade Chadli to resign, then canceled the second round of elections and banned the FIS.[55] It is easy to see that this was a travesty by any democratic yardstick. But it is also easy to understand that many ordinary Alge-rians were pleased with the outcome. Chadli was widely disliked, and the FIS was feared by many, especially the emerging middle class, educated women, secularists, Berbers, the few committed democrats, and intellectuals. For these latter, a FIS victory might well have spelled disaster or civil war. Secularists were quick to note that Hitler had come to power in a democratic election in 1933, but had never held another election. The same thing, they claimed, might have happened if the FIS had come to power.

The army's motives in intervening are apparent on one level.[56] They were protecting their institutional prerogatives, throwing over an un-popular president in order to survive. The senior officers were pro-tecting a comfortable way of life as well, since many had gotten rich from power. But it is unfair to dismiss nationalist sentiment as a mo-tive. Many in the military had fought for Algeria's independence and genuinely felt that they had a legitimate role to play in the political life of the country. The FIS was a threat to all that they had fought for and, like the Turkish military, they would not stand by and watch the principles of the state be trampled. This was not like the Shah's regime, where the generals ran for their Swiss bank accounts as soon as it was clear that Ayatollah Khomeini was going to return. The Algerian generals were prepared to fight—for their lives, their families, their privileges, but also for the country.

Many have asked if the military might not have been wiser to allow the second round of elections to take place and then put the FIS-dominated parliament on notice that it should be careful not to tamper with the constitution or cross the line to political violence. If Chadli and the generals had stuck together, such a strategy might have worked, and the FIS would either have had to accept a strong position in a weak institution—a bit like running the municipal councils—or provoking a coup by threatening the constitutional order. But the flaw in this scenario was precisely that Chadli and the military were not on the same wavelength. Indeed, many suspected that Chadli was about to make a deal with the FIS.[57] If he could remain president, they could run the parliament and he would oust the hard-line generals. So, once again, divisions within the regime undermined one possible strategy that might have postponed, if not entirely avoided, a showdown. Instead, the army stepped in and removed both Chadli and the FIS.[58]

While most critics have focused on the injustice of canceling the elections in mid-course, the greater error was to hold them at all under rules that could only produce a distorted—and therefore heavily contested—outcome. Elections per se were not the problem; winner-take-all rules were. Once that decision was made, the election was bound to be divisive rather than a step toward genuine sharing of power based on relative popular support. In the end, no one could trump the army's power, but the question immediately arose of how to get out of the crisis that was consuming the country. The next several years showed that the military was less adept at ending the crisis than they were at putting an end to Algeria's first fling with democracy.

5

Reversion or Interlude?

THE CANCELLATION of Algeria's flawed parliamentary election in January 1992 represented a major watershed in Algerian politics. But what would lie on the other side of that divide? Apologists for the new order—a regime clearly dominated by military officers—saw the army as the savior of the country, putting an end to a reckless experiment that might have allowed Islamist fascists to come to power by means of democratic elections that would never be repeated. One need not accept such a selfless view of the motives of the Algerian military to acknowledge that there was some risk that the Islamic Salvation Front (*Front Islamique du Salut*, FIS), had it really gotten its hands on the instruments of power, would have been harshly authoritarian and intolerant of those who disagreed with it. By all evidence, the majority of Algerians were not solidly in the FIS camp, despite the election results.

Still, it is hard to credit the military with democratic inclinations as it stepped in to end Algeria's first, troubled experiment with competitive elections. What comes through most clearly in the comments of Algeria's post-1992 rulers is a deep resentment at the FIS for calling into question their nationalism and patriotism. After all, many of those who were part of the governing structure had fought hard, at great risk, for Algeria's independence. To be told by a new generation that this sacrifice counted for nothing, that their central claim to legitimacy was no longer valid, was not just a threat to privilege. It was also a deeply felt insult. By labeling many of the generals as part of the *Hizb Fransa*, the French Party, the FIS was questioning the nationalism of men who felt they had nothing to answer for in that regard.

As an opposition party, the FIS had done remarkably well in its short lifetime in mobilizing and channeling discontent. It had won municipal elections with an impressive vote in 1990. It had succeeded in creating conditions that toppled one prime minister, Mouloud Hamrouche, and had even put an end to the regime of Chadli Benjedid. But the FIS had vastly misread its power vis-à-vis the military. Instead of trying to win over the military as a potential partner, as Hassan Turabi did in the Sudan, it threatened to eliminate the top generals when it came to power. Not surprisingly, the military establishment saw the danger to itself and its corporate interests and it fought back with the means at its disposal. The FIS could flood the streets with demonstrators, but the military had the tanks. Unless the FIS could force a split in the military, as Ayatollah Ruhollah Khomeini had done in Iran in 1979, there was little doubt about the outcome of any armed confrontation. And the military did not split, at least not at the senior level.

When military establishments intervene in politics, they usually seem to have little idea of how they will proceed. They know what they want to avoid, but not how to govern or how to return to the barracks without once again losing control. True, the Algerian military had long been the real power behind the scenes, but there is still a difference between being puppet master and being on stage. So, the post-Benjedid era did not start with a master plan, but rather with a few simple precepts.

First, the FIS would be banned and its leaders arrested or neutralized. It was simply too dangerous to let the FIS continue to operate freely. Within months, the FIS had been declared illegal. Abdelkader Hachani was arrested, as were a number of other leaders. This did not mean, of course, that the Islamist challenge disappeared, or that the social category that had thrown its support to the FIS could be safely ignored. But the FIS leaders were no longer free to agitate and mobilize opinion.

The next step was to find a transitional authority to front for the military. The generals were not ready to seize power in their own names. In fact, they had almost a scholastic sense of laying down timetables and rules and carrying on consultations, all of which gave the impression that Algeria would soon return to a semidemocratic order, but this time with more discipline and less violence. The top-down view of political restructuring left little room for the feelings or interests of the masses of the population. In that sense, the military was thoroughly predictable. But in other ways they were capable of surprises.

One of the first surprises was the announcement of a High State Council that would govern for a transitional period of two years, to the end of 1993, the head of which would be veteran nationalist Mohammed Boudiaf. Boudiaf was a surprising choice. He was one of the genuine fathers of the revolution. His nationalist credentials were impeccable. He had been arrested by the French in October 1956, along with Ben Bella and Ait Ahmed, and at independence had broken with the new government and gone into exile. He had spent most of the previous thirty years in Morocco. Now in his seventies, he agreed to return to serve as interim president. Ordinary Algerians may not have had a clear idea of who he was, but at least he was not associated with any of the regimes of the previous thirty years. Possibly he would bring fresh hope to the disillusioned younger generation.

Boudiaf turned out to be a surprisingly dynamic leader. He agreed with the military's ban on the FIS, but he also wanted to have little to do with the National Liberation Front (*Front de Libération Nationale*, FLN). Instead, he seemed determined to build a new political movement that would be responsive to his blend of populism and nationalism, untainted by the corruption of recent years. He had the unusual habit for an Algerian politician of actually talking to the people, and doing so in their own language—the Arabic of everyday life, not the formal, classical language that was so often used in public. Many Algerians responded positively to this genuinely popular touch.

Boudiaf had little time to make his imprint on Algeria. In June 1992, while speaking in Annaba, he reflected on mortality, uttered the word "Islam," and at that moment a bullet ended his life. One of his security guards was arrested and charged with the assassination. But on whose behalf? This has remained a mystery. Asking Algerians the question "Who killed Boudiaf?" is like a Rorschach test. Some will answer the Islamists, pointing to the alleged Islamist sympathies of the assassin. Others are convinced that the military, fearful that Boudiaf was about to open the dossiers on corruption, decided to eliminate him. Others point the finger at elements in the FLN, who saw him undermining their positions. No conclusive evidence has ever been presented, although the assassin was imprisoned. Those in the military who ought to know point out that they would hardly have let the killer live if they had ordered the execution. But such arguments do little to convince those with other views. The Boudiaf affair will remain a source of controversy for some time.

Could Boudiaf have made a difference? Perhaps. He seemed to be "clean" and he seemed to have the beginnings of a popular following, especially among the young. But his popularity may have been greater after his death than during his brief moment on the stage of Algeria's suspicion-ridden politics. At best Boudiaf was a politician who knew how to speak to the people; he was a populist more than a democrat.

What came after Boudiaf resembled bureaucrats seeking to solve Algeria's crisis by the dual strategy of repression and economic reform. It was not a happy time. The High State Council continued to wield power, but a new prime minister, Belaid Abdesselam, was appointed and charged with tackling the economic problems of the country. Abdesselam had been the architect of Algeria's policy of concentrating on heavy industry in the late 1970s. He was intelligent, experienced, a Kabyle, and quite outspoken about the errors of the Benjedid era.[1] He had a good reputation for personal integrity. He had fought corruption when in office and he had remained in Algeria, living modestly, after Chadli had ousted him from the cabinet after Boumediene's death. But Abdesselam had no popular base and depended entirely on the military. And the economic problems he had to confront were formidable. Among other challenges, the repayment on the debt in the coming years was bound to absorb almost all of Algeria's export earnings, leaving nothing for new investment.

Something had to be done. In the international climate of the day, with emphasis on market economies and privatization, Abdesselam seemed a strange choice. He was adamantly opposed to debt rescheduling, since it would require major economic reforms, and he simply did not believe that Algeria was ready to shift to an export-oriented industrial strategy.[2]

1993 turned out to be a terrible year for Algeria. Not only was the economy in deep trouble and the government without legitimacy in the eyes of the population, but also the security situation took a dramatic turn for the worse.[3] As many had anticipated, the FIS would not just fade away after the arrest of its leaders and its banning. Instead, it became radicalized and splintered, making it a less credible political actor but a more formidable armed opponent. One wing of the FIS seemed intent on emulating the FLN in its days of glory fighting the

French. It took to the hills, set up armed groups (*maquis*) in the countryside, tried to build political networks there, and occasionally carried out armed actions against the regime and its supporters. This strand of radical Islam took the name of the Armed Islamic Movement (*Mouvement Islamique Armé*, MIA), later the Armed Islamic Group (*Armée Islamique du Salut*, AIS). It acknowledged its ties to the FIS leadership.

Beginning in 1993, but more noted in later years, a number of small armed gangs began to appear, especially around Algiers. These groups were known as the Armed Islamic Groups (*Groupes Islamiques Armés*, GIA). They recruited from the ranks of the marginalized, sometimes criminal elements in Algiers' sprawling suburban slums. Usually the bands were made up of young men who knew each other, clustered around a self-appointed "emir." In many ways, they seemed to be little more than gangs, but with the extra zeal that may have come from fighting in a religiously sanctioned campaign against a regime that was considered to be illegitimate and non-Muslim. No one seemed to have control over all these groups, and many suspected that the regime had penetrated some of them and manipulated their activities. But they were lethal, whatever they may or may not have represented in the larger society. They targeted intellectuals, women, journalists, as well as regime figures—and each other.[4]

As the violence grew in 1993 and 1994, most Algerians simply tried to stay out of the way. There were occasional demonstrations calling for civil peace, but there was no sign that either the regime or the armed Islamists had won the battle for public support. The masses, in whose name all this violence was being carried out, remained remarkably silent. The death toll was astonishing. From 1992 to 1998 about 200 Algerians each week lost their lives in this form of violence, only some of it politically motivated. In all, more than 75,000 died and many more were wounded. The killing was often of the most intimate and grisly kind, the kind that perhaps only happens in civil wars where the enemy has to be totally demonized in order to legitimize the killing.[5] No one could be sure of whether the regime or the Islamists were responsible for most of the deaths. Such was the state of mind of many Algerians that they often blamed one when the other seemed more obviously involved. But the lack of evidence, or contrary evidence, was often seen as proof of the diabolical workings of either the regime or the Islamists. Charges of terrorism and atrocity were heard on both sides. By early 1997, however, it seemed clear that some groups in the GIA were engaged in the wholesale slaughter of civilians, without any explicit political agenda, and even the FIS leaders in exile were regularly condemning their actions.

The regime kept promising that the fight against terrorism was proceeding, and that it would all be over soon. But the military had clearly been caught off guard. They were not prepared to fight a guerrilla war against their own people. They were not trained for it, they did not have the equipment, and they did not have special units available. By 1995, when the regime began to get the upper hand, the fight seemed to be conducted more professionally, but no less brutally. Aircraft and napalm were regularly used, and accusations of torture and extrajudicial killing were widespread. That this was happening in Algeria, after all that Algeria had gone through to win its independence, was stunning and demoralizing.[6]

Economic Reforms

While the security situation was deteriorating from 1992 on, it was hard to be optimistic about the economy. Indeed, Abdesselam was not long in his job. He was replaced in September 1993 by a member of the High State Council and former diplomat, Redha Malek. Facing the impossibility of meeting Algeria's debt payments, Malek accepted the inevitability of debt rescheduling and all that went with this. Algeria was pressed by the International Monetary Fund (IMF) to carry out a package of reforms—deficit reduction, exchange rate reform, interest rate adjustments, reduction of subsidies—in order to get the clean bill of health that would open the way for debt relief.[7]

Malek had good contacts in Paris and Washington, where he had served as ambassador, and with the help of an able economic team, he quickly managed to convince the IMF to endorse Algeria's reform program. Debt relief was forthcoming, and by 1994–95 Algeria was past the worst of the economic crisis. Modest positive economic growth took place in both 1995 and 1996, helped by the debt relief, abundant rain, and a higher-than-expected price for oil.

By mid-1996 Algeria reached the next difficult step in economic reform, the privatization of state-owned enterprises. The regime seemed reluctant to move quickly with privatization, perhaps worrying that one of its few bases of support—the trade unions—would protest any forced layoffs or wage reductions. Indeed, there was ample reason to worry about declining wages. According to the IMF, real wages dropped by 35 percent from 1993 to 1996, a period when many macroeconomic reforms were being successfully carried out.[8]

Political Developments

As the transitional period neared its ostensible end in late 1993, it became clear that Algeria had a long way to go before normal politics could be resumed. But rather than simply extend the transitional period indefinitely, the regime decided to name a new figure to head the country, General Liamine Zeroual, most recently the minister of defense.[9]

Little was known about Zeroual's political stance. He had broken with Benjedid over reorganization of the military and had been sent abroad as an ambassador in the late 1980s. During his brief stint as minister of defense, he had reportedly been in touch with the FIS leadership in prison, giving rise to the view that he might favor dialogue (*dialoguiste*) rather than "eradication" (*eradicateur*), to use the jargon of the time. Whatever his views, it was clear that he did not enjoy personal legitimacy. He was president merely because the military establishment had decided to back him, not because of broad popular support. In this sense, he began his tenure like Chadli Benjedid.

The inner circle around Zeroual consisted of a number of other generals—Mohammed Betchine, Mohammed Lamari, Tewfik Mediène, and Abbas Gheziel were the most frequently cited.[10] Civilian figures rounded out the cabinet and played important roles in the economic sector, but security and political matters seemed to be in the hands of the generals. Among them, Lamari and Gheziel had the reputation of being strongly anti-Islamist (the most visible eradicators) and Betchine presented himself as more moderate. Any major move seemed to require consensus among these top figures in the regime.

The political question during much of 1994 and early 1995 was whether some sort of deal could be reached between the FIS and the Zeroual regime that would bring Algeria's crisis to an end. Any such agreement would presumably have to allow the FIS to reconstitute itself as a legal party on the one hand, and on the other the FIS would have to denounce the use of violence by the radical Islamists and demonstrate that it was using its influence to end the activities of the armed groups. While easy to describe, this outcome was extremely difficult to negotiate. First, the hard-liners on each side were unwilling to accept the basic premises of the deal. For the eradicators, nothing should be done to rehabilitate the FIS. The issue would be settled by force. It was a security issue, not a political one.

On the FIS side, the demand that the FIS denounce Islamist violence was met by hard-liners with the assertion that it was the regime that was responsible for the violence. It had canceled the elections, depriving Algerians of the right to choose their representatives. The FIS was only responding to the violence of the regime. A solution had to start with the military's acknowledgment that it was in the wrong for intervening in politics. The FIS leaders should be released, the parliamentary elections should be respected, and the army should return to the barracks and purge itself of those responsible for the coup.

On the face of it, there seemed to be little chance for common ground between the hard-liners. The more moderate elements in each camp would most likely find it difficult to make the necessary compromises because of their dependence on their own hard-liners for support.[11] Still, despite the odds, and in the highly unequal circumstance of the regime negotiating with FIS leaders in prison, Zeroual and his associates pursued a dual strategy for about eighteen months of periodic talking, combined with intensive security measures designed to crush the armed Islamist elements. The FIS responded by talking, while simultaneously urging the armed elements to keep up the struggle.[12]

Meanwhile, the political landscape had begun to shift among the legal political parties. The FLN, now under the somewhat shaky leadership of both Mehri and Hamrouche, became an opposition party, regularly criticizing the government, but also strongly condemning all acts of violence. As an opposition party, the FLN might be able to restore some of its tarnished reputation, while also holding out the promise that its experience could be useful in rebuilding the governing structures of the country whenever the transitional period of military rule came to an end. Among its most controversial positions was its support for the release of the FIS leaders in return for their pledge to condemn violence and respect the constitution. By contrast, the General Union of Algerian Workers (*Union Générale des Travailleurs Algériens*, UGTA), formerly aligned with the FLN, remaining hostile to the FIS and the idea of eventual accommodation with the Islamists.

The other political movement that had garnered significant votes in 1991 was the Socalist Forces Front (*Front des Forces Socialistes*, FFS), and it too called for the release of the FIS leaders. Since the FFS was a rather secular party and its Berber supporters were not keen on the FIS political agenda of Arabization and Islamization, the position of the FFS might seem anomalous. But Ait Ahmed, its leader, was convinced that the only way to tame Islam as a political force was to give it some political expression. He came down squarely in the camp of the dialoguistes, while Said Saadi, the younger Berber leader of the Rally for Culture and Democracy (*Rassemblement pour la Culture et la Démocratie*, RCD), was resolutely aligned with the eradicators.

Even on the extreme left there was a split between those willing to talk to the FIS and those opposed. The Communists were against, and the Trotskyists, led by a dynamic woman, Louissa Hanoun, were in favor of dialogue.[13] Neither had much popular following.

While the regime carried on its dialogue with the FIS in secret, some of the opposition parties—notably the Mehri wing of the FLN, the FFS, Ben Bella's party, and the overseas leadership of the FIS— met under the auspices of the Sant'Egidio community of Catholic laymen in Rome to try to work out a platform for reconciliation. To the surprise of many, this group of old adversaries managed to produce a common set of principles in January 1995.

The Sant'Egidio Platform

The essential points of the Sant'Egidio platform, which was designed to serve as a basis for negotiations with the regime and the return to multiparty elections, were the following:[14]

—Respect for human rights, support for contested elections, popular sovereignty, the rule of law, and the constitution of 1989.

—Rejection of violence as a way of gaining or maintaining power; opposition to dictatorship of any kind; and the return of the army to the barracks.

—Recognition that the Algerian personality is made up of Arabism, Islam, and "amazighité" (Berber cultural identity) and that both Arabic and Berber are national languages that should be promoted.

—Before negotiations begin, the FIS leaders should be released and all political parties should resume their activities.

—Press freedom should be restored; torture should cease, along with extrajudicial killings; and all political prisoners should be released.

—Attacks on civilians and foreigners should be condemned.

The Sant'Egidio platform attracted considerable attention in Algeria and Europe. It was quickly reported that the FIS leaders in Algiers, namely Madani and Ben Hadj, had both approved the document. In fact, they were able to communicate quite freely from their confinement, and the FLN leader, Abdelhamid Mehri, had been allowed to visit them just before the Sant'Egidio meetings. This led many to believe that the regime was easing up on the FIS and that in return it was beginning to moderate its position.

The regime's reaction to Sant'Egidio, however, seemed to indicate that Zeroual and his associates were unhappy with the outcome. The platform was rejected in principle and in detail by the regime. The ostensible reason was that it had been worked out under foreign auspices and therefore was unacceptable from the outset. But many of the points in the platform actually mirrored the regime's own language—the support for elections, for "alternance," or the change of government by elections, condemnation of violence, respect for the constitution, and so forth.

Zeroual's reaction to the platform showed a certain lack of political imagination. It would have been easy to question the auspices of Sant'Egidio as unnecessary; to raise questions about the sincerity of the FIS at a time when its followers were carrying out armed attacks and calling for the overthrow of the regime; and to indicate the many points on which the opposition was adopting the language of the regime itself. But instead Zeroual simply turned his back on Sant'Egidio without ever providing a convincing explanation for his action. Many suspected deep disagreements within the regime.

Still, the secret talks continued, and by mid-1995 there were many rumors that a deal was about to be announced. Madani was believed to have signed a paper denouncing political violence and calling for a peaceful solution to the conflict. But he insisted that Ben Hadj associate himself with it for it to become an official FIS position, and he also wanted a chance to meet with the members of the party's Consultative Council, some of whom had earlier been released from prison, in order to sound out the more radical groups about the possibility of a cease-fire.[15]

This chance for a political agreement to end the crisis collapsed suddenly in mid-1995. Ben Hadj refused to associate himself with the call for an end to violence, perhaps aware from his contacts that the GIA was in no mood to stop fighting just because the FIS leaders appealed for a truce. By now the FIS had little influence over the GIA, if it ever did. This posed a problem for both the regime and the FIS. For the regime, the only motivation for dealing with the FIS was to enlist its support in bringing the violence to an end. If it would not, or could not, it was worthless. For the FIS, if the GIA would not stop fighting, the FIS might look like it was in collusion with the regime if it called for a truce, and its own legitimacy might erode. Either it would look weak or like a collaborator in the eyes of the young militants. Neither posture would help it recover its once unassailable position of premier opposition movement. So, on both sides, there were reasons for the deal not to work. And it did not.

In early July Zeroual announced the failure of the talks with the FIS, putting all the blame on Madani and Ben Hadj. The FIS leaders were then transferred to solitary confinement and over the next two years no more was heard of them or of secret talks between the regime and the FIS.[16] Instead, Zeroual set about reconstructing political institutions without the FIS, while giving carte blanche to the military to eliminate the armed groups.

Presidential Elections

The centerpiece of Zeroual's strategy was to hold a series of elections to restore a semblance of legitimacy. The first would be presidential elections in November 1995. The FIS would not be allowed to participate, but candidates from other parties could. In the end, four candidates were judged to have collected enough signatures nationwide to qualify. One was Zeroual himself; the others were Mahfoud Nahnah, head of the legal Islamist party Hamas; Said Saadi, head of the RCD; and Noureddine Boukrouh, an intellectual Islamist of the Malek Bennabi school, respected but with little following.

The fact that the FIS was not allowed to participate was the most obvious limitation on the democratic nature of the election. But otherwise it was surprisingly free. There was a real campaign, although the candidates running against Zeroual complained that they were not given much time on television or radio. Still, this was a contested election, a rarity in the Arab world, and the elections were monitored by the parties and by a small number of international observers.

Despite the appalling security conditions in the country generally, the period of the election was remarkably calm. The exact count has been a matter of dispute, but virtually everyone agrees that turnout was very high. The official figure put the number at 12 million voters out of 16 million registered voters, or 75 percent participation. Of those who voted, the official figures showed that about 61 percent voted for Zeroual, 25 percent for Nahnah, 9 percent for Saadi, and 4 percent for Boukrouh. Even if the numbers were off by a bit, no one doubted that Zeroual had won more votes than anyone else. It was a significant, but not overwhelming, victory, carried out in reasonably honest conditions. For a brief moment, it brought hope to many Algerians who thought that Zeroual would now be able to move toward a solution of the crisis.

As president, Zeroual named a new government made up of young technocrats. He seemed to be counting on them to continue the economic reform program while he and his inner circle would carry out the rebuilding of political institutions and the fight against the armed Islamists. What seemed missing in all this was a credible political strategy for healing Algeria's wounds. The regime used all the right words—democracy, human rights, pluralism, consultation, free elections, and popular sovereignty. But it seemed obsessed with maintaining tight control from the top down over the political process.[17] During most of 1996 Zeroual squandered much of the goodwill he had gained with the presidential election in a series of formalistic "consultations" with various political groups. Without exception, those consulted felt that their voices had barely been heard, let alone listened to.

New Institutions

The regime seems to have had in mind a scenario of reconstituting political institutions and was mostly going through the motions in talking to the parties. Early on, the presidency produced a proposal for constitutional reform and for new elections and invited a wide array of political figures to consult with the president. Endless meetings were held. Counterproposals were offered by many political figures, and finally the regime came forth with a draft of a new constitution that was presumably the result of the consultations. It bore a remarkable resemblance to the original document drafted at the presidency. In short, for all the consultation that had taken place, little had changed in the regime's plan.[18]

The draft constitution seemed designed to ensure that the events of 1991 could not happen again. Several positive reforms were included, such as a provision for a limit of two presidential terms of five years each. In addition, the regime was on record as supporting a new electoral law that would use proportional representation to select the next parliament, thus reflecting the actual distribution of political sentiment in the country better than the previous winner-take-all majority system.

The constitutional reforms also included significant measures to strengthen the hand of the president. A second parliamentary chamber would be formed that would be partly elected and partly appointed. It would have the power to veto legislation passed by the lower house. In addition, the president would have important emergency powers. And he retained the right, as under the 1989 constitution, to name and replace the head of government. The Constitutional Council would continue to exist to rule on the constitutionality of laws.

The text of the new constitution was submitted to a referendum in November 1996. A number of the political parties called for abstentions or boycotts. In any case, the public hardly seemed interested in the arcane details of the constitutional text. Turnout was reported by journalists to be relatively low, but there were no monitors and therefore little way of verifying the figures produced by the regime. Those numbers were amazing. Supposedly more people voted in the referendum than in the presidential election of the previous year—some 80 percent—and of those about 80 percent voted in favor of the new constitution. Suffice it to say that few Algerian commentators believed the figures. Whatever the case, Algeria had a new, presidentially centered constitution, but the situation in the country was as bad as ever.

Early 1997 was a terrible time in Algeria. For several years, Ramadan, the month of fasting, had been a period of intensified violence. This was again the case in 1997. In the area around Algiers in particular, the GIA carried out an appalling series of murders. The regime seemed unwilling or unable to do anything to halt the carnage. Soon after Ramadan ended, however, the military launched a brutal counteroffensive designed to crush the GIA before the holding of parliamentary elections in June 1997. The impending elections, however, seemed to strengthen the determination of the Islamist extremists to show their presence.

As elections approached, Algeria was a Janus-like country. In some areas, the regime seemed absent, leaving the GIA able to strike in villages and along the roads, with terrible results. The inability—or unwillingness—of the state to provide basic security was shocking.

The other face of Algeria was that of a country proceeding with the organization of elections, with considerable technical mastery. A UN mission that visited the country in the spring came away quite impressed with the arrangements being made. Slowly but surely, parties seemed to be readying themselves to participate in an electoral process about which they presumably harbored grave doubts.

In the midst of these preparations for elections, the Constitutional Council showed a streak of independence by finding that the electoral law violated the constitution by saying that parties could not base themselves on Islam. Since the constitution stated that Islam was the religion of the state and an integral part of the Algerian character, a party could not be prohibited from referring to Islam as a part of its political platform. The only thing that it could not do was to claim that it was the sole representative of Islam (or Arabism or Berber culture, since these were attributes of the entire people). This gave something of a lift to the hopes of Hamas, the party best placed to win the support of former FIS voters.[19] Hamas (the Movement for Islamic Society) and Nahda both agreed to remove the word "Islam" from their names. Hamas became the Movement for a Peaceful Society (*Mouvement pour une Société de Paix*, MSP).

The FFS, which had strongly disapproved of the entire consultative process and the constitutional referendum, nonetheless decided to participate in the elections. One of the losers in the game, however, was the FLN. Zeroual had acted to ensure that the reformers—Mehri and Hamrouche—would be pushed aside in early 1996, but even the newly tamed FLN was not to the president's liking. So a new party was formed. It was originally to have been led by Abdelhak Benhamouda, the experienced head of the UGTA, the labor union, but he was assassinated, supposedly by an Islamist group, in early 1997. The party, named the National Democratic Rally (RND), was nonetheless established, and was immediately labeled the regime's party.

The Parliamentary Elections of 1997

The cancellation of the second round of parliamentary elections in 1992 was a central moment in Algeria's unfolding crisis. Whatever one thought of the wisdom of that act, it left the cloud of illegitimacy over subsequent governments. Zeroual's election in November 1995, followed by constitutional changes, a new electoral law, and then parliamentary elections, were events meant to reestablish the legitimate institutions of the state. But legitimacy is a fuzzy notion, very much in the eye of the beholder, and therefore it mattered a great deal whether Algerian voters actually saw these new institutions as providing channels for addressing their concerns. The answer to this question was not obvious and would probably be long in coming, but early assessments tended to be pessimistic.[20]

What can be said with some certainty is that the regime counted heavily on the parliamentary elections, but it was not prepared to risk an outcome similar to that of 1991–92. One step toward assuring an outcome acceptable to the regime was the banning of the FIS and obliging Hamas and Nahda to drop the word "Islam" from their names. In addition, proportional representation by willaya was adopted, which ensured that no single party would sweep the elections. In addition, the regime, despite its professed neutrality, lent support to the RND in a variety of ways, including disproportionate time on state television for RND candidates, use of government vehicles for campaigning, and other controversial measures. Still, the 1997 election was contested; a large number of parties fielded candidates throughout the country; and the major parties had a chance to present their points of view. By regional standards, this was a reasonably competitive election, even if there was little doubt that the regime would remain in control, since the parliament, whatever the outcome, was a relatively weak institution.

When the votes were counted June 5, the results were immediately criticized by many, but not always on fair grounds. For example, about two-thirds of all registered voters actually cast their ballots, which some saw as a low turnout, although it was considerably higher than in 1991. More pointedly, some wondered how a party like the RND, created so recently, could have won 156 of 380 seats, capturing some 32 percent of the vote. While this outcome was no doubt somewhat inflated, it is not implausible to think that many people simply voted for the regime in the hope that it could find a solution to the country's problems.

Nearly all the major opposition parties filed complaints about the elections, but none that actually won seats refused to participate in the new parliament. The MSP (the former Hamas) came in second with 69 seats; the FLN won 62; the other Islamist party, Nahda, won 34; the FFS and RCD, the two predominantly Berber parties, won 20 and 19 respectively, Independents (some aligned with the MSP) won 11, the Trotskyists won 4, and 5 other seats went to small parties. A fairly large number of votes were also cast for small parties that failed to win any seats at all. (See Chapter 9 for a more detailed analysis of the election.)

The net result of the election was the creation of a coalition government based on the RND, the FLN, and the MSP. Ministerial portfolios were doled out roughly according to party strength within the parliament; Prime Minister Ahmed Ouyahia, loyal to Zeroual but not very popular, was reappointed by the president, and many immediately concluded that nothing had really changed. Indeed, the pattern of killings in rural areas continued apace, along with occasional terrorist bombings in urban areas.

Shortly after the election, there were also hints of change. The FIS leader, Abdelkader Hachani, who had led the party to victory in 1991, was put on trial, given a five-year sentence (he had been held in prison without trial for more than five years), and immediately released. Soon thereafter, in mid-July 1997, with little forewarning, Zeroual removed his hard-line head of the police (*gendarmerie*), Abbas Gheziel, and the leader of the FIS, Abbassi Madani, was released from prison, shortly to be placed under house arrest for allegedly violating terms of his release. Whether these were signs of a more conciliatory attitude, or greater self-confidence on the part of Zeroual, remained to be seen, but they evoked a positive response from most of the opposition parties in parliament. Slowly, it seemed, political life was evolving in Algeria toward greater acceptance of pluralism. But it would take more elections, and better ones, to convince skeptical Algerians that democracy was more than a slogan.

Unfortunately, Algeria's next try at elections in October 1997, when local and provincial leaders were chosen, was accompanied by widespread accusations of fraud. All major parties except the RND voiced outrage, and demonstrations were called. As 1997 came to an end,

Algeria was still far from being even a limited democracy, but at the same time it had a surprisingly vigorous political opposition, much of it represented in parliament, whose debates were televised live and attracted a considerable following. Also encouraging was the relative freedom of the press. But the continuing violence, and the deep social and economic problems that faced the country, cast a dark shadow over the country.

Conclusions

The Zeroual regime's approach to resolving Algeria's crisis seemed to suffer at crucial moments from insufficient political imagination, a bureaucratic and security-driven view of the world. Algeria throughout its crisis of the past decade has had a paucity of politicians able to forge widely supported compromises. Instead, clans deal with one another outside the public view. What takes place in the public arena is formal and uninspiring. And on the ground, the killing goes on.

Still, one has to acknowledge certain realities based on the developments of the past decade:

—The tenor of Algerian politics has changed in perceptible ways. The early emphasis on a unified people, on a government that claimed to embody that unity and reflected in its institutions, has given way to a discourse dominated by a vision of Algeria as a country made up of several currents, necessitating pluralism and some degree of political competition. One may doubt the sincerity of some who utter these new principles, but the fact that most politicians feel compelled to speak of democracy, human rights, popular sovereignty, and pluralism suggests that they believe the population will respond better to these themes than to messianic calls for unity.

—The army remains an essential part of Algeria's political life. From the beginning, it has been the mainstay of each regime. Other political groupings have fragmented, but the military has never split in the same way. Its coherence and hierarchy have given it staying power, even if it lacks popularity. Those in the FIS who thought it could be brushed aside, seduced, or split misjudged its corporate sense of identity. It will continue to play a role in Algerian politics for the indefinite future. The question is whether that role will be at the expense of other parties or will be more discreet, more in the shadows, similar to the role of the military in Turkey, Chile, or Pakistan.

—Political Islam in one form or another is part of the Algerian scene. The FIS showed that it could command support from several million voters, as did Hamas in 1995 and two legal Islamist parties in the 1997 elections. It is probably fair to conclude that at least one-fourth of the electorate will identify with a credible political movement that is seen to uphold Islamic principles. But the FIS as an organized movement seems to be finished; its place has been taken, at least for the near future, by a much tamer movement that reflects the Muslim Brethren strategy of building Islamic institutions from the ground up rather than seizing power as a prelude to Islamization.

—The two other major currents in Algerian society that show staying power, if not in any pure institutional form, are the nationalists— who identify with the revolution and have been represented by the FLN, the UGTA, and perhaps now the RND and a number of smaller parties; and the democrats, who are also part of the nationalist mainstream but reject the idea of a monopoly of power by any one group and who have worked to introduce ideas of human rights, civil society, the rule of law, and free elections. The FFS is probably the best organized of the parties representing the democrats, but others would associate themselves with this current as well. Together, these two tendencies probably outnumber the Islamist current.

—The bulk of the Algerian population seems suspicious of politics and politicians. The frequent reference to *hogra*, or arrogance, as a major problem with the government, suggests a widespread dislike for those in authority. Algerian slang also portrays the rulers as remote, apart from society—the *nomenklatura, le pouvoir, le serail*. Even in the midst of the most intensive mobilization the country had ever known in 1990–91, a large percentage of Algerians simply did not vote. That could be seen as a sign of apathy, contentment, or, more likely, distrust of all politics.

—Algeria is not about to become an Islamic republic. Neither the Iranian scenario—an Islamist revolution—nor that of Sudan—a military takeover with backing of the Islamists—seem likely in Algeria. Some have argued that a period of *régression féconde* ("fruitful regression") is needed, a period when the Islamists rule and are exposed as having no better answers than the FLN did in its prime. Then, the argument goes, the country will be rid of its utopian projects in the name of nationalism and religion and can turn to the democratic alternative that will allow this pluralistic country to be governed.[21] There is merit in the idea that messianic projects must be discredited if Algeria is ever to have a chance at rule-based democracy, but it is less certain that Islamic messianism can only be tempered by a chance to govern. It may be that those who were most attracted to the Islamic project as a solution to the country's ills will be sobered by the price that Algeria has paid since 1992. Perhaps the high cost to their societies of the Islamic regimes in Iran and Sudan will also be cautionary notes, especially when contrasted with the more successful bids for a role in government by Islamic moderates in Turkey and Malaysia.

Even in the hands of bureaucrats and political amateurs, elections and institutional engineering can have some effect on politics. As improbable as the Zeroual strategy seemed to many at the outset, the elections of 1995 and 1997 suggest that top-down steps toward liberalization and democratization can be carried out, despite opposition protests. Whether this will move Algeria eventually toward sustainable democracy, to say nothing of stability and prosperity, remains to be seen. For the short term, one can be skeptical, but Algeria's crisis has provoked a political reaction that eventually may drive both the regime and its opponents to some form of pact to share power as the only way to end the violence—short of full-scale civil war.

PART TWO

Political Analysis

6

Analyzing Algeria's Political Development

TO UNDERSTAND Algeria's troubled transition away from its authoritarian past since the early 1980s requires both a grounding in the major political events of this era—provided in Part I—and the insights that can be gained by a variety of analytical perspectives. The Algerian case is sufficiently rich and complex that it cannot easily be reduced to a single grand explanatory scheme. Any effort to argue that economics, or class structure, or cultural values can account for all the major moments in Algeria's political trajectory is bound to be artificial. Therefore, in Part II we will look in some depth at the patterns of development and the particular features that seem noteworthy. A series of analytical lenses will be used to examine the data that have been uncovered, and we will try to account for patterns and relationships by drawing on theoretical insights from the social sciences. Culture, social structure, the economy, and political institutions will all be put forward as possible explanations. By consciously comparing the Algerian case to others, we will see if insights can be gained.

First, we need to review in somewhat schematic form the main features of Algeria's recent past and focus attention on those parts of the story that seem to need most careful scrutiny. Then in subsequent chapters different analytical perspectives will be applied.

The Authoritarian Model of Boumediene

Houari Boumediene came close to perfecting a certain kind of authoritarianism. Under his leadership, the institutions of the state, backed by the military and security services, and with the aid of a compliant bureaucracy, struck an implicit bargain with the population.

83

The state would provide security, order, welfare, education, and jobs in return for political passivity, or at least controlled access to the political arena. The state would govern in the name of the people, who were portrayed as having a unitary nature and a common set of interests. Nationalism tinged with features of cultural authenticity, such as Islam and Arabism, would be the main ideological reference point, while legitimacy would be claimed in the name of the revolution and the memory of the one million martyrs who died fighting for Algeria's independence.

From the early 1970s onward, this model was complemented by the availability of substantial oil and gas revenues, which made possible a kind of "rentier" economy. The state collected the rents on oil and gas sales and redistributed them in the form of subsidies—for food, housing, education—and to promote state-controlled industries that would be kept afloat regardless of their profitability. Patronage and clientalism became major features of governance. Under this regime, Algeria enjoyed a large measure of stability and civil peace, albeit with restricted freedom, and the economy grew steadily, largely as a result of rising oil revenues.

Compared to other Middle East authoritarian models, Algeria did not have a single leader like Egypt's Gamal Abd al-Nasser or Turkey's Mustafa Kemal "Ataturk"—(Father of the Turks) to preside over the political system and evoke a degree of loyalty. Instead, it had "the revolution" with its own claims, less personal than Nasser but equally compelling for those who had lived it. But since the entire Algerian political establishment could claim legitimacy from participating in the revolution, there was less hierarchy in the Algerian leadership structures than might be found in Egypt or Turkey, for example.

Algeria also was a bit different from other Middle East regimes of its ilk in that the military made fewer claims on the nation's resources than was true in countries like Syria or Iraq. With the exception of a brief border war with Morocco in 1963, Algeria did not face any significant foreign military threat, and therefore it did not spend vast resources on arms. Its military budget was regularly below 3 percent of gross domestic product (GDP), whereas comparable figures for Syria and Iraq were closer to 10–20 percent of GDP.[1]

Finally, compared with Egypt, Syria, or Turkey, Algeria was well endowed with oil and gas resources; but compared with Iraq, Libya, or the Gulf countries, Algeria had relatively modest resources to meet the needs of a fairly large population. Iran was perhaps the closest model of a country with substantial oil resources, but also a large population, although Iran was somewhat better endowed on a per capita basis than Algeria.[2]

Pressures for Change

Soon after Boumediene's death, his successor, Chadli Benjedid, began to relax some of the more stringent economic policies. More imports were allowed—food and some consumer items to satisfy the demands of the growing middle class—and a bit more freedom was allowed for individuals and groups to express themselves. This was designed to win support for the new regime from those who had disliked the austerity and restrictions of the Boumediene era.

A totally predictable response to the loosening of authoritarian controls was the onset of demands for change from various groups that nurtured specific grievances. For example, Berbers called for greater cultural rights; women demonstrated against the oppressive family code; and Islamists campaigned for the application of Islamic law and the rejection of Western cultural influences. Some of this protest turned violent, but mostly not. Still, one could begin to see that the unitary nature of Algerian society that had been posited by the Boumediene model was more myth than reality. As Algeria became a more urban, educated, and complex society, it was beginning to witness group politics as well. As long as the oil revenues flowed, the regime was able to respond with a mix of repression and co-optation. For example, armed Islamists were fought ruthlessly, but mosques were also built at a remarkable rate to appease the demands of mainstream Islamists.

Economic Decline and Mass Protests

A common trigger for economic and political reform is sudden deterioration of the economy. This occurred in Algeria in 1986, as a result of the global collapse of oil prices. All of a sudden the regime faced a real revenue shortfall. It would either have to borrow more, cut services, or reduce subsidies. Borrowing seemed an easy solution if the downturn was likely to be brief and if oil prices would soon recover, but it risked exposing Algeria to intense international pressure to reform the economy as the price for continuing credit. By the late 1980s Algeria was reaching the point where debt repayment was nearly equal to oil revenues, leaving nothing for new investment or financing for imports. An economic crisis was imminent. Some major reforms would be needed if Algeria was to regain a credit-worthy status. One did not need an advanced degree in economics to anticipate that some elements of the Boumediene-era bargain—subsidies, state-sponsored industrialization, controlled exchange rates—would have to be scrapped under the pressure of mounting budget deficits, high unemployment, and rapid inflation. An austerity package seemed inevitable.

Exactly how economic decline triggered the October 1988 protests is still unclear. There was nothing as dramatic as a sudden increase in the price of bread to explain why tens of thousands of young men poured into the streets shouting "Chadli Assassin," "à bas Chadli," and other antiregime slogans. But a link between the deteriorating economy and social protest is not hard to detect, even if there was some element of manipulation by elements within the regime. The economic crisis, after all, did not only increase the alienation of many young Algerians who could find no work. It also intensified the debates within the regime between the reformers, who wanted to dismantle the state-controlled economy, and the old guard, who wanted to return to Boumedienism in its unadulterated form.

The Era of Reforms and the Rise of the FIS

To save himself, Chadli joined the reformers and tried to put the blame for past errors on the old guard in the National Liberation Front (*Front de Libération Nationale*, FLN). As soon as he had secured his own reelection, Chadli moved swiftly to write a new Constitution that would institutionalize reforms. Within a short period Algeria ceased being a one-party socialist state and was on its way to being a multiparty, mixed economy with a remarkably free press. It all happened very quickly and initially produced an explosion of activity as parties and interests groups rushed to occupy space in the newly liberated political arena. It was a heady period, exciting and rather dangerous, but on the whole peaceful.

One of the remarkable features of the post-October 1988 period was the sudden emergence of the Islamic Salvation Front (*Front Islamique du Salut*, FIS) as the major vehicle of protest. Was this an example of religious enthusiasm spilling over into politics or, more plausibly, was this a social protest movement that was taken over by well-organized Islamists? Whichever the case, the FIS became the main alternative to the discredited FLN and the regime that was still associated with it. Many other parties and groups were also present on the scene, but none could really compete with the FIS or pose a credible challenge to the government. Suddenly, the Islamists went from being a major interest group seeking change from within the system to an alternative government demanding its due and threatening violence if it was kept away from the levers of power.

While political life was polarizing between the regime and the FIS, the reformers were desperately trying to get the economy moving again, in the hope that this would give them enough legitimacy to outmaneuver both the hard-liners within the ranks of the government and the opposition FIS and its supporters.

The FIS Seeks Power

Aware of its popular backing and frustrated by gradualism, the FIS began to demand rapid change. It called for Chadli to agree to new presidential and parliamentary elections, which he refused to do, but he did offer to organize municipal and provincial elections, which the FIS handily won in 1990. This whetted the FIS appetite for real power, and perhaps alarmed its leaders as well as they saw their local representatives bogged down in dealing with the problems of everyday life.

The reformers, who seemed to have Chadli's support, were in fact trying to discredit and outmaneuver the FIS, while simultaneously marginalizing the FLN establishment. This was a tricky strategy and it depended on time, improved economic circumstances, and strong support from Chadli and the military to work. Their hope was that the FIS would lose support as it proved to be incompetent in managing local affairs. At the same time, they felt that the extremism of some FIS leaders, especially Ben Hadj, would alarm many ordinary Algerians, who abhorred violence. The reformers also counted on the extremism of the FIS to alienate the military, which could therefore be counted on to back the reformers. (An FIS-army deal at their expense, as in Sudan, would have been a nightmare). The FIS, in its way, might be a useful tacit ally in the struggle against the old guard. The key to Mouloud Hamrouche's strategy, once Chadli had told him to organize parliamentary elections, was to ensure that the FIS would not sweep the elections as it had in 1990. If it boycotted the gerrymandered elections, it would lose out, since most other parties would no doubt participate; if it participated but fell short of dominating the new parliament, it would be forced to compromise its agenda and form coalitions with other groups. Either way, the reformers might remain in control.

The FIS leadership saw the trap and refused to play the game. Instead, they called an unlimited strike in May–June 1991, presumably hoping to topple the regime, or at least force out the reformers, cancel the elections, and demonstrate that they could not be outmaneuvered so easily.[3] The strike was not a great success. It had less resonance than the October 1988 demonstration. But it did provide the military with the pretext to lash out, not at the FIS but at Hamrouche. He was ousted, to be replaced by a less enthusiastic reformer; then the FIS leadership was arrested. Amazingly, the new prime minister went ahead with new parliamentary elections, using a formula of winner-take-all balloting that ensured a large FIS victory. For the third time, the military stepped in, deposed Chadli, canceled the second round of voting, banned the FIS, and declared a state of emergency.

Three times mass political action had been tried to bring about change, first in the partly spontaneous demonstrations of October 1988; then with an organized strike in mid-1991; and finally through parliamentary elections at the end of 1991. Each time, the army stepped in, more to preserve the system than to protect individual leaders. After the first riots, some of the FLN establishment was pushed aside; then the reformers; and then Chadli himself. In a sense, the mass protests had indeed produced change, but not in terms of who held the ultimate power in the country.

The Military Takes Charge

From 1992 onward, the military emerged from its preferred behind-the-scenes position to play a much more obvious role in running the day-to-day affairs of the country. But it would be a mistake to think that this has meant a return to Boumedienism pure and simple. Several differences need to be noted:

—Economic reform has continued in the direction of liberalization of the economy. Those in power seem to count heavily on economic recovery as a path toward stability and a measure of legitimacy. In any case, they have pressed forward with a reform program that has won fairly high marks from the World Bank and International Monetary Fund and has secured for the country a degree of debt relief.

—The security situation after 1992 deteriorated dramatically, forcing the military to restructure itself as a force capable of fighting an internal insurgency and terrorism, while also performing the normal tasks of defending the country. This has placed a great strain on the military, but it has not split and there have not been great defections. A government-sponsored militia has been formed to augment the manpower resources of the regime, with consequences that are difficult to assess. There is a striking similarity in how the Algerian military has confronted the various armed Islamic groups and the way the French fought against the FLN, including the vocabulary used.

—Some of the gains of the liberal reform era have been preserved, although they are under pressure. There are a number of legal political parties; the FLN has not recaptured the dominant place that it once had; a legal Islamist movement does exist; the parliament elected in mid-1997 has within it some outspoken political figures who freely criticize the regime; and the press is less constrained than elsewhere in the Arab world. Human rights groups, women's groups, and Berber cultural associations are active. The excitement and optimism of the 1989–91 period are missing, but even so many Algerians express confidence that the country will eventually move in a democratic direction, that it has a potentially bright future, and that they are prepared to stay and fight for their political convictions. Algeria is not about to succumb to Islamic revolution, and probably will not return to the pure authoritarian model either.

—Political institutions have been laboriously put in place and may in time become part of the workings of the political system. Certain principles that could be important building blocks for Algeria's future have been adopted: limits on presidential terms; proportional representation for parliament; multipartism; the banning of religious, sectarian, or regional parties; the establishment of a second chamber of parliament; and monitored elections.

—The unitary, populist model of development, along with state socialism, has been widely discredited. Whoever governs will now have to accept Algeria's pluralist vocation and mixed economy.

The Key Questions for Analysis

From this summary of Algeria's political development, several key questions must be answered:

—Why did the first reform effort fail so dramatically? Does this mean that major change is impossible? If so, why?

—Why has there been so much political violence since 1992?

In addition, the Algerian case allows us to explore these issues:

—What was the key to the success of the FIS, and can the Islamist tendency be channeled into a less radical current?

—Can economic development and repression dry up support for the armed Islamists, or is some form of political pact between the regime and the FIS needed to end the violence?

—Can institutional changes produce significant changes in political behavior on the part of the regime and its opponents?

—What can we learn from the Algerian case about the prospects for democratization in the Arab world?

These questions will be addressed in the remaining chapters.

7

Cultural Perspectives

ANYONE VISITING the Middle East or North Africa for the first time has the sense of encountering a different culture. This can be seen in matters of everyday life—the way people dress, the food they eat, the language they speak, the way they pray—and it may also be found in the beliefs and values that people seem to share. It is this last dimension of culture—the common beliefs, ideas, and values of a people—that may help us to understand some aspects of their political universe. After all, politics is a human activity and we should expect to find that it mirrors the deepest convictions of those who practice it. Here we are interested in something more than individual opinion on the one hand and universal values on the other. We want, instead, to see if there is anything, because of history and circumstances, that makes an Algerian different in political behavior from an Egyptian, or an Arab from a Turk, or a Muslim from a Jew. On the surface, it is plausible to believe that culture matters. But the question is how much—and how can we be sure.

Culture is an elusive concept, much used but not always artfully. In the hands of a great novelist, culture can be woven together with personal history to produce profound insights. No one can read Jane Austen without feeling the weight on her characters of upper-class English views of what is proper. Nor can one read Thomas Mann without a feeling for patriarchal authority in Germany; nor Naguib Mahfouz without appreciating the awareness of what the neighbors are thinking as the characters of Cairo's neighborhoods go about their everyday lives. The great Algerian novelist, Kateb Yacine, managed to convey a powerful theme of a culture of violence in colonial Algeria as various characters fantasize about Nedjma, the elusive heroine of his best-known book.

91

In the hands of lesser artists, and too many social scientists, culture can become a seemingly sophisticated shorthand for stereotyping or caricature. Culture can explain both too much and too little. Cultural explanations are often applied uncritically to heterogeneous groups—"Arabs believe. . . ." or "Muslims think. . . ." It becomes all too easy to ascribe behavior to cultural values—"They act the way they do because of their culture. That's just the way they are. . . ." We have learned to be wary of those who deal in national character studies, who pretend to peer into the "Arab mind."

It is not just western social scientists who are prone to the misuse of cultural categories. Any visitor to the Middle East will find conversations laden with such cultural images: Iraqis are tough and brutal; Egyptians are easygoing and have a good sense of humor; Israelis are arrogant and aggressive; Saudis are reserved and haughty; and so forth. This game is played from town to town and village to village, as stereotypes and images are attached to one's neighbors, friends, and adversaries.

Gender is another great topic for "biocultural" discourse. Women and men are often described as thinking and feeling in different ways. We are all familiar with these kinds of comments, and on occasions we nod in agreement as a grain of truth can be found hidden behind the sweeping generalization. But more often we pause and think of all the exceptions and the way in which the speaker is telling more about himself than about those he purports to describe.

Still, culture is a category that cannot simply be dismissed because it has been abused. Ideas, values, and beliefs, after all, do matter. People do not just act in response to material advantage, or as members of social classes, or according to rules laid down by those with power. They carry with them ideas and beliefs that lead to actions that cannot be understood without probing the kinds of values that we think of when culture is mentioned.

Many powerful assertions have been made using culture as an explanatory variable. For example, Max Weber attributed the rise of capitalism, in large measure, to the specific values that grew out of the Protestant Reformation.[1] More recently, Robert Putnam examined democracy in Italy and found that a crucial ingredient explaining its spread in northern Italy more rapidly than in southern Italy was the greater prevalence of interpersonal trust in the north. This cultural trait, he argues, has deep historic roots.[2] We encounter the argument that culture matters for economic performance in another context when analysts evoke Confucian values of respect for hierarchy, hard work, education, and family as the keys to the Asian economic miracles.[3] And, of course, we now hear that future world conflicts will be between distinct cultural groups in the "Clash of Civilizations."[4]

What, if anything, in our account of Algeria's recent politics can be ascribed to culture? Some would argue a great deal. One of the most sophisticated analysts of Algeria, Lahouari Addi, sees a political culture of populism as one of the main factors contributing to Algeria's crisis.[5] It is this populist vision of a unified people, shared by nationalists and Islamists, that presents a barrier to the acceptance of pluralism and compromise—crucial ingredients of a democratic alternative for the country. Those who hold such unitary, populist views see in Algeria's multiple identities—Arab, Berber, Islamist, modern, secular, French—a source of deep confusion that has contributed to internal disputes and national weakness. Language, which is central to any cultural argument, can be viewed as reflecting these ambivalences. Does an Algerian express herself in classical Arabic, Algerian dialect, French, or Berber? Or does it all depend on circumstances? Algeria's first president, upon returning to his country after six years in French prisons, insisted that "Nous sommes Arabes, Arabes, Arabes. . . ." But the language he used to affirm Algeria's Arab identity weakened the force of what he said. The struggle over language and education policy suggests that these cultural issues affect politics in some form.

Algerians, some would argue, have also been socialized into a set of values and beliefs that have instrumentalized violence as a means of achieving political goals. The revolution, after all, was not a peaceful adventure. Independence was won after legal methods had been tried and discredited, and it is an article of faith that France would never have given up its prize colony if Algerians had not taken up arms. Does that same belief hold for today's opponents of the regime, that only violence will dislodge illegitimate rulers?

If these are some of the ways that culture may help explain Algerian politics, what must we first do to rescue the concept from those who have misused it? The most crucial point is to accept that cultural values are not genetically imprinted or fixed for all time. They must be seen in historical context. They must not be treated as unchanging essences, or "essentialized," in the jargon of postmodernists. We must also recognize that cultures include multiple, often conflicting values, and that any given individual will carry a whole repertoire of beliefs and values that are found within the broad culture and yet can lead to divergent behaviors, depending on which values are evoked at any given moment. And values can change—not as quickly as attitudes or opinions, but over time values do not remain fixed.

Even if we use the notion of cultural values carefully, we must be aware of several additional traps. First there is the question of causality. It may be true that democracy and interpersonal trust are highly associated. But that does not prove that trust "causes" democratic behavior. In fact, it can be reasonably argued that democratic practices "cause" trust to develop.[6] Even when we think we have the causal relationship between values and behavior correctly stated, the question will arise, for some, of the source of the values themselves. This can lead to a search for "deeper" explanations. Marx did not deny that values and ideas matter, but he saw them as reflecting the more important realities of one's social class, which in turn were rooted in economic structures. Others, such as Barrington Moore, saw the relationship between landlords and peasants over hundreds of years as crucial to understanding why democracy emerged in England in the nineteenth century.[7] Germaine Tillion, in research on the suppressed status of women in Mediterranean cultures, attributed this to cross-cousin marriages, which in turn stemmed from the paucity of arable land.[8] In short, values may matter, but they cannot be taken for granted. They, in turn, need to be accounted for and they need to be put in context.

Finally, the prevalence of certain values in a group cannot just be asserted; there should be some evidence of the extent of the beliefs in question. No community is so uniform that all its members believe precisely the same things. If they did, we would not have politics. So, values have to be specified for subgroups within the larger culture to be useful analytically.

With all these caveats and qualifications, one might think it better to reject cultural analysis altogether. It is, after all, very subjective; it tends to be used to bolster conservative agendas; and it can be misleading. But these are not sufficient reasons to reject culture as a useful concept a priori. They are reasons to use it carefully and for limited purposes.

Several issues in the Algerian story seem to require a cultural lens to see things clearly. These include such crucial matters as the definition of the political community—who is in and who is out; the view of the state and its proper role; beliefs about the use of violence in politics; and views of Islam and its role in the political arena.

Defining Who Is Algerian

A problem for many modern states is that their citizens do not identify with the state, are not loyal to it, and do not think of themselves as forming a political community with other citizens of the state. Sometimes the problem is identification with smaller units—tribes, families, ethnic groups, and religious sects. Sometimes one's political loyalties transcend state boundaries, as with some Arabs and Muslims and many Kurds in the modern Middle East.

There was a time not so long ago when many observers thought that the lack of identity with the Algerian nation would preclude the emergence of Algerian nationalism among that country's Muslim population. But Algeria's struggle for independence settled the questions of national identity for most Algerians. The entire Muslim population, with the exception of those who had collaborated with the French— the *harkis*—is considered by the state to be Algerian, and think of themselves in those terms. The vast majority of the French citizens who lived in Algeria up until 1962 left and have no claim to Algerian nationality today. So Algeria does not suffer from the kinds of internal divisions that rend the Sudan, or the multiple identities that seem to be a problem in Iraq and Lebanon. Algerians have a fairly robust sense of their identity, anchored in recent history.

The one substantial ethnic minority in Algeria, the Berbers, have had relatively little problem identifying with the nation, and generally they have been well represented in all the political movements and institutions of the country. There are Berber populations in Morocco, in particular, but there is no pan-Berber movement and the communities are not geographically contiguous. Although there is a Berber cultural movement, and some interest in fostering respect for Berber language, there is no separatist movement among Berbers. Berbers can be found in many different political movements, including the Islamic Salvation Front (*Front Islamique du Salut*, FIS).

When Algeria first won its independence, Arab nationalism and Gamal Abd al-Nasser were strong. Some thought that Algeria might subordinate its state identity in favor of a broader Arab identity, and some of the debates over the introduction of Arabic as the language of education and government have had overtones of this theme. But few Algerians ever became proponents of Nasser-style pan-Arabism. Even Boumediene, who had studied in Cairo and was very much the product of an Arab-Islamic formation, was more of a rival to Nasser than an advocate of Arab unity. Arabism in the Algerian context always took a back seat to "Algerianness."

Such was also the case with Islam. Algerian nationalism had at its core a strong Muslim identity. Religion, after all, had been a fundamental badge of identity during the colonial period. In 1870, with the infamous Cremieux Decree, France had offered French citizenship to Algerian Jews but not to Muslims. Later, Muslims had been allowed to elect members to their own assemblies, but not to the institutions that represented proper Frenchmen. To be a Muslim in French Algeria was not to be French. In this regard, Berbers and Arabs were treated equally. Islam as a political phenomenon in Algeria did not develop initially in opposition to nationalism, but rather as a part of it. While Algeria did not have the institutions of higher learning that produced great Islamic scholars in Cairo, and even in Tunisia, there were nonetheless Algerian Islamists, such as Ben Badis, who contributed to the Algerian national movement. A few Algerians have been influenced by Islamist currents in the eastern Arab world, and with the experience of *jihad*, or religiously sanctioned struggle, in Afghanistan, but Algerian Islam is striking in its Algerian focus.[9] Indeed, the FIS was commonly described as being split between its Algerian wing and its more "fundamentalist," or *salifiyya* wing.[10]

While Algerians are more or less agreed on the shape of their country and who belongs and who does not, there is another aspect of Algeria's historical experience that shows up in its national identity. Understandably, Algerians are sensitive to any hint of foreign intervention in their affairs, especially if France is suspected of being involved. While many Algerians travel to France, work there, speak French, watch French television, and are often quite enamored of things French, they are terribly touchy about being told what to do by the French. Thus the Islamists have used the French connections of a number of top generals—some had once served in the French army—to discredit them. They are regularly labeled the "French Party." To prove the contrary, those same generals have gone to great lengths to show their independence of France by imposing the Arabic language, building mosques, and generally downplaying any visible French connections they may have.

Similarly, the regime has tried to imply that the Islamists are supported by foreign powers. At one time, no doubt Saudi Arabia provided money to the FIS, but more recently it has been Iran and Sudan who have been portrayed as interfering in Algeria's internal affairs. So the charge of foreign intervention is made by both major protagonists in Algeria's drama, an indication that they both believe that ordinary Algerians are still sensitive to the specter of foreign intervention, whatever the source.

Despite what many observers have said, Algerians do not seem to be deeply divided over cultural issues. They mostly share an identity as Algerians; there are no separatist movements; and the subnational regional and family identities, while strong, have not precluded the emergence of countrywide political movements. Even language, which is a hotly contested cultural issue, is not as divisive as one might think. Nearly all Algerians can communicate in their own dialect without much trouble, and it is sufficiently different from other variants of Arabic to make them aware of their distinctiveness. Although much of the current political contest sounds like a clash of cultures—nationalists versus Islamists—that is only partly true. The nationalists think of themselves as good Muslims, but do not subscribe to the same politicized version of Islam as the Islamists; Islamists are intent on proving that they are the true inheritors of the revolution, ·the real patriots. Many of the FIS leaders were active at one time in the National Liberation Front (*Front de Libération Nationale*, FLN). This has led some to see little real difference between the old FLN and today's FIS—*le FIS est le fils du FLN* (the FIS is the son of the FLN). It is not quite that simple, but the cultural divide is more apparent than real. Other roots, more obviously political and generational, will be found for the conflict that are more persuasive than a presumed cultural divide between those inspired by religion and those inspired by nationalism.

On the whole, Algerians have a robust sense of who they are, largely because of the nature of their struggle for independence. This makes their disputes particularly intense since both sides of the argument claim to be speaking for the Algerian people. Conflict is in abundance, but it is not of the same variety that pitted Algerians against the French colonizers in what can be seen as a clash of different cultures.

Political Violence

No one living in the twentieth century should need to be reminded that people of all cultures have shown themselves capable of extraordinary political violence and barbarism. It is not just "less developed" people in Cambodia and Rwanda who have engaged in genocidal excesses, but also the "civilized" Germans and Russians. And we do not have to go very far back in history to find the English, Americans, and French, now all good democrats, engaged in their own versions of civil war and violence. Nor is Islam the only religion that has spawned extremist fringes. Christian, Jewish, and Hindu zealots have also contributed their share to the world's misery.

While it is doubtless true that humans have the capacity to act violently in specified circumstances, there are moments in the history of a people when violence is seen as a particularly legitimate form of collective behavior. Thus we hear of subcultures—such as gangs— where acts of violence are glorified. In a more disciplined and "legitimate" setting, military establishments the world over inculcate norms that prescribe the use of force in specific circumstances and reward those who are particularly adept at using violence. Normally, however, broader society is not socialized into the use of force and violence for settling quarrels, if only because no regime wants to have to deal with armed and militant citizens who demand their rights with guns in hand.

But what happens in a society where the state, for many decades, is seen as an illegitimate enemy, and where the entire population is mobilized to support the violent overthrow of the oppressive colonial regime? In those circumstances, which resemble the Algerian case, might not a "culture of violence" take hold of an entire people?[11] And once these patterns take hold, might they not prove difficult to change?

Nothing in this line of argument suggests that Algerians are more prone to violence in some genetic sense than other people, but it may be argued that their bloody history has had an impact on how political opposition is likely to be expressed. After all, many Algerians glorified the revolution.[12] Some who supported the Algerian cause, such as the radical thinker Frantz Fanon, became convinced of the therapeutic value of violence, and Fanon's impact on intellectuals was profound.[13]

The Algerian war for independence exacted an enormous human toll—Algerians speak of "one million martyrs," which may overstate the actual numbers, but by all accounts hundreds of thousands were killed. No family was spared. What the official version of events neglects is that many Algerians were killed by other Algerians, some serving in the French army, other victims of internecine struggles. This is a side of Algeria's past that may account for some of the violence in the present. For example, during the war for independence, the FLN dealt harshly with suspected collaborators; in one terrible episode the inhabitants of an entire village, Melouza, were massacred. Years later Algerians from this region cast their votes in the municipal elections for the FIS. And one would hardly be surprised to find support for Islamist radicals in such quarters. This understanding of Algeria's recent struggle has never been systematically researched—it touches too closely on a taboo topic—but there are reasons to suspect that some element of history-related blood feuding and revenge lies behind the regime-*Groupes Islamiques Armés* (Armed Islamic Groups, GIA) confrontations of recent years. But even if this is true, it does not demonstrate that Algerians have cultural values that predispose them to violence. At most it means that the political violence of today may have deeper and more shadowy roots than is often suspected. Behind the screen of ideological battles may lie more prosaic causes.

Finally, if Algerians are particularly prone to violence, how can one explain the long period from 1963 to 1993 when Algeria was relatively free of domestic violence? Did the values change during this period? Possibly so. After all, Algerians now had a government of their own to deal with, not foreign oppressors. But more likely the answer lies in the circumstances of the time, the degree of governmental control, the emergence of the authoritarian welfare state, and the need to balance repression and subsidies to win the acquiescence of most people. Although the system did not work to the satisfaction of all, it provided a modicum of well-being to many. It was not until later, when the system was radically changed late in the 1980s, when new forms of opposition had emerged, and when those were suddenly repressed, that a small number of Algerians—probably numbering in the tens of thousands—took up arms. When the chances for insurrection faded, an even smaller number resorted to terrorism, increasingly without any apparent political purpose.

At most, one might conclude that in the initial stage of the Islamists' challenge to the regime, many ordinary Algerians were inclined to accept the legitimacy of the Islamists' resort to violence, modeled as it seemed to be on the FLN's struggle against a repressive regime in the 1950s. But unlike the war for independence, the bulk of the population has never come down decisively on the side of those who took up arms. In fact, the striking feature of the post-1992 period is how silent the "silent majority" has remained through all the horror. Neither the government nor the opposition has been able to mobilize the kind of popular support that proved decisive for the FLN in its claim to speak for the Algerian people, even when it had been defeated on the battlefield by superior force. By the late 1990s most Algerians seemed sickened by the violence that was becoming endemic.

How the State Is Viewed

One of Algeria's leading sociologists, M'Hammed Boukhobza, traced the origins of the October 1988 uprising to a deep-seated distrust on the part of Algerians toward the state.[14] This sentiment preceded the colonial period but was intensified by the "quasi-permanent violence" of the colonial system. The Ottoman authorities were remote and predatory; the French intrusive and disruptive. As a result, Algerian society turned back on itself, tried to avoid dependency on the state, and developed the habit of local self-sufficiency and distrust of central authority. In the countryside Sufi religious orders provided some measure of integration among these autonomous units.

Side by side with this view of the state as a dangerous predator one finds the view, nurtured by the revolution, of the just state, righting all wrongs, providing for the needy, dispensing justice—in short, doing all the things that the colonial order failed to do. This meant that when Algerians finally had a government of their own, expectations were high—unrealistically so—that it would solve the country's manifold economic and social problems. And if it could not do so immediately, then everyone should at least be treated equally. This combination of historically rooted distrust of the state and a certain idealization born of the revolution was bound to make governing a tricky business. Even with good will, any government would find itself privileging some and neglecting others. With limited resources, choices would have to be made and some were bound to be disappointed.

The idealization of the role of the state was also encouraged by what Robert Malley describes as "Third Worldism."[15] This sentiment posited a strong state in the Jacobin mold, responsible for forging a sense of patriotism and sacrifice for the nation among the citizens of the state. A strong state would be required to bring about the massive social changes that were needed—improve health care, modernize the country, build schools, end poverty, and create the new society. Further, a strong state, allied to others in the Third World, would be necessary to wrest from the rich, exploiting former colonial powers the resources and technology that would speed the transition to modernity. Algeria, for a moment, was a leading proponent of the "new international economic order," which essentially called for a redistribution of resources from north to south.

The economic and social model that lay behind Third Worldism was largely derived from the Soviet experience. There a poor rural state had managed to industrialize and become a great power within a generation; it had managed to help defeat the Nazis and went on to build powerful rockets and send astronauts into space. Russia had shown the way, but China was another model of socialist power. Both were believed to have strong governments and strong economies. Planning replaced the chaos and unfairness of the market. The state ensured that no one would be abandoned and no one would get too rich. Algeria, with a few variations on these themes that were distinctive, signed on to this model with enthusiasm.[16]

The risk with this "total state project," as the Algerian experience could be described, was that it had no safety net built in. Given the high expectations and the residual distrust of the state, there was likely to be a moment when ordinary people would be disappointed and they would have no one to blame for their unhappiness other than the state. Even if the state managed to do quite well in providing education and basic services, some were bound to get rich while others stayed poor. Boukhobza argues that in fact all social categories did improve their status through the 1970s into the 1980s, but not all at the same rate.[17] Those who got less from the system were bitterly resentful, blaming the state and suspecting that those in power had used their positions to help their cronies. This had the added power of often being true, as is bound to happen in any state that receives a massive inflow of "rents" from the export of oil and gas. Corruption was not seen as an inevitable by-product of development, a sign of human imperfectability, but rather it was an affront to basic notions of justice and equity.

For a while, the Algerian state probably enjoyed some benefit of the doubt simply because it represented the triumph of the revolution over colonialism. Most people thought their lives would improve once independence was won. But soon the legitimacy of the regime, the very commitment of the citizens to the state, depended on its performance. The state was everything. There was no sizable private sector that could share the burden and the blame for economic problems that might arise. As the state was forced to retreat from some of its commitments as a result of dwindling oil resources in the mid-1980s, popular anger quickly turned on the system that had betrayed the people. The FIS successfully tapped this sentiment, holding out the promise that "Islam is the solution." Once they took charge of the state, they would set things right. Needless to add, with such a "total" project of what the state would do, the Islamists also might well have suffered the fate of their predecessors had they come to power.

Politics and Islam

One of the running debates in the Middle East and among analysts of the region is about the compatibility of Islam and democracy. At the extremes, the positions are stated forcefully. Some see in Islam—with its assertion of the sovereignty of God in all spheres of life, including the political—a necessary contradiction with the notion of popular sovereignty that is essential to democracy. At the other extreme are those who argue that Islam contains within it important principles, such as the rule of law and the requirement of consultation, that are barriers to one-man rule and can be quite compatible with an Islamic form of democracy.

The Algerian case is not conclusive with respect to the debate over Islam and democracy. Relatively few convinced democrats can be found in either the ranks of the Islamists or among those who have governed Algeria since independence. At the same time, we can detect some voices in each camp who have begun to use the language of pluralism, free elections, and multiple parties.

As elsewhere in the Islamic world, there is no single interpretation in Algeria of what Islam requires of its followers. As has been frequently noted, there is no formal hierarchy in Sunni Islam, nothing comparable to the papacy as a source of infallible interpretation. This has meant, historically, that many different interpretations have coexisted within the broad confines of Islamic orthodoxy. From the Middle

Ages on, these differences were even codified in several distinct schools of law. In Algeria, however, nearly all Muslims follow the same Maliki rite. What differences there have been are not legal, but rather concern the political role of Islam.

It is difficult to be a sincere Muslim without believing that the ideal form of government should be one that is based on Islamic laws. This does not necessarily mean that Muslims agree on any particular form of government—in fact there is little discussion of political institutions in Islamic political theory—but Islam does hold out an ideal representation against which any government can be judged. The fact that the prophet Muhammad actually governed the Islamic community of his day has provided a real-world example of how secular and religious authority can be combined.

Even with this much consensus among Muslims on how they should ideally be governed, there is much divergence in practice. The main differences have been between a conservative tradition that has accepted the authority of the state as long as it provides order and upholds Islamic law and a more radical tradition that recognizes the right of any believer to reject unjust authority. Needless to say, most states in the Middle East have tried to encourage the former; most radical opposition movements have evoked the latter.

Several themes stand out in the radical Islamist critique of the conservative tradition. First, if the state is in the hands of nonbelievers, or insincere Muslims, the society will never become a true Muslim community. The radicals reject the notion that a Muslim community can be built from the ground up, and that the state is only marginally relevant to that process. The radicals draw on the Quranic injunction "to forbid evil and to require the good" to justify their right to use political power to impose their views on others. Taking a theme from the Egyptian radical Islamist, Sayyid Qutb, they argue that it is the duty of a good Muslim to unmask the insincere among them, to engage in *takfir*—to expel someone from the ranks of believers to that of the unbelievers. Once a regime has been denounced as non-Muslim, it is legitimate to use force against it, including the declaration of a *jihad*. This may or may not include the use of force, but once *jihad* is invoked, taking up arms is legitimate.[18]

In the Algerian context, the portion of the FIS that formed around Ali Ben Hadj was much influenced by the radical interpretation of Islam. Ben Hadj was outspoken in his criticism of democracy. If free elections were to produce an outcome contrary to his interpretation of Islam, the results would be invalid, since no expression of popular will could be viewed as superior to God's will. In his extensive writings, he is obsessed by the vision of overthrowing tyrannical government and replacing it with a just Muslim order. He is against alliances with so-called moderate Islamist parties, seeing them as pawns of the regime.[19] Nothing in his discourse suggests a man of moderation or tolerance.[20] Those who suspected that his view of elections would be "one man, one vote, one time" in the event of a FIS victory had plenty of evidence on their side.

Other Islamist leaders, by contrast, adopted a more nuanced view of Algerian society, the role of violence, and of how best to proceed with the Islamic project. Many of them were opposed to Ben Hadj, and even a number of the founders of the FIS soon broke with him. Since 1995 his voice has been stifled, but some of those who were most inspired by him drifted toward the militant GIA.

The more moderate wing of the Islamist movement in Algeria has been expressed by Hamas, An- Nahda, and a small party led by Noureddine Boukrouh. This tendency is relatively close to the Muslim Brethren, arguing that Islam can and should be constructed from the bottom up. If the society can be made Islamic, regardless of the regime in place, then eventually the political system will also become Islamic. This is the tendency that has concentrated on building clinics and orphanages, providing scholarships, tutoring students in Arabic, providing disaster relief, and so forth. A portion of the FIS seemed to be of this persuasion when it was first established. By most measures, including recent elections, a sizable part of the electorate, perhaps one-fourth, seems drawn to Islamists of this orientation.

Hard-liners within the regime and their supporters argue that there is no real difference between the so-called moderate Islamists and the so-called radicals. There is a seamless web, they argue, that links the two faces of political Islam. And neither of them, the hard-liners would add, has much to do with Islam as a religion, as a faith, as values guiding people in everyday life. They are simply different tactics for pursuing political objectives and do not deserve the prestige of religion that they try to appropriate. For this reason the Algerian government, like those in Turkey and Egypt, does not allow political parties to lay claim to Islam as their particular property. They can acknowledge that Islam inspires their positions—Islam is after all the religion of the state in Algeria—but they cannot assert a monopoly over the common heritage of Algerians.

From this brief overview, it is obvious that Islam is at the center of a crucial debate in Algeria. But is it a debate about religion and culture, or power and how it will or will not be shared? Are those who are drawn to the Islamist message primarily motivated by the religious message, or by the promise of radical change in society? There is no conclusive evidence on these questions, but there is ample reason to suspect that more than culture and religion is at stake in these debates, as will be shown in the chapters that follow.

Conclusions

What importance do we place on culture in our account of Algeria's political development? Some, but not too much. The most crucial role of culture is in the definition of the political community. The colonial era and the war for independence answered that question clearly. Algeria, unlike South Africa, would not be the common home of colonizers and colonized. It would be uniquely the nation of the indigenous Arab-Berber-Muslim people. That remains a core conviction of nationalists and Islamists. For both, the revolution and its overthrow of the colonial system are fundamental to Algeria's identity.

Another set of values derived from the revolutionary struggle was the myth of the mobilized people. The revolution was not portrayed as a class war of the peasants or workers against the aristocracy. Colonialism had destroyed Algeria's aristocracy; what remained was not quite the "human dust" that some Frenchmen spoke of in the early part of this century, but was still a fairly segmented, atomized, and egalitarian society without much hierarchical structure. When the FLN managed to mobilize the bulk of the population behind the idea of independence, it recruited from all sectors—peasants and workers, educated and illiterate, men and women, Arabs and Berbers. This strategy meant that at independence everyone felt he or she had a claim on the fruits of victory. No one should be excluded a priori from power and its perquisites, except for collaborators. This meant that the political arena was crowded with claimants for a piece of the pie. Few were prepared to acknowledge the superior credentials of others. All had fought in some form; all had suffered. History left Algeria with a egalitarian set of norms, a populism rooted in the notion of common sacrifice. The problem was that no one wanted to accept the authority of anyone else. And, to a large degree, that has remained true.

History also seems to have willed to the Algerians a profound ambivalence about the state. On the one hand, they look at the state with mistrust and distaste, complaining of the arrogance and contemptuous attitudes (*hogra*) of those who rule them. Sometimes it seems as if the colonial era never ended. Rulers are still seen as remote, foreign, and self-serving. But at the same time, the populist model of development that has been the cornerstone of independent Algeria has put the state at the center of everything. People have come to expect a range of services, jobs, security, and justice from the state, and when they do not receive them, their negative attitudes are reinforced. This stance vis-à-vis the state may help to account for how quickly the FIS was able to mobilize large numbers of people against the FLN in 1990–91.

Less convincing, or at least less far-reaching, are cultural explanations of Algeria's troubled transition from authoritarianism and the prevalence of political violence in recent years. Algerians are probably no more prone to violence than any other people, but their history predisposed some of them to conclude that violent resistance to illegitimate authority is justified. But the vast majority of Algerians have been onlookers, not participants, in the bloody battles of the 1990s, so it is hard to see that a pervasive cultural norm is at work when a small minority resorts to violence. At most, we may find that certain subgroups have been socialized to resort readily to violence.

Similarly, Islam as a body of beliefs is too all-encompassing to be a satisfying explanation for Algeria's political troubles. After all, Algerians were Muslim when there was order and stability in the Boumediene years; they were Muslim during the chaotic, but mostly nonviolent democratization period, and they were Muslim in the 1990s when hundreds were being killed each week. In using the category of Islam to explain political behavior, we must, at least, ask "whose Islam"? And this question will bring us more to politics than to religion, especially when looking at leaders of Islamic movements.

Islam as culture, as a widely shared set of cultural norms, may help to explain the receptivity of broad sectors of the population to the appeal of Islamist militants. After all, the sudden emergence of the FIS as a popular movement demands some explanation. It seems plausible that for many ordinary Muslims, a party using the name of Islam, promising an end to tyranny and corruption, and using the slogan that "Islam is the solution" would have a particular appeal that could not readily be met by non-Islamic parties. But the receptivity of the population to the Islamists does not seem to have been merely a matter of culture, but also a matter of deep socioeconomic grievance, plus the particular role that mosques played in disseminating the FIS message.

So, culture helps us to understand the shape of the political community and its fiercely egalitarian ethos. It may contribute to understanding the negative view of the state. But it does not provide fully satisfactory answers to the questions of why Algeria has had such trouble moving away from authoritarian rule and why there has been so much political violence. For answers to these questions, other perspectives must be examined.

8

Social and Economic Perspectives

THE STUDY of politics has always involved the study of society and the economy. The reason is obvious. Individuals do not participate in political life in isolation. Most often, they are part of a group, sometimes small, sometimes extensive. Those groups are often, but not always, defined by common economic interests. Success in politics often depends on the coherence and size of one's group support, the ability to forge cross-group coalitions, and the control over economic resources.

Here we will not focus so much on the nature of Algerian society per se, or examine the economy in depth. Rather, this chapter will highlight those social and economic features of the country that have a direct and convincing impact on its political development. We will examine Algeria's troubled transition from authoritarianism, its initial failure to democratize its political system, the emergence of radical Islam as the predominant form of protest, and the perennial factionalism in Algerian politics by focusing on social and economic developments.

State and Society

While a link between politics and society is apparent, the precise nature of that link is hotly debated. Scholars working on the Middle East have come up with two diametrically opposed images of the relationship.[1] One posits that in this region the state is typically strong, the society weak. According to this school of thought, the roots of the strong state divorced from underlying social structure can be traced to Ottoman days when the ruling elite was literally imported from outside the Ottoman domains and imposed by force upon society.

Order was maintained, the borders were protected, and the components of society—the various language and religious groups—were pretty much left to go about their business as long as they did not challenge the prerogatives of the state. This gap between state and society was then reinforced by the colonial era, when again the ruling class did not emerge from society, but rather was imposed upon it. Power, in this model, was maintained by those who could master the game of "divide and rule." Social groups were pitted against one another to ensure that a unified social movement would not confront the state with its political demands. Modern nationalism was the first trans-group movement that posed such a challenge.

A different argument is made by those who see the state in the Middle East as essentially weak, little more than the expression of one or another of the powerful solidarity groups in the society. From this perspective one should focus on the social building blocks—family, tribes, ethnic and religious groups, the military—to see which ones manage to capture the state apparatus for their own benefit.[2] The journalistic phrase that catches this perspective is that the states of the Middle East are "tribes with flags." This is not meant to imply that those who control the state have little power; rather, they have little legitimacy. They rule by coercion, since they cannot count on the loyalty of the bulk of the population.

The artificial division of the Middle East into modern states is believed to have aggravated this problem of the lack of a fit between society and state. Even apparently strong states, such as Saddam Hussein's Iraq and Hafiz al-Asad's Syria, on careful inspection have a narrow social base. Saddam rules with family members from his home region of Tikrit; Asad's key allies in the security services are his Alawite co-religionists. The weakness of the state in this "strong society, weak state" paradigm is the weakness that comes from the widespread perception of most citizens that they are excluded from the political arena and thus owe no loyalty to the institutions of the state. The state may be able to coerce, but it cannot easily persuade.

Which, if either, of these images best fits Algeria? Further, what can be explained by looking at the structure of Algerian society as it impinges on political life? At first glance, the Algerian case would seem to resemble the "strong state, weak society." After all, the colonial period had a devastating impact on Algerian social structure. Much of its traditional elite was driven into exile; the best land was seized by

Europeans; few Algerians prior to the 1950s received anything more than a rudimentary education. This meant that men of very modest social backgrounds led the revolution. Algeria arrived at independence without a powerful land-owning aristocracy, without an indigenous elite of privilege and wealth, and without great disparities between one region and another. The population was relatively homogeneous, poor, and illiterate, with most speaking the same language and practicing the same religion. The national struggle had settled the issue of national identity; the state was viewed as a legitimate entity, even if its institutions and leaders might be challenged.

In many ways this relative uniformity in Algerian society—even the one major ethnic minority, the Berbers, saw themselves as Algerians first—was an advantage. Algerians did not need to have a social revolution to end the rule of the old aristocracy. The colonial regime was the equivalent of the old order and as of 1962 it was gone. Nor were there intense class differences pitting industrial workers against agrarian interests. At the moment of independence, there was only a minuscule working class in the country. Most Algerians were of rural origin, some peasants, others town dwellers. The big cities of Algiers and Oran had been heavily European, although Constantine was more of an Arab city. Apart from these three large cities, the rest of the country consisted of small towns and villages. There were no great institutions of learning comparable to Al-Azhar in Cairo; no strong tribal leaders; no single national hero except for Abd al-Qadir, who had been forced into exile in 1847, never to return.

All in all, Algeria began its life as a free country with a remarkable degree of equality. As time went on, however, the state presided over a restratification of society, and the political consequences of that fact were far-reaching. In particular, those who saw their relative position decline blamed the state. There was no one else to blame.

The Restratification of Society

With independence, the state and its policies were the agents for rapid social transformation and the emergence of a new elite of privilege, power, and wealth. During the first three decades of Algeria's development, the state provided most of the opportunities for economic advancement. Those who became wealthy did so because of the state.[3] The state also adopted policies that fostered a massive move from the countryside to the cities. Agriculture was collectivized, and many peasants as a result simply gave up and moved to the urban areas. Also, it was there that services were most readily available. For the first to arrive there was cheap housing, as the state redistributed the abandoned French housing stock; there were jobs in the new state industries and in the massive bureaucracy. Young men could join the military and hope for improvements in their lives. Education was offered for the first time to almost all school-age children.[4]

Two inevitable results of these policies were rapid urbanization and a population boom. By the late 1980s, 40 percent of Algerians were under the age of fourteen. Most lived in cities, often in crowded housing, with few social amenities and bleak prospects for finding gainful employment when they would reach the age to enter the labor force. The state, mostly through inadvertence, brought into existence a social category in the 1980s that threatened to unseat the existing order.[5] It was from the ranks of these recent migrants to the cities—these young, marginal, unemployed men—that the Islamic Salvation Front (FIS) found its most ardent recruits. The FIS leadership may have had different roots—more educated, higher social status—but the Islamists' shock troops were from the sprawling slums on the outskirts of Algiers, suburbs with names like Eucalyptus, Hussein Dey, El- Harrach. In these impoverished areas an underclass formed, black markets and crime flourished, drug trafficking occurred, gangs formed, and political recruitment took place. In these areas the state was almost absent.[6] Those at the pinnacle of the pyramid of power had little idea of what was going on at the base.

The Egalitarian Legacy

The century-long disruption of Algeria's traditional social structure that came with colonialism left the country without strong social groupings from which new, more modern formations might emerge. When one looks at other newly independent countries, one often finds some remnant of the old order but in modern guise. For example, in both Morocco and Jordan the institution of the monarchy has been adapted quite successfully to the demands of the modern state, preserving an element of legitimacy and structure in societies that have otherwise changed in many ways. Or take the case of South Africa, where leaders such as Nelson Mandela and Mangosuthu Buthelezi transformed their fathers' tribal roles into those of party leaders, while preserving much of the unquestioning loyalty that goes with the former. Or look at neighboring Tunisia and the role played by the small, educated elite that graduated from the Zitouna school, mostly sons of privilege, but capable of leading a national movement against colonialism.[7]

The Algerian case stands apart in the Middle East in the extent to which the old social order was destroyed rather than transformed. Some aspects of development in Egypt are similar under Gamal Abd al-Nasser—much of the elite came from modest backgrounds and forged links to one another in the military—but elsewhere modernizing regimes were much more likely to rely on the social structures they had inherited. Turkey's Mustafa Kemal was a relentless modernizer, but he drew heavily on the urban, educated elite that had been formed in Ottoman times.[8]

Trying to govern a society that is broadly egalitarian and lacks strong, powerful vested interests sounds easier than it is likely to be in reality. Two models might seem to work. One would be a very decentralized, relatively weak government, which would allow for extensive self-government in diverse regions. Tribes and village leaders would play a large role at the local level; at the national level the government would limit its role to a few key matters such as maintenance of order, protecting against foreign intervention, and so forth. The problem is that such a weak state, while perhaps suitable for a strongly egalitarian society, would not be good at promoting economic and social change or warding off external pressures. It sounds a bit too much like the old Ottoman system, which was remarkably durable in its time, but failed precisely when it encountered dual pressures for change from within and without.

The alternative to the weak state in such circumstances would seem to be a strong state that did not play favorites among the various social categories of the nation. To some extent, this is what both Nasser and Houari Boumediene tried to do. There was a kind of egalitarian austerity that surrounded them as leaders—others might be corrupt, but they were not. All sectors of the population were treated more or less equally, at least in a formal sense. There was mass education for all, health care for all, subsidies for all, and austerity for all. Everyone had the right to vote—for the single party! Everyone complained, but everyone was essentially in the same boat, so the privations were tolerable. At least there was order and security. This was the classic authoritarian model in an egalitarian social setting, more egalitarian in Algeria than Egypt, but similar in theory.[9]

The problem with this model is that the state regulates everything, so that the moment things begin to go wrong, the struggle for the state assumes enormous importance. For example, if some groups in society feel they are getting less than their fair share—even if they are objectively better off than they used to be—they are likely to blame the state. When enough discrete groups all feel relative deprivation— such as at a time of economic recession—the potential may exist for a rapid mobilization of protest.[10] Protest movements, when they become powerful enough, will not be satisfied simply with forcing a change of policy. They will want to control the state.

So, somewhat paradoxically, an egalitarian social structure with a strong state may well set the stage for intense political competition. The lack of intermediary groups—strong tribal leaders, regional influentials, economic brokers, or religious dignitaries—may in fact mean there is no safety net when things begin to go badly. It may be easier to find balances and compromises in political systems that are more structured, where various communities have recognized leaders who have an interest in preserving their own leadership positions, and where compromise with other powerful leaders is a more feasible means of redressing grievances than seizing power over the entire system.

Lebanon, which is much less egalitarian than Algeria, has a complex sectarian and communal structure. At worst, this can lead to intense civil war, as in the decade after 1975. By the same token, when the war was over, it was relatively easy for Lebanon to reconstitute its political system around the major social building blocks.

Algeria's internal violence has resulted in fewer deaths than Lebanon's, but has also been harder to bring to an end. The dozens of small, militant Islamic groups are only answerable to themselves. The Lebanese militias, by contrast, were in the business of defending and advancing the interests of their communities. When the communal leaders decided to end the conflict, the militiamen stopped fighting and returned to civilian life. The fighting was terrible while it lasted, but it was somehow understandable and the ingredients for a deal were not too hard to detect. No one had to give up everything. Instead, adjustments were made, power was divided a bit differently, space was made for excluded communities, and then people went back to work. The difference in social structure between Algeria and Lebanon accounts for at least some of the difference in the way the political systems have dealt with severe crises and chronic political violence.

The Algerian nationalist movement and the Algerian Islamist movement bear more than a few similarities, most likely rooted in the nature of Algerian society and the egalitarian norms it has spawned. First, the nationalists and the Islamists were both populists, claiming to speak for all the people, a common feature of egalitarian discourse. Second, each became convinced that the only way to achieve its goal— independence and *sharia* (Islamic law)—was to control state power. The French had to be evicted for the nationalists to succeed; similarly, the corrupt National Liberation Front (FLN) establishment had to be ousted for the Islamic project to succeed. The Islamists were not always as blunt in stating this clearly—after all, their adversaries were also Muslim and Algerian—but in moments of stress their totalist ambitions became apparent. They felt entitled to power and were prepared to take it by elections if possible and by other means if not. This is the only sense one can make of the comments by FIS leaders on resort to *jihad*, or religiously sanctioned struggle, if the regime stood in the way of its coming to power by peaceful means.

The potential social base for both the national movement and the Islamists in Algeria was essentially the entire society, and the actual social base proved to be extensive, anchored in similar social milieus at the outset. If anything, the FIS leaders, coming a generation after the nationalists, were better educated, but the followers were still those on the margins of the modern sector, those who did not quite manage to make it in the existing order, but whose aspirations for a better life had been whetted. These were not so much movements of the dispossessed as they were of young, marginalized men who had been exposed to modernity but had been denied its advantages.

Both the FLN and the FIS were broad fronts that emerged quickly in circumstances of crisis, with a strong theme of rejecting all that had come before. True, many of the FLN founders had gotten their start in Messali Hadj's Algerian People's Party (*Parti du Peuple Algérien*, PPA) and the Movement for the Triumph of Democratic Liberties (*Mouvement pour le Triumphe des Libertés Démocratiques*, MTLD), but Messali himself, along with all other political parties, were rejected by the revolutionaries of November 1, 1954. Similarly, the FIS included many who had been associated with the Algerian Association of Ulama and its off-spring, but it also represented a break with the more traditional Islam-ist associations.[11] The FIS, much like the FLN before it, was reluctant to enter alliances with other parties. Instead, it wanted them to dis-band and then join as individuals in the new movement.

Since both the FLN and FIS reflected broad social movements, they were able to dominate the political arena soon after their creation. They seemed to come from nowhere overnight. Lacking much clear-cut hierarchy and little in the way of established tradition, these broad movements were given to factionalism and personality quarrels. Al-most as soon as they formed they began to split, sometimes in debili-tating ways. Maintaining internal discipline was a constant challenge. The FLN split into a number of clans, argued over whether the political or military wing of the movement should prevail, and immediately dissolved into bitter disputes the moment that independence had been won.[12] The FIS was divided between its *salifiyya* wing and the Algeri-anists. Madani and Ben Hadj provided a degree of leadership at the top of the organization, but at crucial moments decisions had to be postponed because a consensus could not be reached. According to one version of what happened, the regime's effort to negotiate with the FIS in 1995 ended when Madani and Ben Hadj could not agree on calling for a truce in the armed struggle. When the FIS split again in 1997, the ostensible issue sounded very much like debates within the FLN forty years earlier.[13]

This factionalized structure is not surprising in broad, egalitarian, populist movements. Such a structure has the effect of breeding a contentious form of politics, characterized by defensive maneuvers, manipulation of others, ideological sloganeering designed to discredit one's adversaries, and little trust among supposed political allies. The existence of a charismatic leader like Ayatollah Khomeini in Iran can ensure some discipline in such a movement, and Khomeini was quite masterful in playing a balancing role among the various factions. But in the absence of such a figure, factional struggles can become intense.[14]

Both the FLN and the FIS rose quickly, and began to splinter quickly. The social movements that they represented were strong enough to survive the instability that infected the top leadership, but neither proved to be a match for the more disciplined structure of the Algerian military. It was Boumediene, the head of the armed forces of the exterior, not the FLN, who managed to seize power in independent Algeria; it is his descendants who still run the country, while the FIS has been disbanded and its followers have drifted to other political movements like Hamas and the gang-like bands of the Armed Islamic Groups (*Groupes Islamiques Armés*, GIA).

Social and Demographic Change

To appreciate the extent to which Algeria as an independent state has witnessed a remarkable transformation of the society, we need to look at the aggregate statistical picture in 1960 and in the early 1990s. What was once a relatively egalitarian society with a strongly egalitarian ethos has become much more differentiated and stratified, much more "modern," without necessarily changing its normative values. This is typical, of course, of rapidly changing societies, and in time one would expect more congruence between social structure and values.

Simply put, Algeria today has a much larger population than at independence; it is younger, more literate, healthier, and more urban. The population at the time of independence was about 10 million. By the year 2000, it will exceed 30 million. In 1962 the average Algerian could expect to live to the age of forty-seven; life expectancy in the early 1990s was sixty-seven. Literacy for adults went from 25 percent in 1970 to about 60 percent in the early 1990s. Per capita income in purchasing power terms tripled from 1960 to the early 1990s, from about $1,200 to over $3,500.[15] Infant mortality has fallen from 168 per 1,000 to about 55 per 1,000 over the same period of time. Most primary and secondary-age students are now actually in school, and a significant number go on for higher education as well.[16]

Much of this change has been the result of state policy. Government spending on health went from 1.2 percent of gross domestic product (GDP) in 1960 to 5.4 percent in 1990; on education, from 5.6 percent to 9.1 percent. (Military expenditures, by contrast, were about 2.7 percent of GDP in 1992.) State policy also reduced the size of the agricultural sector of the economy from 57 percent of the labor force in 1965 to about 12 percent in 1990. Meanwhile the industrial sector expanded to provide jobs for about 45 percent of the labor force; the remainder were in service jobs, many in the government bureaucracy.[17]

During the 1980s estimated income distribution showed that Algeria's lowest 40 percent of households received about 18 percent of its income. The top 20 percent was almost seven times better off than the bottom 20 percent. These disparities seem striking in a supposedly socialist country, as Algeria was until 1989, but they place Algeria among the relatively egalitarian countries on a global scale.[18]

Numbers of these sorts never tell a satisfying story by themselves. But they do give an overall picture of quite substantial change over a thirty-year period. When placed in comparative perspective, several points stand out. Other countries with less wealth actually did better in producing "human development" with their resources. Algeria placed number 82 in the world on the Human Development Index in 1997, a composite measure of wealth, education, and life expectancy.[19] By contrast, it is seventeen ranks higher on GDP per capita. At that level of per capita income, in other words, other countries have done considerably better on social indicators. This probably means that Algeria has overinvested in industrialization at the expense of education and health, even though it has done well on those measures. It also shows a typical pattern of oil-rich countries' failure to translate that wealth into social progress.

By looking at these patterns over time, another crucial point stands out. The rate of change, and of economic growth in particular, was relatively rapid from 1965 to 1980, some 4.2 percent annually. But from 1980 to 1992 average GDP annual growth fell to -0.5 percent. Only since 1994 has growth turned positive again, with 1996 showing about 4 percent growth. With population increase now at about 2.2 percent yearly, this means that per capita growth is quite low, and was actually negative for some of the worst period of Algeria's recent crisis.[20]

Nearly all theories of revolution point to the danger of upheaval when a growing economy and rapidly changing society suddenly lose forward momentum.[21] Expectations of a better life are suddenly dashed, causing enormous and wide-spread resentment that can be readily channeled into protest movements.[22] Sometimes the result is little more than demonstrations and riots; sometimes it is the emergence of a new political force, as with the FIS; and sometimes it contributes to revolution, as in Iran. It is not just coincidence, by these standards, that Algeria's severe crisis coincided with the sudden downturn in the oil market in 1986. This shows how vulnerable an oil-based economy can be to developments beyond its borders.

Another point that stands out from a glance at Algeria's demo-

graphic profile is that the population boom—that period when repro-
ductive habits have not yet changed but infant mortality has begun to
drop rapidly—ensured that a large number of new entrants to the
labor market would arrive just as the Algerian economic model was
coming under enormous strain. From 1960 to 1970 the population
growth rate in Algeria increased, then leveled out and began to decline
later in the 1970s. But all those born in the decade of the 1960s, during
the period of rapid increase, would be entering the labor market in the
1980s. One could anticipate that this would be a particular period of
heavy demand on the regime to provide jobs. But even though growth
rates began to decline in the late 1970s, the absolute number of new
entrants into the labor market will continue to grow steadily until about
2005, at which point it will begin to level out and then slowly decline.
Sometime around 2025 more people will most likely leave the labor
force by retirement than enter it. But for the coming generation, dealing with the consequences of the postindependence population boom
will be a major challenge. Uncertainties about women's participation
in the labor force may cloud this picture somewhat. Algeria has been
at the low end of the scale for the Middle East region in terms of
women working, but that could conceivably change. Indeed, the issue
of women "taking men's jobs" was featured in the FIS election cam-
paigns and was one justification for the party's call on women to stay
at home.

Philippe Fargues, whose research is the basis for these generali-
zations, sees a demographic imbalance that will last about one generation in its acute form. It will end within the next generation, but
not before having contributed to political disorder, as the younger,
more literate cohort rebels against its elders.[23] In short, social and
economic trends combined to produce extremely difficult conditions
for the Algerian regime in the late 1980s, and will continue to do so
for some time. That does not mean that no other path than the one
taken was available, but it does suggest that no easy choices were
at hand to deal with the country's simultaneous socioeconomic and
political crises.

Oil and the Rentier State

Social and economic trends in the 1980s help to explain the emergence of the FIS as a mass-based protest movement. The unraveling

of the old authoritarian order was in large measure due to its inability to cope with the consequences of its earlier successes—large numbers of partly educated young men in the cities looking for jobs—aggravated by the decline in the crucial ingredient of the economic system, oil revenues. Algeria's oil economy certainly made it vulnerable to external shocks. But it also gave the regime more staying power in the 1990s than many expected.

One of the common explanations for the persistence of authoritarian regimes in the Middle East is the prevalence of "rentier states."[24] The central concept here is "rent" revenue that a regime derives from sources external to the society. This can take the form of oil and gas revenues paid directly to the government by foreign companies or economic aid that goes directly to the state budget. In either case, the rents go directly to the regime and can then be used for investment, redistribution of wealth, personal consumption—or it can end up in Swiss banks.[25] However the revenue is used, wisely or unwisely, it does relieve the regime of having to amass capital by other means, namely taxation or borrowing. In the most extreme form—the rentier states of the Gulf region, such as Kuwait and Saudi Arabia—there is almost no direct taxation on incomes. In a play on the American revolutionary slogan of "no taxation without representation," oil-rich regimes seem to be saying "no taxation, therefore no representation." It seems to be true that when a regime needs to tax its population directly, particularly on income earned from other than the government payroll, citizens begin to ask for a role in how the revenues are used. This can be the start of political pressures to make government accountable for how it spends money, a crucial moment in the building of accountable institutions.[26]

Rentier states are not only likely to be able to ward off demands for popular participation by engaging in targeted payoffs; they also inevitably spawn a large public sector. This means that businessmen and the educated middle classes, which are often sources of pressure on regimes for change and accountability, are much more likely to be coopted into the state-controlled sector. Rentier states frequently try to reduce mass demands for participation by offering generous subsidies on food, housing, and electricity. They also typically subsidize unprofitable industries, and they manipulate exchange rates to ensure that imports of crucial items are kept at low prices, which can act as a direct subsidy to state industries that depend on those imports. Businessmen, instead of becoming vigorous proponents of free markets, end up as "crony capitalists," making profits because of their connections to those in power, which gives them access to subsidized goods, cheap credit, and guaranteed prices for their products. In these circumstances, the last thing a businessman wants is real competition.[27]

An obvious corollary of a rentier state is the likelihood of extensive corruption. When access to power is the key to wealth and there are few mechanisms of accountability and little transparency in how financial transactions are handled, corruption, and perhaps more important, the perception of corruption, is likely to become a major political issue.[28]

Algeria is by no means a perfect case of a rentier state, even though it shares some of those features. The most dramatic difference has to do with the role of oil and gas revenues—the rents—in the overall economy of the country. With its population of nearly 30 million, and rents of around $10 billion, Algeria can count on about $350 per capita from oil and gas exports. A country like Saudi Arabia, by contrast, earns much more and has a much smaller population, yielding rents of closer to $5,000 per capita. For Algeria, rents provide a cushion but cannot substitute for a productive economy outside the hydrocarbon sector.

Algeria, as a partial "rentier state," was also particularly vulnerable to the fiscal crisis that hit in the mid-1980s when oil prices plummeted. Faced with a sizable drop in revenues, the Algerian regime had only four choices: cut expenditures significantly in order to avoid a major budget deficit; borrow abroad, as it had been doing for much of the decade; increase taxes; or print money.[29] Each posed different problems. Austerity and tax increases could generate significant social and political protest. Additional borrowing, at high interest rates, could saddle the country with a crushing debt burden, with consequences for the future. Printing money would be inflationary and would lead to a loss of confidence in foreign partners of Algeria.

Faced with this type of fiscal crisis, many regimes have resorted to a tactical opening of the political and economic system. By allowing more participation and freedom, they think they can deflect some of the criticism that will otherwise be directed at them. They may force other political groupings to share some of the responsibility for the economic choices that are made.[30] If an opposition party agrees to support painful economic reform, it may be given more scope for its activities by the regime. Similarly, by opening up the economy, allowing black markets to prosper, regimes give some means for people to earn a living outside the state-controlled sector. In Algeria, the post-1986 period saw an explosion of "trabendo" (black) markets, where goods imported from Europe by individuals, bypassing customs levies, would then be sold at open markets.

Algeria's serious commitment to economic reform began in 1988–89. A new investment code was adopted to encourage foreign participation in the hydrocarbon sector; the dinar was devalued; tax reform was enacted; subsidies were removed; multiple exchange rates were eliminated; and agricultural prices were set by the market. All this was done under the pressure of a severe economic crisis, with a reform-minded team, which was convinced that the old state-centered economy should not be revived.[31] Giacomo Luciani maintains that Algeria carried out in two years reforms that had taken Egypt twenty years to implement.[32] After some hesitation in 1992–93, Algeria pressed ahead with reforms as the necessary price to receive the International Monetary Fund's seal of approval for debt rescheduling. Debt repayment was absorbing nearly all of Algeria's income, and relief was desperately needed. By 1994 Algeria gained a breathing space during which growth resumed. This trend was helped in 1995–96 by higher oil prices, some new investment capital, a good agricultural year, and somewhat greater confidence that the regime would not be ousted by militant Islamists.

With an expanding hydrocarbon sector, some Algerians believe that a return to a variant of a rentier state is possible. But Luciani has persuasively argued that increased hydrocarbon rents "will not allow for enough public investment—and of the right kind—to reabsorb a pool of unemployed which is constantly fed by population dynamics. Stimulating agriculture and labour-intensive industrial projects . . . can be obtained only by encouraging private investment, from within the country as well as from abroad. The path of economic liberalization will therefore need to be resumed, immediately positing the question of a redefinition of the roles of the state and the private sector, and of taxation. The return to authoritarian rule can thus be a parenthesis in Algerian history, and the question of democratization will continue to figure prominently on the political agenda."[33]

Conclusion

By looking carefully at Algeria's social and economic realities over the past several decades, the origins of many facets of Algerian political reality become more clear. Social and economic factors seem more powerful than cultural influences. They help explain the emergence of the unitary, populist state, with its claim to represent all the people; the clannishness and factionalism of Algerian politics as a by-product of extreme egalitarianism within the society. To a great extent the state as a whole became the target of opposition demands as the state presided over the restratification of society. The sudden emergence of the FIS as a protest movement is not surprising when we look at demographic and social trends. Nor is the survival of an unpopular regime, which can maintain itself, in part, by controlling rents from the hydrocarbon sector.

Still, it cannot simply be concluded that Algeria's recent history was entirely determined by these underlying social and economic developments. Somewhat like culture, but with greater precision, these factors helped to frame the choices that political leaders, both in government and in opposition, made. They set boundaries, provide contexts, structure choices, but they did not determine outcomes in a mechanistic way. Even Marx, one of the great economic determinists, acknowledged that "men make their own history, but they do not make it just as they please; they do not make it under circumstances chosen by themselves, but under circumstances directly encountered, given, and transmitted from the past."[34]

If culture, society, and the economy set the stage for, but do not determine, political action, what is the missing piece of the puzzle? In the next chapter, it will be argued that political choice, reflected in the political institutions that have been constructed by Algerian politicians, must be added to any explanation of Algeria's recent history. Politics is not just an epiphenomenon that can be explained by "deeper" structures; it has an autonomy of its own and an impact on those supposedly deeper structures. Indeed, understanding politics— the struggle for power, for who gets to control the allocation of scarce resources in a society, for who monopolizes the use of force—is crucial for an understanding of Algeria. This approach will result in a complex view of Algerian history, one in which politics interacts with social, cultural, and economic change, with political institutions often causing changes in other sectors, rather than merely reflecting those changes. It will also be shown that choices were available at crucial moments that might have opened up alternative outcomes. And, by extension, choices still exist for Algerians looking for a way out of their country's crisis. Political leadership, in this perspective, becomes a crucial ingredient that is often in short supply, but much needed if the future is not simply to resemble the past.

9

Political Perspectives: Institutions and Choices

POLITICAL INSTITUTIONS embody the rules by which the game of politics is played. Those rules may be explicit, embedded in a constitution, widely observed, and respected. Or they may be informal, tacitly understood, susceptible to change, and hotly contested. The more the rules are set and accepted, the more we speak of "institutionalized" political behavior.

It takes time for new institutions to sink roots in society, and recently independent states generally start off with weak institutions, which are often mere facades. This had led many to dismiss the obvious formal institutions of government as not very important. Instead, especially in the Middle East, analysts are generally tempted to look at informal political groups—families, tribes, ethnic groups, powerful individuals and their networks—and to focus on "vertical" linkages between patrons and clients rather than "horizontal" linkages such as class and party.

In much of the Middle East political parties are weak, as are parliaments and interest groups. Power is generally concentrated in the hands of the king or president, backed by the military and supported by a compliant bureaucracy. Civil society—the network of autonomous voluntary groups that often mediate between the state and the individual—is often kept weak and dependent by those in authority. Even businessmen, who might be expected to constitute a pole of opposition to government, instead become dependent on regime subsidies and handouts.

When the old authoritarian model begins to erode, much of the debate over what should come next focuses on institutions. It is not just by chance that the early signs of democratization involve the creation of new political parties and contested elections. These institu-

124

tions may provide the means for making a smooth transition from authoritarian rule to a more open, democratic system. But there is no consensus on which models will work best. Choices are made, and those choices have consequences. The choices have an element of trial-and-error improvisation about them.

The early stages of transition to democracy often have an experimental quality, as contending forces propose various institutional arrangements before settling on ones that meet the multiple criteria of representativeness and coherence, responsiveness and continuity, strength and flexibility. As Adam Przeworski has argued, the challenge is to create institutions that are seen by all major participants as fair and that assure uncertain outcomes. If the institutional arrangements are discriminatory against any major group, they will not pass the test of fairness; if they assure a certain outcome, those who cannot hope to win will not enter the game.[1]

Students of politics have found their way back to the study of institutions. The "new institutionalism" starts with an assumption that the rules of the political game do matter. Therefore, one needs to pay attention to constitutions, electoral systems, the formal structure of presidential or parliamentary systems, the nature of the party system, pacts among parties, the legal system, and so forth. While institutions alone do not assure any particular outcome—they may in fact turn out to be empty shells—there is a chance that agreed rules will influence behavior, especially when institutional arrangements are the outcome of negotiations. It is increasingly believed by many analysts that institutionally constrained behavior will eventually produce a change in norms and values.

From this institutional perspective, one need not wait for democratic norms to exist in a society before democratic politics can take hold. If the institutional arrangements are sound, the values needed to sustain democracy over the long run may well develop as people participate in the new arrangements. Whatever one's skepticism about elections may be at the outset, if one sees the chance for peaceful change over a period of time as a result of elections, then attitudes and values will begin to change. That, at least, is the bet made by those who emphasize the importance of institutions.

Institutionalists also assume that the state matters. While some free-market economists may talk as if the role of the state is simply to get out of the way so that the invisible hand can work its wonders, few political analysts see much virtue in the withering away of the state. The images from Lebanon, Somalia, Rwanda, and Bosnia are too deeply etched in our minds to allow any romantic notions of what might be expected if the state were to collapse. States can certainly be too strong and can inhibit the development of civil society and democracy. But a weak or failed state is a recipe for anarchy and civil war. If there is to be a successful transition from authoritarianism to more accountable political systems, then the state will continue to play an important role in setting the rules of the game, providing security for the population, upholding the rule of law, and opening the political arena to new social forces.[2]

Algeria's Institutional Legacy

The newly independent state of Algeria began with the National Liberation Front (*Front de Libération Nationale*, FLN) and the military. Soon a bureaucracy was formed, a constitution was adopted, and a parliament was elected. Under Houari Boumediene, the presidency became the center of the political system, with the military and security services as the major pillars of the regime. The "troika" that ruled Algeria in the heyday of authoritarianism was the president, the military, and the party. Of these, the party was least important, although it embodied whatever legitimacy was carried over from the revolution.

By the 1980s the authoritarian system was under pressure. The October 1988 explosion of popular discontent set the stage for the first significant change in Algeria's institutions of government. The new constitution allowed for free association and free speech and removed all references to socialism. Very quickly new political forces emerged, parties were formed, newspapers were founded, interest groups were organized, and Algerian political life seemed to change dramatically. If anyone had any doubts about the importance of institutions for political behavior, a glance at what happened after the adoption of the new constitution in 1989 would show that people quickly responded to the new rules.

Algeria's first wave of democratization succeeded in shattering the old FLN. It was unable to adapt to the requirements of competitive politics. Even the presidency was shaken, as Chadli Benjedid was forced to resign. But the military stayed on, demonstrating, if there were any doubt, that it was the key institution in the entire political system.

It is tempting to conclude that the story of Algeria's political development really ended in January 1992 when the military asserted its power. Ever since, the military has held the upper hand. Some would argue that all the institutional developments of the 1990s have been nothing more than window dressing for a military junta. But that would miss the complexity of the Algerian scene, where a number of the institutional experiments from the late 1980s are still alive. The military may well have the central role in politics, but it is not uncontested and it is not alone on the stage. We need to look more carefully at the institutional changes made since 1988. Out of these experiments elements of a pluralistic polity may yet emerge.

Constitutions

Each decade since Algeria's independence has seen a new constitution. This shows quite graphically that there has been little consensus on political rules. In each case, the constitution was imposed from the top, although in 1976 there was considerable debate within the party before a new charter and constitution were adopted.

In 1989 a small group of reformers drafted the constitution. In 1996 the presidency put forward a set of guidelines to amend the constitution, then consulted with most political figures in the country and proceeded to implement its original plan with almost no variation. In short, constitutional rules have never been the result of real negotiation among contending forces, of compromise, or of accommodation. They have been dictated ex cathedra, which has reduced their value as a means of building consensus and legitimacy. Still, they embody a certain number of principles that have influenced the course of politics.

The 1989 constitution reflected several important choices made by Prime Minister Mouloud Hamrouche and his team of reformers. First, the FLN and socialism were nowhere mentioned in the body of the constitution. Second, the all-powerful presidency was somewhat reduced in dimension, although it remained the central institution. The constitution itself was meant to be the supreme law, not subordinate to the national charter as in 1976. A Constitutional Council was established to interpret the document.

With the end of the FLN's role as "état-parti" (state and party), executive power was separated from any mention of political parties. In fact, the constitution only went so far as to acknowledge the right to form "associations of a political nature," along with other rights. The president was to be directly elected for a term of five years. He would no longer have to be nominated by the FLN. Although no mention was made of competitive elections, the door was open to them in the constitution.

Presidential powers were far-reaching, a legacy from the past. The president had the power to name the head of government and to depose him at will. He could name the ministers on recommendation of the head of government. He could dissolve parliament whenever he wanted to. He could oblige the assembly to come into session for a second vote on a law that he did not approve. He had extensive powers to rule by decree in emergency situations. He was not answerable to parliament in any way.[3]

The head of government, or prime minister, was a considerably weaker figure. He had the right to propose legislation and to preside over the Council of Government. Each year he was to present his program to the National Assembly for approval.

The parliament, which was elected to a five-year term, could overthrow the government in two ways. First, it could refuse to approve the program of the government during its annual presentation to parliament. If the program were rejected, the head of government had to resign and the president would name someone else. If the assembly again refused to endorse the government's program, then it would automatically be dissolved and new elections would be held. A second method for ousting a government was by a vote of censure, which required a two-thirds majority.

There were several problems left by this constitution. For example, if the president dissolved the parliament and then resigned, who would have power? This is precisely what happened in January 1992 when Chadli Benjedid was persuaded by the military to step down after dissolving the parliament. The constitutional vacuum was filled, but not without a dispute. In addition, there could be a constitutional vacuum if the parliament refused to vote for a government's program. Until a new head of government was chosen and his program approved, there would be no legal cabinet.

These were just some of the gaps that the constitutional revision of November 1996 set out to fill. Overall, the thrust of the revisions was to strengthen significantly the already strong presidency and to create a second house of parliament that could provide a check on the National Assembly. In addition, the new constitution set out to ensure that no party would be based on any one of the three "fundamental components of national identity"—Islam, Arabism, and *Amazighité* (Berber cultural identity). This provision was clearly aimed at preventing the emergence of parties that identified themselves as Islamist or Berberist.

In terms of powers, the only limitation on the president compared to 1989 was the provision that he could not serve more than two terms. The head of government was also given a somewhat stronger role. If the parliament voted against his program and the parliament was then dissolved, the head of government would stay on until the new parliament had approved a new government.

The other major innovation of the 1996 constitution was the creation of a Council of the Nation, a second house of parliament. Two-thirds of its seats would be chosen by indirect elections by, and from among, members of the communal and provincial councils; one-third would be named by the president. Their terms would be six years. The president of the council would serve as interim president in the event of the dissolution of parliament and a vacancy at the presidency. Legislation passed by the National Assembly would go to the council for approval. There it would have to pass with a three-fourths majority. If the two houses of parliament could not agree on the finance law within seventy-five days, the president could approve it by decree.

The 1996 constitution was the subject of a great deal of debate during the latter half of that year. The president met with most leading political figures, asked them to submit memos on the proposed reforms, and then the final constitutional revisions were submitted to a referendum. Remarkably, after all the so-called dialogue, the government ignored nearly all the suggestions made by the various parties it consulted. As a result most parties expressed reservations and called for a boycott of the referendum or for a negative vote.

A public opinion poll taken before the referendum showed that about 64.7 percent of those polled planned to vote and that about 71.8 percent approved the proposed changes. (In light of these numbers, it is odd that only 29 percent said they were satisfied with the policy pursued by the government since the presidential elections of November 1995.[4]) When the actual vote was reported, many Algerians found the figures incredible. Anecdotal evidence suggested that turnout was in fact rather low, as one might expect in a referendum on complex constitutional matters. It strained credulity to believe that more people had turned out in the constitutional referendum than in the previous year's presidential election. So, Algeria began its experience with a new constitution without it being widely viewed as a legitimate document. Still, the first parliamentary elections under the new system saw the participation of nearly all legal parties. And the new Constitutional Council even made a determination that the attempt by the government to force parties to remove all references to Islam from their party platforms was unconstitutional.[5]

It will take time to see what the results of the 1996 constitution are in practice. One can anticipate a number of problems with the current system. So much power is in the hands of the president that the parliament may turn out to be little more than a debating society, if that. Its potential function of channeling participation from all the major currents of opinion and providing an arena for the peaceful resolution of disputes could be lost. Voters may turn cynical and cease to take parliamentary elections seriously.

Fortunately, the early signs indicate that the parliament elected in 1997 is playing a significant part in Algeria's political life. Debates are lively and are broadcast directly on the national television network. Freedom of speech within the assembly is guaranteed—and exercised. In late 1997, a lengthy debate on security was followed with great interest by a public long excluded from such deliberations. Young parliamentarians, speaking easily understood dialectical Arabic, are developing a following as they routinely criticize the government for its shortcomings. Still, real power is lodged elsewhere.

Since the presidency is almost all-powerful, it will remain the primary focus of political competition. If the opposition some day wins the presidency, the military will have to decide whether to intervene again to prevent change or to allow a major shift in the locus of power, without any obvious constitutional check on a new president. The temptation for the regime may be to allow relatively free parliamentary and local elections, which will not affect real power considerations, and to manipulate the more consequential presidential elections. In short, the political struggle over Algeria's basic institutions of government is likely to remain unsettled for some time.

Electoral Laws

It is fairly well understood that different electoral laws will produce significantly different results. For example, pure proportional representation (PR) tends to be good at reflecting the distribution of opinion in a population. It encourages a high turnout, since every vote counts, even those cast for small parties. Since parties draw up the lists of candidates, they have more clout than in single-member constituencies where the individual candidate may count for more. The typical problem with proportional representation is that it tends to produce a fragmented outcome, with no single party able to form a majority. This can make governing difficult, as stable majorities can be hard to form. Israel, which uses PR for elections to the Knesset, has never had a majority party. All Israeli governments have been coalitions, often with considerable power lying in the hands of small religious parties that offer their support to larger parties in return for specific payoffs to their constituents. In Turkey, PR produced in 1996 an outcome where the top three parties each received about 20 percent of the vote. The Islamist Party was briefly able to win the prime minister's office in coalition with a secular party, which alarmed the military, as well as many of the nearly 80 percent of Turks who had not voted for the Islamists.

The value of effective representation, which PR assures, is high in early stages of democratization. If people are to take voting seriously, they should see that their vote counts, which it does under this system. Algeria used PR for the first time in the parliamentary elections of June 1997. Since parties drew up the lists of candidates, and each voter had the choice of selecting one list, the parties themselves were strengthened. Correspondingly, the idea of individual representatives being responsible before their constituents was weakened. No one voted for an individual candidate, only a party list.[6]

For reasons that are not entirely clear, a decision was made by Hamrouche early in 1991, and then reaffirmed by the National Assembly prior to the December 1991 elections, to use two-round majority system in the parliamentary elections.[7] This system was designed to favor large parties, or those whose votes were concentrated in specific districts. Small parties had little chance of winning any seats, and there was a good chance of significant overrepresentation. If one party prevailed in each district by a few percentage points, it could theoretically win all the seats in parliament with only slightly more than 50 percent of the vote. This system, popular in France, was specifically designed to overcome the fragmentation of the French Fourth Republic by producing stable governing majorities.

Hamrouche's reasoning for opposing PR was that it would prevent the renewal of the FLN. The old guard would dominate the process of drawing up party lists. Instead, he wanted to encourage new party activists who had grass-roots support and might be able to win single-member constituency races because of their local popularity. This goal may have been worthy, but the results were catastrophic for the FLN.

In the Algerian case, where parties were not yet well institutionalized, and no one had a clear idea of what the effect of this voting system would be, the results helped the Islamic Salvation Front (*Front Islamique du Salut*, FIS), not the FLN. First, turnout was low, with only slightly more than 50 percent of voters casting valid ballots. Not surprisingly, many who might have supported small parties or independents realized that their candidates had no chance of winning, so they stayed home. With splits in the ranks of the non-Islamist parties, the FIS was well on its way to a crushing victory.

Try to imagine what the electoral outcome in December 1991 might have been with PR. More people probably would have voted, mostly those who supported candidates other than those of the three fronts—the FIS, the FLN, and the Socialist Forces Front (*Front des Forces Socialistes*, FFS). That might have amounted to another 15–20 percent of the electorate. Assuming no other change than that, the outcome in terms of parliamentary seats would have been approximately as follows: 35 percent FIS, 20 percent FLN, 10 percent FFS, all others 35 percent. Even if these figures are off by plus or minus 5 percent, the general picture does not change. No single party would have been able to claim a majority of the public on its side; any government would have required the support of a coalition of parties. The FIS would have a strong voice (in a weak institution), but it could not expect to impose its views on everyone else. At best, coalition politics might have encouraged compromise. At worst, new elections would have been called and some of the smaller parties might have forged alliances with the larger ones. But there would have been no crisis, no panic, and no need for the military to consider intervention. This one change in institutional arrangements might have helped salvage Algeria's first, tentative experiment with democracy.

Political Parties

When Algeria first made the transition from one-party state to a multiparty one, the law on parties was remarkably lax. Any group of a dozen individuals could declare themselves a party and could qualify for government subsidies. Not surprisingly, this led to an explosion of parties, some fifty within the first two years. Many were little more than a prominent name and a few of his friends. Only a handful had any real roots in the society. The reformers seemed so intent on undermining the FLN old guard that they were prepared to allow almost any group to call itself a party.

The most remarkable decision made after the new party law in 1989 was the decision to recognize the FIS as a legal party. This decision was viewed by many as contravening the law on parties, which excluded any party based exclusively on religion. In most countries of the Middle East, parties like the FIS were not legal, or were at least forced to remove Islam from their name and to refrain from claiming that they were the sole spokesman for Muslims. Some have noted that Prime Minister Merbah had already recognized the Rally for Culture and Democracy (*Rassemblement pour la Culture et la Démocratie*, RCD), a Berber party, which had helped maintain calm in Kabylia during the October 1988 riots. How could the Chadli regime refuse to recognize the FIS, which had played a crucial role in bringing the riots to an end? In any case, the FIS was a significant force in society by this time, and it would have been costly to try to exclude it from a role in politics.[8] It is remarkable that the decision to legalize the FIS without conditions was never debated or made the subject of government deliberation. It was simply done, most likely at the direction of the president.

The new party law approved in 1997 set out to ensure that the "errors" of 1989 would not be made again. To be recognized as a legal party, stringent requirements had to be met. Members in all parts of the country had to be registered; a party platform had to be approved; a probationary period of one year had to be passed; and no partisan use could be made of Arabism, Islam, or Berberism. This latter provision was controversial, but was used to force legal parties such as

An-Nahda and Hamas to change their names. In the case of An-Nahda, the word "Islamic," originally part of its name, was dropped; Hamas changed its name from the Movement for Islamic Society to the Movement for a Peaceful Society (*Mouvement pour une Société de Paix*, MSP). The FIS remained banned.

With such tight constraints on party organization, there is some risk that voters will write off the parties as creatures of the regime. The National Democratic Rally (*Rassemblement National Démocratique*, RND), in particular, will be seen as the president's party, which will ensure it support in some quarters, but not in all. Part of the appeal of the FIS as an opposition movement was the resolute stance that it took against the old order. By forcing the parties to accept so many conditions, the regime might well deprive them of legitimacy in the eyes of their members. In trying to prevent the emergence of a future FIS, the regime may simply prevent the emergence of any strong parties. At the same time, the new party law precludes the emergence of a legal party that might try to overthrow the constitutional order, which the FIS had come quite close to doing.

The Role of the Military

No one will dispute that the Algerian military has played a dominant role in the country's political development. At the moment of independence, it helped to prevent the outbreak of civil war. It has essentially determined who would govern the country at each moment of transition, from Ahmed Ben Bella to Boumediene, from Boumediene to Chadli Benjedid, from Chadli to Mohammed Boudiaf, from Boudiaf to Ali Kafi, from Kafi to Liamine Zeroual. For those who try to understand Algeria's opaque politics today, much of the discussion turns on generals such as Tewfik Mediène, Mohammed Lamari, Mohammed Betchine, Khalid Nezzar, and a few others.[9] Some profess to see complex factional struggles among these powerful figures, and this is quite likely true. But this is a realm of Algerian politics that is closed to ordinary Algerians and to most of the outside world.

Those who defend the role of the military say that it saved the country from an Islamic revolution in 1991, a revolution that would have inevitably led to a civil war, with higher costs than those that have ensued. But even those who see the need for a strong role for the military are quick to comment on the political limitations of generals in politics. Boudiaf, who was not a military man, was seen as a politician who had something of a common touch, who spoke to people in their own language, and who tried to persuade. Zeroual, by contrast, is remote, rarely tries to explain his policies, and seems content to surround himself with other generals. Many have noted that during the spate of terrorist killings of villagers during 1997, Zeroual never visited the scene of the massacres to extend condolences to the surviving family members or visit the wounded in the hospitals. Instead, he issued televised statements saying that the military was on the verge of eliminating "residual terrorism."

Given the strong role of the Algerian military in politics today, is there any way for it to withdraw from day-to-day governance and adopt a more distant role as guardian of the state and protector of the Constitution—a role more analogous to that of the military in Turkey, Pakistan, or even Chile? It is probably unrealistic to think that the military can quickly be brought under full civilian control as in Argentina, Spain, or Greece.[10]

Skeptics will argue that the Algerian military and its civilian allies have no incentive to step aside from the commanding positions they now occupy. Not only do they see themselves as the guardians of the nation, but they have also profited handsomely from their powerful position. Many observers, especially in France, have detailed the extent to which members of the establishment have financially profited from their positions. It did little to enhance the prestige of Ali Kafi during his brief tenure as head of the High State Council when his son was seen driving an expensive car around the wealthy districts of Algiers. One notable case of financial corruption in the military did come to light, that of General Mustafa Benloucif, but many suspect that other cases exist as well.

Several possibilities seem to exist for reducing the dominant role of the military in Algerian political life. First, at some point a strong civilian candidate may run for the presidency, perhaps in the election to be held in 2000. A victory at the polls by a civilian would place enormous constitutional power in the hands of someone other than a military officer. How that power would be used, and what sorts of assurances could be given to the military to convince them to return to the barracks, would be major tests of the new president.

Almost certainly, the military will seek guarantees of its corporate interests in exchange for any dilution of its political role. It will want to continue to control promotions and personnel policy.[11] It will also insist on immunity from prosecution for any excesses committed during the long campaign against the armed Islamists. Experience in other countries shows that this is often a delicate issue. Democrats are reluctant to grant immunity to those believed to have engaged in serious human rights abuses. But unless such immunity is offered, it may be impossible to convince the military to step aside. Chile offers one model where guarantees were offered, to the dismay of some democrats; South Korea shows another model, where former heads of state, including generals, have been prosecuted for their abuses when in office.

Turkey provides another example of giving the military an important role, while extricating the officers from day-to-day political management. After three overt interventions in political life in as many decades, and frequent rewriting of the constitution under pressure of the military, Turkey today has a National Security Council on which the generals sit and where they set overall defense and internal security policy. The president of the country is relatively weak, and the prime minister must rule with a parliamentary majority. In recent years, this has meant that Turkish democracy has developed without the direct threat of military intervention, although the military continues to act as the guardian of the constitution and of the legacy of Ataturk. It was not shy in warning the Islamist prime minister in mid-1997 where the lines were that he must not cross. And eventually, a non-Islamist coalition was forged. But this time the military did not send tanks into the street; the outgoing prime minister was not arrested; and the changes were made according to the constitution, albeit with the heavy hand of the military leading the way.

The last alternative for altering the role of the military would be a major purge of the top-ranking officers. The Iranian case shows that this can happen, but only in extreme circumstances. Short of a revolution or military defeat, this seems highly unlikely in Algeria.

This leaves some form of pact between new political forces and the military as one option. At one point, the FIS was clearly tempted by this idea in 1991, hoping that it could enlist the military's support against the FLN. Any realistic politician from outside the ranks of the military will have to figure out whether some sort of deal or pact is possible that gives guarantees, but not a veto, to the military. The other possibility is something like an institution that gives the military a role in protecting the state and the constitutional order—a security council of some sort. Whichever institutional arrangement is pursued, it seems clear that managing the military's return to the barracks may well be the most difficult challenge for an Algerian democrat. Yet without such a development, democracy cannot really be expected to flourish.

Pacted Transitions

The remarkably successful transition in Spain from authoritarian rule to well-functioning democracy, followed by a number of comparable cases in Latin America, has raised interest in the notion of "pacts" as a device for managing transitions to democracy.[12] The idea here is that the various political groups contending for power need some assurances about the rules of the game before they enter the uncertain world of democratic politics. This may take the form of some guarantees of representation of minorities (some seats can be set aside in parliament), assurances that a federal system will be adopted that allows a degree of decentralization of power, term-limits to ensure that power will not indefinitely be monopolized by one faction, transparency in budget decisions, the presence of international observers during elections, guarantees of equal access to the media, and so forth.

What has been seen in Algeria to date are largely efforts at transition without pacts. When the FIS was legalized in 1989, there might have been an opportunity to work out a pact of some sort. The regime would agree to recognize the FIS in return for assurances from the FIS that it would not challenge the constitution by extra-legal means, would commit itself not to use inflammatory language about *jihad* in the domestic arena, and would agree to respect the outcome of elections in which it participated. The nature of the election law could have been worked out between the FLN and FIS, with both parties agreeing on proportional representation as the fairest means to test their strength. But none of this was done. The entire preparation of the communal and parliamentary elections was done without consultation with opposition parties, or with very little. It was the FLN-dominated National Assembly that voted the election law, without the benefit of an electoral commission made up of several parties.

Another opportunity for a pact between the government and the main opposition parties arose in early 1995. The government had been in contact with the FIS leaders in prison to see if a deal could be made whereby the FIS would condemn the radical Armed Islamic Groups (*Groupes Islamiques Armés*, GIA) violence and rein in its own followers. At various moments in 1994 it seemed as if a deal might be struck. Then, in January, the FIS lined up with the FLN and the FFS, as well as several other parties, behind the Sant'Egidio principles. The regime had clearly known that this attempt at a common platform was going on, and had even made some of the contacts possible. But when confronted with the actual document, its response was unequivocal. It rejected the document "in detail," even though much of the language in the document was not much different than its own. It might have been possible to see Sant'Egidio as a basis for discussion, or to at least point to those specific parts that were problematic. But instead, this bid for a pact between the regime and its opponents was totally rejected.

Again in 1996–97, the government proposed constitutional reforms, a new party law, and a new electoral law without much attempt at reaching an agreement with the opposition. While consultations took place and there was some discussion of alternatives, the end result did not represent a consensus based on compromise. Indeed, it is striking how similar the initial proposals of the regime were to the final result. One wonders if any of the suggestions made by political figures and parties were paid any attention.

Based on recent evidence, there seems little interest on the part of the Algerian regime in the model of a pacted transition. Instead, the rules for a new political order will be laid down from the top and the opposition will be given the choice of joining in or boycotting. The determination not to lose control over the process is perhaps understandable in light of what happened in 1991, but insistence on maintaining control is ultimately in conflict with the goal of opening up the system. Some risks must be taken in return for the benefits of democratization in the form of legitimacy and commitment to peaceful competition. But this notion of a pact to ensure that democracy will not mean winner-take-all outcomes is still not widely accepted in Algeria.

Electing a New Legislature

The Algerian government went to considerable lengths to ensure that the parliamentary elections in 1997 would not be a repeat of 1991.

This led some observers to conclude that they were "sham elections."[13] But that judgment is too harsh. The elections were flawed, but not to the point of lacking all credibility.

First, the technical organization of the elections was meticulous. Voters were carefully registered, with voting lists publicly displayed well in advance of the elections. An electoral commission consisting of representatives of the major parties was created, and the regime welcomed international monitors, including about one hundred under United Nations' auspices. In addition, the parties were allowed to have poll watchers in the voting stations and during the count and compilation of the vote.

Several abuses were widely mentioned during the election. For example, the security forces all voted in special locations without observers present. Not surprising, most of these votes went to the pro-government party, the RND. As many as 100,000 votes might have been affected. In addition, in rural areas the government provided mobile voting booths to reach remote locations, and these were not always under the supervision of observers. Again, these votes went heavily to the government (as the vote generally does in rural areas). In addition, there were some instances of observers being denied access during the vote and the compilation of the vote. Many of these abuses were reported to the electoral commission, and a few investigations were made, but many complaints were simply ignored. All the opposition parties protested.

The international observers sent under UN auspices were divided in their opinions. They did not declare the election "free and fair," but they did not condemn it as fraudulent either. Some of the observers were impressed by what they saw; others were not. One of the harshest critics, who felt that the election "lacked soul" and that people were simply going through the motions, nonetheless judged that fraud could not have changed the outcome by more than plus or minus 5 percent.[14] Assuming that such an estimate is not too far off, the numbers cannot be taken literally as an expression of Algerian sentiment, but can nonetheless be seen as rough indicators of popular sentiment.

Of the 16.767 million Algerians registered to vote, 10.999 million went to the polls, and all but about 500,000 cast valid ballots. This yields a turnout of about 65 percent, lower than the presidential election of 1995 but higher than the 1991 parliamentary elections. Table 9-1 provides the official results.

Table 9-1. *1997 Parliamentary Results*

Party[a]	Seats[b]	Votes[c]	Seats[d]	Votes[d]
RND	156	3.53	41	32
MSP	69	1.53	18	14
FLN	62	1.49	16	14
Nahda	34	0.92	9	8
FFS	20	0.53	5	5
RCD	19	0.44	5	4
Independents	11	0.48	3	4
PT	4	0.19	1	2
Others	5	0.15	1	2

a. Nearly 1 million votes were cast for parties that failed to win any seats and for unsuccessful independents. RND = *Rassemblement National Démocratique* (progovernment); MSP = *Mouvement de la Sociéte de Paix*; FLN = *Front de Libération Nationale* (nationalist); Nahda (Islamist); FFS = *Front des Forces Socialistes* (Democratic, Berberist); RCD = *Rassemblement pour la Culture Démocratique* (Berberist, Secularist); PT = *Parti des Travailleurs*. The Sant'Egidio platform was signed by representatives of the FLN, FFS, Nahda, and PT.
b. Number.
c. Millions.
d. Percent.

The strong showing of the RND raised serious questions since the party was so young and the regime was not generally believed to be very popular. Still, the habit of voting for the government is often strong in late-authoritarian regimes and the RND doubtless benefited by being seen as the government's party. It had advantages of privileged access to television, extensive coverage in the press, and expectations of future patronage. The other proregime party, the FLN, also did somewhat better than expected. Together, the FLN and RND controlled about 57 percent of the seats in parliament (not far from the 61 percent of the vote that Zeroual won in November 1995). The two Islamist parties controlled about 27 percent of the seats; this increased slightly when a few independent Islamists were added. An-Nahda did well in the Constantine area; Hamas (MSP) claimed to have been cheated, but readily took the seats offered. The two Berber parties held slightly more than 10 percent of the seats, which tracks well with their previous votes.

What happened to the FIS voters of 1991 in this election? No one can be sure. The FIS urged its followers not to vote, but said that if they did they should vote for parties like An-Nahda or even the Trotskyists who had supported the Sant'Egidio platform. Presumably the FIS voters went several directions—some must have abstained, some voted for Islamist alternatives to the FIS, and some for independents.

The election, even with its flaws, shows the difference electoral rules can make. The number of seats won by each party corresponded much more closely with the number of votes actually received than in 1991, as one would expect with PR voting. The resulting government was a coalition, with significant representation from three parties. (Some of the most difficult ministries were given to the MSP and FLN, no doubt so that they would be blamed for shortcomings.)

The next stage of institution building was the organization of local elections for *willaya* and communal councils in October 1997. Those leaders would then elect from among their midst two-thirds of the members of the new second chamber, the Council of the Nation. (The remaining one-third is appointed by the president.) When all these institutions were in place, the challenge would be to see if they made any difference in the way the country was run—and, as important, in the way ordinary Algerians felt about their government.[15]

One early sign that the postelection environment might produce surprises was the release of two prominent FIS leaders: first Abdel-kader Hachani and then, briefly, Abbassi Madani in mid-July. Coupled with the retirement of several hard-line generals, this action could be seen as a gesture toward the parliamentary opposition, and more generally the Islamists, who all urged that the FIS leaders be released. Whether the FIS could be revived in some form, or whether its leaders could play a role in ending the chronic violence in the country, re-mained to be seen.[16] But it appeared to be a step in the right direction and was welcomed by most Algerians.

Just as there seemed to be some prospect for an improvement in the political environment, however, the extremists of the GIA launched an all-out campaign of terror in the countryside around Algiers and even in the outlying slums of the city. Hundreds of innocent civilians were slaughtered. Whatever the motives behind these grisly attacks, the inability, or unwillingness, of the government to provide basic security was a direct challenge to its legitimacy. Many Algerians went so far as to accuse the government of complicity in the killings. The regime tried to deny the seriousness of the new round of violence, which further eroded its credibility. With local elections on the horizon in October 1997, the violence was bound to have political implications, even if the strongest reaction of most Algerians was a feeling of re-vulsion toward the perpetrators of the massacres. Hatred for the extre-mists would not automatically mean support for the government, how-ever, since some believed the GIA was a creation of the regime. At a minimum, it was likely to deepen the feeling of many Algerians that there were no good alternatives on the horizon, adding to their alien-ation and cynicism about politics.

As the security situation in the country seemed to deteriorate in fall 1997, another surprising development took place when the armed wing of the FIS, the Islamic Salvation Army (*Armée Islamique du Salut*, AIS), announced a truce, to go into effect on October 1. This clearly seemed to be a result of some form of negotiation between the regime and the FIS leadership, both presumably hoping to bring an end to the GIA-led slaughter. Whether the FIS, perhaps under a new label, would be allowed to return to the political arena, and whether it could help restore civil peace if it did, remained an unanswered question.

Completing the Institutional Architecture

From the outset, the Zeroual regime had doggedly pursued a strat-egy of rebuilding political institutions to its own specifications. Parlia-mentary elections in June 1997 had been the first step, followed by local and provincial ones in October. While there had been charges of fraud in June, there was a much more vocal protest from opposition parties when the one-sided results of the October elections came in. According to official statistics, the RND won 55 percent of the seats in the communal assemblies; the FLN won 22 percent, the MSP won only 6.8 percent, the FFS about 5 percent, and independents another 4 percent. The results for the provincial assemblies were about the same, with the RND receiving 52 percent of the seats, the FLN with 20 percent, and the MSP with 14 percent. With such results, the regime was sure to control political life at the local level, but at the cost of further damaging its credibility. Almost no one seemed to believe that the elections had been free and fair, and no international observers had been allowed to monitor the proceedings.

One reason the local elections were important was that the upper house of parliament, with considerable powers, would be elected by and from these local and provincial delegates. And in order to be able to pass any legislation at all, the government would need three-fourths of the votes, because of a constitutional provision. To get such an outcome, the regime seems to have resorted to widespread manipulation. When the results of the election for the Council of the Nation were announced in December, 80 of the 96 seats that were chosen by ballot went to the pro-government RND. Another 48 seats were appointed by the president, mostly from among known political personalities of the past. Nothing in the composition of the upper chamber did anything to dilute the reality of power concentrated in the hands of the president. So, after all the effort to create institutions during 1997, Algeria seemed no closer to having a government that was genuinely representative of its people. What had begun as an exercise to restore legitimacy and bring civil peace had done neither.

Conclusions

When a country is in deep crisis, one way out is a reshaping of the political system. By doing so, new social forces can be accommodated, a new sense of commitment may be generated, and peaceful means of handling conflict may be found. But much depends on the new institutions that are chosen and on how those choices are made.

There is no correct institutional model that suits all countries. Nor is there any way to be certain in advance what the consequences of specific choices will be. Uncertainty is endemic in rapidly changing societies with high-stakes political contests. No one should be surprised if institutional choices have unintended consequences and need to be revised in light of experience. When institutions are well designed, they should include mechanisms for their adaptation and revision in light of new circumstances. The point is that such changes of rules—which may be needed—should be made according to rules if parties are to learn to compete within a legal institutional framework.

In looking at the Algerian experience of the past decade, the period when conscious efforts to change the political system have been made, one is struck by two points: almost all efforts of institutional change have been made from the top down, with little apparent consultation or negotiation among contending parties; and the specific institutional models that have been adopted have been biased in favor of a strong executive, with little attention paid to the importance of representation and decentralization. These two features of Algeria's approach to institutional change are perhaps understandable in light of historical experience. Algerians of all backgrounds have been convinced of the need for a strong state, and only recently have they begun to talk of their society as a complex, pluralistic one that could not easily be fitted into a single mold. The populist, unitary, even messianic view of the state has not entirely faded, although experience has taught most Algerians to be suspicious of those with power and with claims to speak for them.

Apart from this tendency to privilege institutions of control and order over those of representation and accountability, the Algerian experience has been marked by a series of unfortunate decisions along the way to creating new institutions. First among the questionable decisions was that of legalizing the FIS without any apparent quid pro quo in 1989. Presumably the FIS was eager to be recognized; it had adopted a relatively moderate platform and might have been persuaded to adopt even more explicit commitments to a nonhegemonic project. Second, one can question the wisdom of starting the democratic experiment with local elections. In principle, this may have seemed to minimize the risks, but it in fact whetted the FIS appetite, while ensuring that the regime began to lose control at the grass-roots level where services were delivered. Third, the FIS made a major error in calling an unlimited strike in May–June 1991. Many FIS leaders were opposed, but Madani and Ben Hadj went ahead nonetheless. If the strike had been called primarily to protest the election law, or to demand an end to gerrymandering or any other limited goal, it might have been possible to negotiate an agreement. But an unlimited strike sounded like a bid for power without elections, and this provided the pretext for the military to oust the reformist prime minister, who was actually prepared to work with the FIS, and then to arrest the FIS leaders themselves. Fourth, the choice of a winner-take-all electoral system in 1991 was certainly a mistake. Had the elections been held under proportional representation, the results might have been accepted by most groups in society, including the military.

It is hard to say whether the military's decision to cancel the 1991 elections was an error of the same magnitude. It had enormous consequences, and it ushered in a terrible period of violence. But by the time the election was held, no easy choices were left. If Chadli Benjedid had been a stronger president and the military had had more confidence in him, it might have made sense to let the elections take place, live with their results, and only move against the FIS if it sought to overturn the constitutional order. But those conditions did not exist in January 1992.

More recently, the regime's hasty rejection of Sant'Egidio looks ill-considered. This might have provided a way out of the crisis before the GIA had become such a violent part of the scene. Again, after the impressive presidential election in November 1995, the Zeroual regime lost an opportunity to turn public support in the direction of reconciliation and a political settlement. Most of the parties were offended by the mechanical way in which Zeroual went through the motions of consulting them. Reformers in the FLN resented the regime's heavy hand in dragging the party back into conformity with its views. The FLN loyalists were resentful when the regime promoted a new party, the RND, to carry its flag in the parliamentary elections in 1997. The apparent rigging of the October 1997 local elections angered all opposition parties, including the FLN.

All these choices might have been made differently. There is no guarantee, of course, that they would have ensured a different outcome to Algeria's crisis. And the choices already made, even if flawed, do not preclude an eventual breakthrough in Algeria's search for a solution to its political and economic problems. But the first attempts at democratization have been troubled, to say the least, and one cannot be overly optimistic about the future. If democracy is to lie anywhere in Algeria's near future, better choices will have to be made by those in power—and by those in opposition.

10

A Democratic Algeria?

A LGERIA IS rarely thought of as a country with a possible democratic future. Instead, if democracy in Algeria is mentioned at all, it is usually in the context of the canceled election of 1992. Was this evidence that democracy would never be allowed to take root in an Arab country, especially if it was accompanied by a militant Islamic opposition movement? Or was this a case of the military acting to prevent a fascist-like movement from hijacking democracy? Whichever the answer, Algeria seemed stuck with a nondemocratic regime.

Algeria does not look much different from other authoritarian regimes, especially those in Latin America and Central America, that have moved hesitantly toward democracy. Many of them had to deal with powerful military establishments that were used to having a strong say in government. Some, such as Colombia and Guatemala, had endured prolonged domestic violence. Most had serious problems of income distribution and social inequality. By comparison, Algeria's problems do not seem insurmountable.

The Essence of Democracy

Democracy has the disadvantage of being defined by the rules it provides rather than the ends that it promises. No one can credibly say that democracy guarantees good government, economic well-being, an end to corruption, equality, or justice. Democracy is the solution to one major problem in politics—the problem of tyranny. Democracy, if it means anything, means that people can rid themselves of truly bad government without going to the barricades, without revolution, and without the gun. Ballots, not bullets, can remove the tyrant.

An important corollary of this central point about democracy is that people have the right to change their mind. They may make a mistake—elect a tyrant or an incompetent—but that should not deprive them of the right to choose again and to oust a leader that they previously embraced. People may not always be able to articulate exactly what they want from their government, but they can usually be counted on to know when they do not like what they are getting.

The precise institutional arrangements that can guarantee these basic rights to select one's leaders and to hold them accountable for their acts can take many forms. But central to the exercise of democracy is the holding of elections.[1] This is the primary means for the expression of popular sovereignty.

Not all elections qualify as fully democratic. Here, as in most things political, there are degrees by which democracy can be evaluated. Robert Dahl identified the two key dimensions of democracy. One is participation: Do all citizens have equal access, in a legal sense, to the political process? Today, the norm in democratizing countries is universal adult suffrage, but that has not always been the case. England and America claimed to be democratic before they allowed universal suffrage, and indeed much of the nineteenth and early twentieth century involved struggles over extending the franchise. With a restricted franchise, it is easier to open up the political arena to contending forces. In the Middle East today a country like Kuwait still limits the vote to certain categories of male citizens. But elsewhere, the norm of universal adult suffrage has taken root. If elections are to be held, then every citizen has the right to participate. Algeria fits this profile.

Dahl's second dimension is contestation. What issues in society are resolved by competition? Are some topics off limits, such as the role of the military? Does the elected parliament have real control over the budget? Are certain issues considered taboo for politicians, such as the status of religious institutions? Generally, the more issues that are open to contestation, the more that can be debated and decided by deliberation and voting, the more democratic a political system is considered.[2] So the questions to be asked when assessing the degree of democratization present in an electoral system are these: Who participates? What issues can they and their representatives decide?

Przeworski asks the basic question about democracy: Why would losers in a democratic election accept the outcome? After all, there will be winners and losers, and it is not intuitively obvious why those who fail to win power will continue to abide by the rules.

The Algerian case shows that an election that upsets the old order without assurances of what the new order will bring can impel the losers to cancel the results of the election, as they did in 1992. Przeworski answers his question about why the losers should abide by the results in the following way: "Some institutions under certain conditions offer to the relevant political forces a prospect of eventually advancing their interests that is sufficient to incite them to comply with immediately unfavorable outcomes. Political forces comply with present defeats because they believe that the institutional framework that organized the democratic competition will permit them to advance their interests in the future."[3] In other words, a time dimension can become important in the calculus of politicians in a democratic setting. By playing by the rules, they may improve their situation in the future, compared to the consequences of rejecting the rules entirely and seeking other means to advance their interests.

This nuanced understanding of democracy—of the appreciation for its open-endedness, of the value of rules and institutions—does not develop overnight. There is a great deal of evidence to suggest that these features of democracy are not much appreciated by those eager to bring about rapid social and economic change. The common complaints about democracy are that it does not produce a strong government, that well-organized interests can prevent change, that coalitions are often unwieldy, and that money can buy votes. For those who want clear direction and are impatient with the old order, democracy may not be very appealing. But when it is, the perception of fairness and open-endedness, and the existence of institutions that ensure a second chance to losers are crucial. Without them, democracy has little chance to win over the skeptics.

Fareed Zakaria has written of the rise of illiberal democracy where freely elected regimes ignore minority rights, the rule of law, and limits on their power.[4] He argues that too much attention has been paid to the holding of elections, without parallel efforts to emphasize those aspects of democratic theory that make for "liberal" democracy—the most important being constitutional balances and respect for basic human rights. While valid, this emphasis on the importance of liberal values should not be used as an argument against the holding of elections until such values are already well established. It is, after all, the interplay of institutions and values that eventually helps consolidate democratic practices. The point about elections in postauthoritarian settings is that they should be fair and should be held on a regular basis, and that simultaneous efforts should be made to strengthen the institutions needed to make democracy work—the press, courts, parties, voluntary organizations, and so forth. But elections still remain a crucial part of the democratic architecture and should not be devalued because they do not by themselves ensure liberal constitutional order.

Transitions

A voluminous literature now exists on transitions from authoritarianism to democracy. The democratic wave of the 1980s, which brought most of Latin America, Eastern Europe, and parts of Asia into the democratic fold, has led to many models and hypotheses. Notably, the Muslim Middle East is almost entirely absent from this literature, largely because of the paucity of convincing democratic cases. Nonetheless, Turkey, Jordan, Lebanon, Yemen, Iran, Palestine, Morocco, Egypt, Kuwait, and Algeria have all experimented with competitive elections and have called into question some aspects of the old authoritarian model. But only in Turkey and Lebanon have incumbent governments been peacefully replaced by means of a democratic election, and even in these cases the process has been uneven. Thus, in talking about the Middle East and democracy, it is reasonable to think that we are seeing, at best, the early phases of transitions away from authoritarian government toward partial democratization. Still, the processes that brought change in Latin America, Asia, and parts of Africa may well have similar effects in the Middle East.

One point that the transition literature makes clear is that change often begins with serious divisions within the elite.[5] This does not always mean that change must come from the top; splits in the regime may be in response to challenges from below, but in virtually all cases of transitions there is a divergence between reformers and hard-liners. The reformers in the regime do not want to commit suicide. Instead, they see the chance of perpetuating their hold on power by allying with some of the emerging social forces. With a broader base, the regime might be able to survive longer.[6]

A classic formulation of how democratization can begin "without democrats" as a result of internal conflicts was provided in 1970 by

Dankwart Rustow.[7] The first stage, in his view, is a prolonged dispute that no single party can win. He calls this a "hot family feud."[8] As summarized by Waterbury, he argued that "positions tend to be polarized, and democracy is espoused tactically, as a means to other ends. Then comes the decision phase in which the major antagonists recognize a no-win stalemate and negotiate compromises. . . . In this phase democratic rules and various quid pro quos are agreed upon. In the third phase, repeated plays of the democratic game produce habituation and, presumably with time, a positive identification of most citizens with the democratic rules."[9] (It is worth noting that Rustow constructed his model after studying Sweden's transition to democracy, among others.)

Pressure for change can come suddenly from external sources, such as a military defeat or as the result of a severe economic crisis. If the economic crisis obliges the regime to borrow from abroad, or to turn to the International Monetary Fund (IMF) for help, it may be subject to irresistible demands for economic reforms. To deflect blame from itself for an austerity program, a regime may think it necessary to bring new elements into government, such as representatives of the workers or businessmen.

Once a transition begins, the specific path that a country will take is likely to be heavily influenced by the nature of the prior authoritarian regime.[10] Here the contrast is between authoritarian regimes such as Franco's Spain, where there was little ideology and some predictability and autonomy for social groups, compared to Mao's totalitarian state, which allowed little autonomy and tried to mobilize society according to an explicit ideology. Another variant is post-totalitarian rule, such as Khrushchev's USSR, where careerism set in, the ideology went stale, and cracks appeared in the previously solid facade of government and society. Finally, the highly personalistic dictatorship of a ruler like Saddam Hussein—termed "Sultanism" by Weber—can be very erratic and tends toward dynastic rule. Using these categories, one might locate Algeria in the Boumediene era somewhere between authoritarian and post-totalitarian. Linz and Stepan argue that this type of regime may find it easier to arrive at a "pacted" transition with guarantees for the military than the other models.[11] Totalitarian or Sultanistic regimes are susceptible to collapse—as in Romania—whereas the milder authoritarian variants may allow for a negotiated transition.

The southern European cases of Spain, Portugal, and Greece are encouraging for those looking for rapid transitions to consolidated democracy after periods of authoritarian rule. But these cases may be less important to our understanding of the Algerian case than those in Latin America, where the role of the military seems comparable. When the military does not collapse or change sides, it has to be dealt with by reformers and democrats as a continuing actor during the transition and beyond. Handling the military is likely to be the most difficult task facing a new democracy, but Latin American cases show considerable variety in outcomes, from strongly institutionalized prerogatives for the military, as in Chile, to civilian control in Uruguay.

In thinking about transitions, one must be careful not to adopt a linear model of change. The Chinese case shows that economic liberalization need not result in democratization, at least not right away. There can and will be reversals of direction, and there is always the possibility of reverting to dictatorship after experimenting with democracy. After all, Hitler came after Weimar.

For a country like Algeria, whose first nationalist government was authoritarian, and where democratization coincided with the emergence of a new political generation of alienated youth, the attempt to reverse directions in 1992 could not be entirely successful. Too many Algerians were aware of the failings of the old order to go back without complaints. Too many had experienced the freedom of the 1989–91 period and had relished the right to protest, say no, and reject the regime's arrogance and remoteness by supporting its mortal opponents. After canceling the 1992 elections, the regime could not return to Boumedienism with popular acquiescence. But it could buy time, hope that passions would cool, prove that the military could not be ousted, and rewrite the rules for a new round of controlled democratization. Whether the next round would be more successful than the first remained to be seen. But the important point here is that the regime saw no alternative but to resume, in some form, the democratization process that had been interrupted. Once the opening of 1989 had taken place, it was hard to pretend that the old one-party regime could ever be comfortably reimposed. In Rustow's terms, Algeria is making the transition between the first stage of the prolonged internal crisis, which cannot be ended by the clear victory of one side or the other, to the second stage of forging new rules of the game. Algeria is still in the midst of its "hot family feud." It is still far from having reached the point of "habituation," where the rules are accepted as legitimate and better than all other possibilities for resolving conflicts. But out of this costly struggle Algerians may learn to value a political order that offers workable compromise instead of utopia, if the price of utopia is always to be paid in blood.

International Pressures for Democracy

It is often argued that democracy in Latin America was encouraged by outside forces. These included the example of Spain and Portugal and pressure for democratic change from the Reagan administration. But what may have been true for Latin America has been much less in evidence in the Middle East.

To the extent that there has been some external impetus for democratic change in the Middle East-North Africa region, it has been largely indirect. For example, the collapse of the Soviet Union and the moves toward democracy in Eastern Europe undermined the credibility of the one-party systems. The so-called progressive states of the Arab world—Syria, Iraq, Algeria, and Egypt—had never been as close to the Soviet Union as Eastern Europe, but they had consciously adopted some models from the Soviet experience, especially in the management of the economy. When those models were suddenly discredited, the Algerian elite was quick to see the need for change.

Closer to home for many Algerian intellectuals was the transformation in the 1980s of the French socialist party of François Mitterrand from a mildly doctrinaire socialist party to a partisan of market economic reforms. If even the French, with their strong tradition of centralized administration, were looking more positively at capitalism, markets, and decentralization, then the French-educated elite in Algeria was at least aware of the debates about the limits of central planning and unaccountable bureaucracies.

France played another indirect role in fostering change in Algeria. By the 1980s many Algerian households were equipped with *paraboles*, small satellite dishes, that allowed them to see television broadcasts from Europe. Without many opportunities for entertainment outside the home, Algerians spent long hours watching French television. One can only speculate about the multiple messages that were taken in. On the one hand, there was intense exposure to material wealth and modernity. Algerians could easily see how far they were from enjoying the material benefits of the ordinary European. Since they thought of themselves as living in a rich country, the gap between their lives and those of Europeans could be explained by government corruption. A second message, no doubt, was that people have the right to criticize their government, even to make fun of it with satire, as a famous French puppet show did of its leaders. A third message, often mentioned with contempt by Islamist leaders, was the moral degradation of the west, i.e., the prevalence of sex and violence on European television. Islamists made a big issue of banning paraboles so that corrupting western values would not infect Algeria. This was one issue on which most Algerians did not side with the Islamists. They were quite attached to their paraboles.

It would be wrong to conclude that international financial institutions deliberately pushed Algeria toward democracy. But by the late 1980s Algeria was facing major problems in repaying its debt, and in 1993 it finally went to the International Monetary Fund to seek a structural adjustment loan and to get a clean bill of health with its creditors so that it could reschedule loan repayments. Algeria was therefore obliged to take the IMF medicine: reducing the budget deficit, removing subsidies, floating the exchange rate, raising interest rates, and facing up to the eventual need to privatize some of the state-owned industries. This pressure forced the state to withdraw from some areas of the economy, making way for new entrepreneurs and investors. Since Algeria still has a sizable debt—around $30 billion in 1997—and repayments will remain an issue for many years, external pressures for economic liberalization are unlikely to subside. Insofar as economic liberalization stimulates demands for political reform, an indirect link can be seen between the demands of the IMF and the process of democratization. But, it must be added, the link is not direct or strong.[12] And no one at the IMF has made it a condition of further loans that Algeria open up its political system. In fact, the IMF is barred from imposing such political conditions.

While some indirect sources from abroad no doubt stimulated a demand for change and opened the way for the protest movements of the 1980s in Algeria, there is no evidence of significant pressure from foreign governments on the Algerian regime to democratize. If anything, the reverse was true. Particularly in France, the fear seemed to be strong that democratization might bring the Islamists to power, and that would be a disaster for French-Algerian relations. When the 1992 election was canceled, there was no protest from Europe. Unlike Turkey, which has been chastised by Europeans for its human rights record, Algeria has rarely been the target of European concern on this score. At the time of the Sant'Egidio platform in January 1995, the French and American governments gave mild support to the ideal of political dialogue and reconciliation, but neither was prepared to go beyond words to the imposition of economic conditionality on aid or credits.

Algeria also found that its immediate neighbors were generally supportive of the regime in its battle with the militant Islamists. Tunisia, in particular, was a strong supporter of the Zeroual regime. Morocco was less enthusiastic, with the king occasionally musing about how much more successfully he was able to handle his Islamists than the Algerians, but Morocco did not become a significant supporter of the Islamic Salvation Front (*Front Islamique du Salut*, FIS). Egypt and Libya were solidly behind the regime, leaving only Sudan, and distant Iran, as critical of the harsh Algerian campaign against the FIS and the *Groupes Islamiques Armés* (GIA). Although FIS leaders in exile were able to operate in Turkey, in a number of European states, and even in the United States, they were more tolerated than encouraged. In France, some intellectuals came down on the side of the FIS, but a remarkable number of the French left, who might have been expected to side with the FIS, were so strongly secular in their views that they refused to support the underdogs; they either wrote off both the regime and its opponents with Gallic scorn or sought to support the embattled democrats who stood between the two extremes, in particular the Socialist Forces Front (*Front des Forces Socialistes*, FFS) and the Rally for Culture and Democracy (*Rassemblement pour la Culture et la Démocratie*, RCD), which were well-represented among the Kabyles in France.

Liberalization

While democratization is still a debatable concept in much of the Arab world, most analysts would agree that a substantial degree of liberalization has taken place since the days of Gamal Abd al-Nasser and Houari Boumediene. The crucial question is whether these measures are an important component of the democratization process, or whether they may become a substitute for it. The opening up of the society and the economy to diverse currents may simply release some pent-up frustrations that had accumulated during the preceding authoritarian era, while leaving power squarely in the hands of the same old guard. More optimistically, liberalization may allow civil society to reconstitute itself, and this may be a crucial step on the way to pluralistic politics and electoral competition.

Wherever authoritarian regimes have begun to liberalize, "the first reaction is an outburst of autonomous organization in the civil society. Student associations, unions, and proto-parties are formed almost overnight."[13] Algeria was no exception. Not only did the FIS suddenly emerge in the late 1980s as the main opposition movement, but so did a host of other groups. The regime went so far as to tolerate, and even subsidize, a proliferation of publications. From one month to the next, topics that had been entirely taboo were being publicly discussed.

The fact that this initial burst of organizational activity can take place tells us something about civil society. The authoritarian regime can try to prevent such autonomous groups from forming, but it cannot crush the underlying sentiments that give rise to them. As soon as the opportunity to organize and express oneself arrives, hundreds of thousands of people are ready to take advantage of the new environment. The prior absence of civil society told us more about the state than about the society itself.[14]

Needless to say, not all the expressions of civil society have deep roots. Some are quite small and some may even be creatures of the regime. Many of the so-called new parties had little following, and some of the newspapers attracted few readers. But out of the proliferation of new groups, some fairly impressive gains were made. First, the press quickly became interesting and showed a flair for both criticism and investigative reporting, despite frequent attempts by the regime to exercise strict censorship, especially over security matters.[15] Second, a number of Algerians wrote books and articles with great insight and subtlety about their country.[16] With freedom of expression came new authors, filmmakers, and poets. Women and students formed groups. Nonofficial trade unions were formed and the number of strikes greatly increased. Berber cultural groups demanded the right to use their language.

Out of all this activity, the language of politics began to change fairly quickly. Instead of talking about socialism and the unity of the people, politicians began to pay deference to democratic values—

whether sincerely or not is more difficult to say—and soon a new vocabulary was common. Multipartism, pluralism, "alternance," the rule of law, human rights—all became catch phrases of politicians in all camps. Some, such as Ali Ben Hadj, were blunt in saying that democracy had no place in Islam, but other Islamists were more prudent and spoke with a moderate voice about democracy.

Somewhat surprising, the cancellation of the 1992 election, which was clearly a blow to Algeria's reputation as an emerging democracy, did not alter the terms of discourse much. The new regime never claimed that it was legitimate. In fact, it acknowledged that it was not and that it could only rule for an interim period. From the outset, the regime promised that there would be a return to multiparty politics with elections, but this time under more controlled circumstances. And, more or less, that is what has happened, although the degree of top-down control has been far-reaching.

The Algerian pattern suggests that liberalization can be an important part of the process of democratization. But liberalization by itself sets in motion so many new elements that it can in fact be destabilizing. Institutions are needed to channel the new forces into agreed arenas of competition. And this is where the first Algerian attempt at controlled democratization failed. By choosing an inappropriate institutional mechanism for the 1991–92 elections—the winner-take-all system—the regime produced a result that it was not prepared to live with. Much of the institutional engineering of the mid-1990s was designed to correct for that flaw, but has gone too far in the other direction. Speaking of the constitution of the Fifth French Republic, one scholar wrote that the regime's "preoccupation with abuses of the past has blinded it to the needs of the present."[17] The same can be said of the Zeroual regime.

The Balance Sheet

Algeria has many things in its favor as it moves hesitantly toward democracy. It has a relatively egalitarian society, a well-grounded sense of national identity growing out of the revolution, widespread literacy, an emerging middle class, and a per capita income that comes close to the minimum at which democratic transitions usually succeed.[18] Many Algerians have been exposed to democratic government directly or indirectly, as workers or students in France, or by means of the

French media. While the French connection is a source of ambivalence, in light of colonial history, one should not underestimate the extent to which the elite of a certain generation picked up political ideas, including that of the strong administrative state, from France. The Algerian constitution bears a remarkable resemblance to France's.

While Algerians have never poured into the streets demanding democracy, there is nonetheless evidence that they want the chance to choose their own government. They complain about the *hogra* of their rulers, their arrogance and aloofness, and the contempt they show for ordinary citizens. This is not the attitude of a passive or complacent electorate. When given the chance to vote, large numbers of Algerians have actually gone to the polls. Those who argue that Algerians do not understand the basic principles of democracy have a hard case to make. Algerians may not demand democracy, but they seem eager to have the chance to rid themselves of rulers they do not like. And that, after all, is one of the core principles of democracy.

On the other side of the democratization balance sheet are an impressive list of negatives. First, Algeria has a strong tradition of the military playing the central role in politics, and it will be difficult to break that pattern. If it can be done at all, it will probably be done gradually, through negotiations that give many assurances and guarantees to the military. Pure democrats will find this galling, but it may well be the price to pay for any opening of the political system, as in Turkey and Chile. Most parties seem to be realistic about the need to accept a privileged position for the military.

Second, Algeria has a strong presidential system, which could mean that voters quickly become cynical about elections and parties as they see that real power remains in the hands of the president and his cronies. Centralization of power in the presidency could also mean intense competition for that position, and if the existing regime stacks the deck too much in its favor, many will understandably cry foul. Relatively fair parliamentary elections, coupled with rigged presidential ones, will not produce a stable political system.

Third, Algerians have had bitter experience with government, from the days of the French to their own postindependence leaders. One finds a great deal of distrust of politics and politicians, coupled with a willingness to believe the worst of those with power. It is striking that the only agreed national hero is Emir Abdelkader, the truly remarkable historic figure who led a seventeen-year resistance to the

French in the early nineteenth century. No one in the past one hundred years even comes close.

Fourth, there are the mixed blessings of oil and gas revenues. On the one hand, these resources ensure a degree of prosperity that makes Algeria the envy of many in Africa and the Middle East. But the money goes directly to the regime, reinforcing its clout, making everyone dependent on those with power. Ample oil revenues may lead politicians to postpone needed economic reforms. It is hard to escape the conclusion that so much money concentrated in the hands of those who are not really accountable to anyone will foster corruption. None of this is inevitable, and Algeria is not one of the big rentier states, but on balance the existence of oil and gas revenues is better for Algeria's future economic health than for its political health.

Finally, there is the problem of persistent violence, terrorism, and the use of force to settle accounts and advance one's cause. In the 1990s at least 75,000 have lost their lives, and this means that most families have been directly or indirectly affected. Often the violence is intimate, and one must fear that revenge killings will continue for years to come. The violence, much of it seemingly more pathological than political in origin, has inevitably had a devastating impact on morale. Some 400,000 or more Algerians have emigrated since 1992.[19] The rural areas around Algiers where many grisly massacres took place in 1997 are being depopulated, adding to the already large numbers of desperate people living on the margins of the city. Even if one does not see the hand of the government behind the GIA violence (and on the whole I do not), there are so many accounts of abuses of human rights by the regime—extrajudicial killings, torture, arbitrary arrest, intimidation of journalists—that there will inevitably be a demand some day by opposition forces for a settling of accounts. It seems unlikely that the South African model of "truth and reconciliation" will be adopted. It is more likely that victims of regime violence will seek revenge, if they ever have the power to do so. Knowing this, the military and its civilian allies are all the more reluctant to loosen their grip.

Lessons from the Algerian Case

What can we learn from Algeria's past decade of flawed political and economic reforms? Several general points can be made, although a single case cannot provide much more than tentative hypotheses.

The most commonly drawn lesson is also the least convincing—that premature democratization in a Muslim country will result in the triumph of nondemocratic Islamist forces. Regimes and scholars alike have drawn this conclusion from the Algerian elections of 1991. In fact, the Islamists, while strong, did not win a majority of the electorate's vote and have never been able to claim the support of more than one-fourth to one-third of the population as a whole. The key to the Islamists' strength lay not in their numbers but in their superior organization as a broad opposition front.

A more analytical conclusion that seems solidly grounded is that Algeria's strongly egalitarian and populist characteristics—products of the colonial era and the revolution—have left a largely negative legacy for managing the transition from authoritarianism to democracy. While equality is a crucial value in democratic theory, democratic politics actually requires differentiation and hierarchy to achieve structured competition among groups representing diverse interests. A fiercely egalitarian society seems to find it difficult to form such broad coalitions. Instead, political life tends to revolve around small clans and cliques. Political parties are often little more than small networks of friends and relatives. In such circumstances, power is likely to end up in the hands of those who are better able to form hierarchical organizations. In the Algerian case, there have been three such organizations—the military, the National Liberation Front (*Front de Libération Nationale*, FLN) in its heyday, and the FIS. The latter two, however, proved to be faction ridden and unable to stand up to the more disciplined military organization. The key to the dominance of the military over Algeria's political life lies not only in its monopoly over the means of violence, but also in its avoidance of the types of splits that weakened both the FLN and the FIS at crucial moments.

Another lesson from the Algerian case is that during transitions the choice of institutions can be of crucial importance. Algeria's elites have made two crucial errors in their choice of institutions. In 1991, in the hope of weakening the conservative FLN, the reformers opted for an electoral system—two-round majoritarian—that produced an unintended and unanticipated landslide for the FIS. Had some form of proportional representation been chosen, the outcome most likely would have been much more tolerable to a wide spectrum of Algerians and would have reflected the underlying distribution of attitudes in Algeria much more accurately. In early stages of transition from authoritarianism, when institutional legitimacy is still in question, it is particularly important to allow for representation of diverse opinions. The Algerian reformists missed this point as they sought to outmaneuver both the old guard of the FLN and the radicals of the FIS. Their failing opened the way for the return of the military.

Since 1992 another set of institutional choices has been made by rulers determined to avoid a repeat of the elections of December 1991. The power of the presidency has been augmented to the point where parliamentary elections, even if they were conducted fairly, would not have much impact on actual governance. As a result, Algeria seems stuck in limbo between its authoritarian past and its democratic pretensions. A better balance between presidential and parliamentary prerogatives—between the institutions of control and order and those of representation and accountability—would have given Algeria a better chance at a successful transition to democracy.

In addition, institutions of civil society and the rule of law are a crucial component of democratization. But they need time to take root and develop credibility in a society that is used to seeing the state as all-powerful. During Algeria's brief democratic opening, there was a burst of activity that suggested the potential for a vibrant civil society, but many of these promising "green shoots" of democratic life withered away after 1992. The press, and some political parties, remain feisty contenders against the state's inclination to control all facets of life. The parliament elected in 1997 has shown signs of vitality, but these potentially democratic forces all operate in constricted space. As Rustow argued in 1970, a habituation period is needed for democratic forces to learn to work together. Algeria did not have enough time for civil society and an independent judiciary to gain strength during its first phase of democratization. During the more recent period, the regime has been too suspicious of any independent groupings to allow for the kind of liberalization that ultimately must be the handmaiden of successful democratic consolidation.

The agonizing problem of violence has ravaged Algerian society in recent years. I do not see this as a reflection on Algerians as a people or as a culture. But I do see it as the result of a disastrous social policy that left hundreds of thousands of young Algerians in dreadful economic and social conditions. Most of these young men did not become terrorists or take up arms. But some did, and the state's harsh and

unimaginative response created even more extremists for whom violence soon became a way of life.

Algeria's violence has many causes. Some violence is politically
motivated, aimed at overthrowing an unpopular regime. Some is
closer to vendetta and blood feuding, with origins that go back many
years, including to the revolutionary period when many Algerians
were killed by other Algerians. Some violence is probably motivated
by greed and prospects for economic gain, as villagers are driven from
their homes in some of Algeria's richest agricultural regions. And
finally, some is the result of action and inaction by a regime that has
become unaccountable for its behavior in the security realm. In the
name of fighting terrorism—and terrorism is a problem that has to be
confronted—the regime has justified appalling abuses of human
rights, violations of judicial procedures, and indifference toward parts
of its own population that is exposed to danger.[20]

With so many sources of violence converging during the recent
period of transition from authoritarianism, Algeria in the 1990s has
been the Middle East state with the highest death toll. In the 1980s
Lebanon, Iran, and Iraq were the most prominent arenas of far-reaching
political violence. Today Algeria has that dubious distinction.

Finally, if there is to be a brighter future for Algeria, it will require
political change. Economic growth will help, as will the anticipated
demographic shift as birth rates subside. But without reform of the
political system toward greater representation and accountability—in
short, toward real rather than facade democracy—Algeria's crisis is
likely to continue. For a while it seemed as if President Zeroual might
be the reformer who could gradually move Algeria toward the twin
goals of order and pluralism. But in his term as president, he has
shown little real leadership, preferring a formalistic process of institution building to a genuine process of broadening the base of the
regime. As a result, Algeria's new institutional makeup, largely com-
pleted during 1997 with the elections of two houses of parliament and
local and regional assemblies, has had little apparent impact on popular perceptions of the legitimacy of the regime. Nor has civil peace
been restored, which, one hopes, was a goal of the entire exercise.

Changing the nature of the political regime remains the most serious challenge facing Algerians. It will not happen by revolution, as
the FIS once hoped. Instead, it can only occur from hard-fought bar-

gaining among the contending forces of Algerian society. If nothing else, the broad outlines of those forces—nationalist, regional, Islamist, democratic, and the military—are fairly well known. Each will need to be given a place in a future democratic Algeria if the violence that has debilitated the country is to be contained and eventually brought to an end. And that can only be done by political action by an elite that shows much more imagination and civic responsibility than we have seen to date. Algeria's crisis, political in its origin, will also have to be solved by its politicians.

Guessing the Future

Political scientists do not have good tools for predicting the future of countries making the transition from authoritarianism. At most, some general tendencies can be identified. But Algerians still have choices to make in determining their country's future, and where there is choice there is uncertainty.

Having watched Algerian affairs for more than thirty years, I believe that Algeria is not about to become the next Islamic Republic in the Middle East; nor is it likely to resemble Bosnia, Afghanistan, or Somalia. Even the high levels of violence have not shaken the main pillars of the state. Algeria is going through a severe internal crisis, but not a civil war. Most Algerians have remained on the sidelines during the clashes between the regime an its radical Islamist foes. The mass mobilization that occurred in October 1988 has been strikingly missing in the 1990s. I would therefore rule out a collapse of the existing order. The Algerian state will not prove to be so fragile that it will be readily swept aside, as the FIS seemed to believe in 1991.

Algeria is not likely to make a smooth transition to democracy on the Spanish model, either. There simply is not enough strength in the opposition parties and in civil society to push the military from center stage in the near future, and as long as the military plays such an important role, Algeria will only be a partial democracy at best.

Nonetheless, Algeria seems to be destined for a more pluralistic future than many would have imagined a decade ago. The old, unitary state model is gone. Both the FLN and the FIS tried to embody this populist myth of a single people that could be represented by a single party. But Algeria has become too complex and the society too differentiated for that.

One can also anticipate that large numbers of today's Algerians in their twenties and thirties will remain permanently alienated from the political system. Many will never find a productive job, will never be able to afford decent housing, and will never be able to raise families. This lost generation—in part the result of successful policies of improved health care—represents the crest of the population boom. Within twenty to twenty-five years, this huge age cohort will be approaching retirement, and the new entrants into the labor force will find it easier to get jobs. This will help to dry up the social base from which extremist political movements can easily recruit. But for some time, even with the best of governments, this generation will pose a major problem. It is no exaggeration to say that Algeria's crisis is in large measure a result of this fundamental social and economic development.

During my visit to Algeria in mid-1996 and again in early 1998, I found most of the people I spoke to fairly pessimistic about the short-term, but surprisingly optimistic about the longer run. The horrific violence of 1997 deepened the pessimism about the immediate future. But if the violence can be brought to an end, I would expect a fairly rapid return to a more optimistic mood. Despite everything, Algerians remain fiercely proud of their country and want a voice in the determination of their future. Even in the middle of their deep crisis, Algerians are quick to agree that their press and parliament are more free than those of their neighbors. It will be years before anything resembling a robust democracy will be seen in Algeria, but it may well come precisely because of the disastrous experience with other alternatives.

The country has not been blessed with great leaders. One could even say that the Algerian crisis, while socioeconomic in origin, was deepened by the mediocrity of its political class.[21] Clannishness and self-interest have won out over civic mindedness. But Algeria's people are tough and not easily pushed around. One of these days they will make themselves heard. With time and experience, their leaders may come to appreciate that social peace can only exist if all the main currents of Algerian society are heard. Then the chance for democracy to flourish will have arrived.

For the moment, Algeria should be thought of as a country in the early stages of a difficult transition away from its authoritarian past. But it will not be surprising if Algeria reaches the goal of accountable, representative government in advance of many others in the region. That is both my expectation and my hope for Algeria.

Bibliography

Books

Abrahamian, Ervand. *Iran between Two Revolutions*. Princeton University Press, 1982.

Addi, Lahouari. *L'Algérie et la démocratie: pouvoir et crise politique dans l'Algérie contemporaine*. Paris: Editions la Découverte, 1994.

Ahmad, Feroz. *The Making of Modern Turkey*. London: Routledge, 1993.

Algérie: briser le silence. Témoin. Paris: Editions Balland, 1994.

Al-Ahnaf, Mustafa, Bernard Botiveau, and Franck Frégosi. *L'Algérie par ses Islamistes*. Paris: Editions Karthala, 1991.

Al-Azmeh, Aziz. *Islams and Modernities*. London: Verso, 1993.

L'Algérie en contrechamp. Peuples Mediterranéens. Paris: Centre Nationale des Lettres, 1995.

Ayubi, Nazih N. *Overstating the Arab State: Politics and Society in the Middle East*. London: I. B. Tauris Publishers, 1995.

Baduel, Pierre Robert, ed. *L'Algérie incertaine*. Paris: Edisud, 1994.

Bakhash, Shaul. *The Reign of the Ayatollahs: Iran and the Iranian Revolution*. Basic Books, 1989.

Beer, Samuel H., and Adam B. Ulam, eds. *Patterns of Government: The Major Political Systems of Europe*. Random House, 1958.

Beinin, Joel, and Joe Stork, eds. *Political Islam: Essays from Middle East Report*. University of California Press, 1997.

Ben Khedda, Benyoucef. *Les origines du 1er novembre 1954*. Hussein-Dey: Editions Dahlab, 1989.

Bennabi, Malek. *Memoires d'un temoin du siecle*. Alger: Editions Nationales Algériennes, 1965.

Bennoune, Mahfoud, and Ali El Kenz. *Le hasard et l'histoire: entretiens avec Belaid Abdesslam*, two volumes. Alger: ENAG, 1990.

Boukhobza, M'Hammed. *Octobre 88: évolution ou rupture?* Alger: Editions Bouchène, 1991.

Bourdieu, Pierre. *Sociologie de l'Algérie*. Paris: Presses Universitaires de France, 1963.

Brynen, Rex, Bahgat Korany, and Paul Noble. *Political Liberalization and Democratization in the Arab World*. Boulder, Colo.: Lynne Rienner, 1995.

Burgat, François, and William Dowell. *The Islamic Movement in North Africa*. University of Texas Press, 1993.

Camau, Michel. *La notion de démocratie dans la pensée des dirigeants maghrébins*. Paris: Centre Nationale de la Recherche Scientifique, 1971.

Camus, Albert. *The First Man*. Knopf, 1995.

———. *L'Etranger.* Paris: Gallimard, 1970.

Chaliand, Gérard, and Juliette Minces. *L'Algérie indépendante*. Paris: François Maspero, 1972.

Charef, Abed. *Algérie: le grand dérapage*. Saint-Amand-Montrond: Editions de l'Aube, 1994.

Claiming the Future: Choosing Prosperity in the Middle East and North Africa. Washington, D.C.: The World Bank, 1995.

Courrière, Yves. *Les fils de la Toussaint*. Paris: Fayard, 1968.

Dahl, Robert A. *Polyarchy: Participation and Opposition*. Yale University Press, 1971.

Dawisha, Adeed, and I. William Zartman. *Beyond Coercion: The Durability of the Arab State*. London: Croom Helm, 1988.

Dévoluy, Pierre, and Mirelle Duteil. *La poudrière Algérienne: histoire secrète d'une république sous influence*. Paris: Calmann-Lévy, 1994.

Eickelman, Dale F., and James Piscatori. *Muslim Politics*. Princeton University Press, 1996.

El-Kenz, Ali. *Algerian Reflections on Arab Crises*. University of Texas Press, 1991.

Esposito, John L. *The Islamic Threat: Myth or Reality?* New York: Oxford University Press, 1995.

Etienne, Bruno. *Abdelkader: Isthme des isthmes*. Paris: Editions Hachette, 1994.

Fanon, Frantz. *Les damnés de la terre*. Paris: Découverte, 1985.

Feuer, Lewis S., ed. *Basic Writings on Politics and Philosophy by Karl Marx and Friedrich Engels*. Two Harbors, Minn.: Anchor Books, 1959.

Field, Michael. *Inside the Arab World*. Harvard University Press, 1995.

Foweraker, Joe, and Todd Landman. *Citizenship Rights and Social Movements: A Comparative and Statistical Analysis*. New York: Oxford University Press, 1997.

Frey, Frederick. *The Turkish Political Elite*. MIT Press, 1965.

Fukuyama, Francis. *The End of History and the Last Man*. Free Press, 1992.

Fuller, Graham. *Algeria: The Next Fundamentalist State?* Santa Monica: Rand, 1996.

Gellner, Ernest. *Muslim Society.* Cambridge University Press, 1981.

Gellner, Ernest, and Charles Micaud, eds. *Arabs and Berbers*. London: Gerald Duckworth and Co. Ltd., 1973.

Ghadbian, Najib. *Democratization and the Islamist Challenge in the Arab World*. Boulder, Colo.: Westview Press, 1997.

Goumezaine, Smail. *Le mal algérien: économie politique d'une transition inachevée 1962–1994*. Paris: Editions Fayard, 1994.

Guazzone, Laura, ed. *The Islamist Dilemma: The Political Role of Islamist Movements in the Contemporary Arab World*. Reading, UK: Ithaca Press, 1995.

Gurr, Ted. *Why Men Rebel.* Princeton University Press, 1970.

Halliday, Fred. *Islam and the Myth of Confrontation: Religion and Politics in the Middle East.* London: I. B. Tauris and Co. Ltd., 1995.

Harbi, Mohammed. *L'Algérie et son destin: croyants ou citoyens?* Paris: Arcantère Editions, 1992.

———. *Le FLN, mirage et réalité: des origines à la prise du pouvoir (1945–1962).* Paris: Editions Jeune Afrique, 1980.

———. *Les archives de la révolution algérienne.* Paris: Editions Jeune Afrique, 1981.

Harik, Iliya F. *Economic Policy Reform in Egypt.* University Press of Florida, 1997.

Hidouci, Ghazi. *Algérie: la libération inachevée.* Paris: Editions la Découverte, 1995.

Hirschman, Albert. *Exit, Voice and Loyalty: Response to Decline in Firms, Organizations, and States.* Harvard University Press, 1970.

Horne, Alistair. *A Savage War of Peace: Algeria, 1954–1962.* Viking, 1978.

Hudson, Michael. *Arab Politics: The Search for Legitimacy.* Yale University Press, 1977.

Human Development Report 1995. United Nations Development Project. New York: Oxford University Press, 1995.

Huntington, Samuel. *The Clash of Civilizations and the Remaking of World Order.* Simon and Schuster, 1996.

———. *The Third Wave: Democratization in the Late Twentieth Century.* University of Oklahoma Press, 1991.

Ignasse, Gerard, and Emmanuel Wallon. *Démain l'Algérie.* Paris: Syros, 1995.

Kaplan, Robert D. *The Ends of the Earth: A Journey at the Dawn of the 21st Century.* Random House, 1996.

Kateb, Yacine. *Nedjma.* University Press of Virginia, 1991.

Kepel, Gilles, ed. *Exils et royaumes: les appartenances au monde arabo-musulman aujourd'hui.* Paris: Presses de la Fondation Nationale des Sciences Politiques, 1994.

———. ed. *Les Politiques de Dieu.* Paris: Editions du Seuil, 1993.

Khalil, Samir. *Republic of Fear.* University of California Press, 1990.

Koroghli, Ammar. *Institutions politiques et développment en Algérie.* Paris: Editions L'Harmattan, 1988.

Labat, Séverine. *Les islamistes algériens: entre les urnes et le maquis.* Paris: Editions du Seuil, 1995.

Lacheraf, Mostefa. *L'Algérie: nation et société.* Paris: François Maspero, 1965.

Lavenue, Jean-Jacques. *Algérie: la démocratie interdite.* Paris: Editions L'Harmattan, 1992.

Lazreg, Marnia. *The Eloquence of Silence: Algerian Women in Question.* New York: Routledge, 1994.

Leveau, Rémy. *Le sabre et le turban: l'avenir du Maghreb.* Paris: Editions François Bourin, 1993.

Linz, Juan, and Alfred Stepan. *Problems of Democratic Transition and Consolidation.* Johns Hopkins University Press, 1996.

Maîtriser ou accepter les Islamistes? Hérodote: *Revue de Géographie et de Géopolitique.* Paris: Editions la Découverte, 1995.

Malek, Redha. *L'Algérie à Evian: histoire des négociations secrètes 1956–1962.* Paris: Editions du Seuil, 1995.

———. *Tradition et révolution: l'enjeu de la modernité en Algérie et dans l'Islam.* Paris: Editions Sindbad, 1993.

Malley, Robert. *The Call from Algeria: Third Worldism, Revolution, and the Turn to Islam.* University of California Press, 1996.

Mernissi, Fatima. *Islam and Democracy: Fear of the Modern World.* New York: Addison-Wesley, 1992.

Milani, Muhsin. *The Making of Iran's Islamic Revolution: From Monarchy to Islamic Republic.* Boulder, Colo.: Westview Press, 1994.

Moore, Barrington, Jr. *Social Origins of Dictatorship and Democracy: Lord and Peasant in the Making of the Modern World.* Boston: Beacon Press, 1966.

Moore, Clement Henry. *Tunisia Since Independence: The Dynamics of One-Party Government.* Westport, Conn.: Greenwood Press, 1965.

Norton, Augustus Richard, ed. *Civil Society in the Middle East.* London: Brill, 1995.

O'Donnell, Guillermo, and Philippe C. Schmitter. *Transitions from Authoritarian Rule: Tentative Conclusions about Uncertain Democracies.* Johns Hopkins University Press, 1986.

Olson, Mancur. *The Logic of Collective Action; Public Goods and the Theory of Groups.* Harvard University Press, 1965.

Pierre, Andrew J., and William B. Quandt. *The Algerian Crisis: Policy Options for the West.* Washington, D.C.: Carnegie Endowment for International Peace, 1996.

Provost, Lucile. *La seconde guerre d'Algérie: le quidproquo Franco-Algérien.* Saint-Amand-Montrond: Editions Flammarion, 1996.

Przeworski, Adam. *Democracy and the Market: Political and Economic Reforms in Eastern Europe and Latin America.* Cambridge: Cambridge University Press, 1991.

———. *Sustainable Democracy.* New York: Cambridge University Press, 1995.

Putnam, Robert D. *Making Democracy Work: Civic Traditions in Modern Italy.* Princeton University Press, 1993.

Quandt, William B. *Revolution and Political Leadership: Algeria, 1954–1968.* MIT Press, 1969.

Rahal, Yahya. *Histoires de pouvoir: un général temoigne.* Paris: Editions Casbah, 1997.

Reporters Sans Frontières. *Le drame algérien: un peuple en otage.* Paris: Editions la Découverte, 1995.

Richards, Alan, and John Waterbury. *The Political Economy of the Middle East.* Boulder, Colo.: Westview Press, 1990.

Rouadjia, Ahmed. *Les frères et la mosquée: enquête sur le mouvement islamiste en Algérie.* Paris: Editions Karthala, 1990.

Roy, Olivier. *The Failure of Political Islam.* Harvard University Press, 1994.

Sadowski, Yahya M. *Political Vegetables? Businessman and Bureaucrat in the Development of Egyptian Agriculture.* Brookings, 1991.

Salamé, Ghassan, ed. *Democracy without Democrats? The Renewal of Politics in the Muslim World.* London: I. B. Tauris Publishers, 1994.

———. ed. *The Foundations of the Arab State.* London: Croom Helm, 1987.

Seale, Patrick. *Asad of Syria: The Struggle for the Middle East.* University of California Press, 1988.

Shahin, Emad Eldin. *Political Ascent: Contemporary Islamic Movements in North Africa.* Boulder, Colo.: Westview Press, 1997.

Sivan, Emmanuel. *Communisme et nationalisme en Algérie 1920–1962.* Paris: Presses de la Fondation Nationale des Sciences Politiques, 1976.

Taguemout, Hanafi. *L'affaire Zeghar: déliquescence d'un état. L'Algérie sous Chadli.* Paris: Editions Publisud, 1994.

Touati, Amine. *Algérie: les islamistes à l'assaut du pouvoir.* Paris: Editions L'Harmattan, 1995.

Viollette, Maurice. *L'Algérie vivra-t-elle?* Paris: F. Alcan, 1931.

Waterbury, John. *Exposed to Innumerable Delusions: Public Enterprise and State Power in Egypt, India, Mexico, and Turkey.* Cambridge University Press, 1993.

Willis, Michael. *The Islamist Challenge in Algeria: A Political History.* Reading, UK: Ithaca Press, 1996.

Articles

Addi, Lahouari. "The Islamic Challenge: Religion and Modernity in Algeria." *Journal of Democracy*, 3 (October 1992): 75–84.

———. "Violence et système politique en Algérie." *Les Temps Modernes*, 50, 580 (January–February 1995): 46–70.

Aouli, Smail, and Ramdane Redjala. "La kabylie face à la dérive intégriste." *Les Temps Modernes*, 580 (January–February 1995): 196–208.

Ardouin, Caroline. "Economie Algérienne: quelles perspectives?" *Monde Arabe Maghreb-Machrek*, 14 (July–September 1995): 13–22.

Babadji, Ramdane. "Le FIS et l'héritage du FLN: la gestion des communes." *Confluences Méditerranée.* 3 (Spring 1992): 105–12.

Bacaille, Laetitia. "L'engagement Islamiste des femmes en Algérie." *Monde Arabe Maghreb-Machr*, 144 (April–June 1994): 105–18.

Bekkar, Rabia. "Taking up Space in Tlemcen: The Islamic Occupation of Urban Algeria: An Interview with Rabia Bekkar." *Middle East Report*, 22 (November–December 1992): 11–15.

Belaid, Lakhdar. "Femmes algériennes: victimes de l'histoire." *Etudes* (January 1996): 15–25.

Benachenou, Abdellatif. "Inflation et chomage en Algérie: les aléas de la démocratie et des réformes economiques." *Monde Arabe, Maghreb-Machrek*, 139 (January–March 1993): 427–34.

Benhaddi, Zemri. "Algérie: origines et aspects géopolitiques de la crise actuelle." *Hérodote*, 65–66 (1992): 50–62.

Benyelles, Rachid. "Les événements d'octobre 1988." *La Tribune* (Algiers), (May 28, 1996): 11–13.

Blin, Louis. "Algérie: les elites politiques." *Les Cahiers de l'Orient*, 25–26 (1992): 237–59.

Brahimi, Mohamed. "Les évènements d'octobre 1988: la manifestation violente de la crise d'une idéologie en cessation de paiement." *Revue Algérienne des Sciences Juridiques, Economiques et Politiques*, 28 (December 1990): 681–703.

Brumberg, Daniel. "Islam, Elections and Reform in Algeria." *Journal of Democracy*, 2 (Winter 1991): 58–71.

Carlier, Omar. "De l'islahisme à l'islamisme: la théorie politico-religieuse du FIS." *Cahier d'Etudes Africaines*, 32 (1992): 185–219.

Chenal, Alain. "La France rattrapée par le drame Algérien." *Politique Etrangère*, 60, 2 (Summer 1995): 415–25.

Chevillard, Nicole. "Algérie: l'après guerre civile." *Nord Sud Export Conseil* (1995): 17–77.

Chhibber, Pradeep K. "State Policy, Rent Seeking, and the Electoral Success of a Religious Party in Algeria." *Journal of Politics*, 58 (February 1996): 126–48.

"Democracy, Islam and the Study of Middle Eastern Politics." *PS: Political Science and Politics*, 27 (September 1994): 507–19.

Djeghloul, Abdelkadar. "Le multipartisme à l'algérienne." *Monde Arabe Maghreb-Machrek*, 127 (January–March 1996): 194–210.

Dix, Robert H. "History and Democracy Revisited." *Comparative Politics*, 27, 1 (October 1994): 91–105.

Etienne, Bruno. "L'Algérie entre violence et fondamentalisme." *Revue des Deux Mondes* (January 1996): 47–56.

Fontaine, Jacques. "Les élections législatives algériennes: résultats du premier tour." *Monde Arabe Maghreb-Machrek*, 135 (January–March 1992): 155–64.

Gadant, Monique. "Femmes en alibi." *Les Temps Modernes*, 580 (January–February 1995): 221–32.

Garçon, José. "L'Algérie: si loin de Washington . . ." *Politique Etrangère*, 139 (January–February 1993): 427–34.

Ghozali, Sid Ahmed. Interview. *Arabies*, 61 (January 1992): 12–14.

Hammoudi, Abdellah, and Stuart Schaar. "Algeria's Impasse." *The Institute for the Transregional Study of the Contemporary Middle East, North Africa, and Central Asia*, 8 (1995).

Hansen, William H., and Rachid Tlemçani. "Development and the State in Post Colonial Algeria." *Journal of Asian and African Studies*, 24 (1989): 114–33.

Harbi, Mohamed. "Algérie: l'interruption du processus électoral. *Respect ou déni de la constitution?*" *Monde Arabe Maghreb-Machrek*, 135 (January–March 1992): 145–54.

———. "Violence, Nationalisme, Islamisme." *Les Temps Modernes*, 50, 580 (January–February 1995): 24–33.

Hidouci, Ghazi. "L'Algérie peut-elle sortir de la crise?" *Monde Arabe Maghreb-Machrek*, 149 (July–September 1995): 26–34.

Huntington, Samuel. "The Clash of Civilizations." *Foreign Affairs* (Summer 1993, Fall 1993, and Fall 1994).

Kapil, Arun. "Algeria." *Political Parties of the Middle East and North Africa* (1994).

———. "Le retour de Boudiaf." *Les Cahiers d'Orient*, 25–26 (1992).

———. "Portrait statistique des élections du 12 juin 1990: chiffres clés pour une analyze." *Les Cahiers de l'Orient*, 23 (1991): 41–64.

Kepel, Gilles. "Islamists Versus the State in Egypt and Algeria." *Daedalus*, 124 (Summer 1995): 109–27.

Khelladi, Aïssa, and Marie Virolle. "Les démocrates algériens ou l'indispensable clarification." *Les Temps Modernes*, 50, 580 (January–February 1995): 177–95.

La Coste, Dujardin. "Démocratie kabyle. Les kabyles: une chance pour la démocratie algérienne." *Hérodote*, 65–66 (1992): 63–74.

Leca, Jean. "Crise algérienne. Le point de vue d'un acteur politique. La recherche d'une voie constitutionnelle." *Monde Arabe Maghreb-Machrek*, 149 (July–September 1995): 23–26.

Leca, Jean, and Rémy Leveau. "L'Algérie: démocratie, politiques économiques et demandes sociales." *Monde Arabe Maghreb-Machrek*, 139 (January–March 1993): 3–52.

Lewis, Bernard. "Islam and Liberal Democracy." *Atlantic Monthly* (February 1995): 89–98.

Leverrier, Ignace. "Le front islamique du salut entre la hâte et la patience." In *Les politiques de Dieu*, edited by Gilles Kepel, 28–51. Paris: Editions du Seuil, 1993.

Martinez, Luis. "Les groupes Islamistes entre guérilla et négoce: vers une consolidation du régime algérien?" *Les Etudes du CERI*, 3 (August 1995): 2–26.

Marx, Karl. "The Eighteenth Brumaire of Louis Napoleon." In *Marx and Engels: Basic Writings on Politics and Philosophy*, edited by Lewis S. Feuer, 320. Garden City, N.Y.: Anchor Books, 1959.

Mortimer, Robert. "Algeria after the Explosion," *Current History*, 89, 546 (April 1990).

Moussaoui, Abderrahmane. "De la violence au djihad." *Histoire Sciences Sociales*, 6 (November–December 1994): 1315–33.

Muller, Edward N., and Mitchell A Seligson. "Civic Culture and Democracy: The Question of Causal Relationships." *American Political Science Review*, 88 (September 1994): 635–52.

Murray, Roger, and Tom Weingraf. "The Algerian Revolution." *New Left Review*, 22 (December 1963).

Nair, Sami. "Le peuple exclu." *Les Temps Modernes*, 580 (January–February 1995): 34–45.

Olson, Mancur. "Dictatorship, Democracy and Development." *American Political Science Review*, 87 (September 1993): 567–76.

Przeworski, Adam. "Democratization Revisited." *Items: Social Science Research Council*, 51 (March 1997): 6–11.

Przeworski, Adam, and Fernando Limongi. "Modernization: Theories and Facts." *World Politics*, 49 (January 1997): 155–83.

172   BIBLIOGRAPHY

Roberts, Hugh. "Algeria Between Eradicators and Concilators." *Middle East Report*, 24, 4 (July–August 1994): 24–27.

———. "The Algerian State and the Challenge of Democracy." *Government and Opposition*, 27 (Autumn 1992): 433–54.

———. "Algeria's Ruinous Impasse and the Honourable Way Out." *International Affairs*, 71, 2 (1995).

Rouadjia, Ahmed. "Du nationalisme du FLN à l'islamisme du FIS." *Les Temps Modernes*, 50, 580 (January–February 1995): 115–36.

———. "L'armée et les islamistes: le compris impossible." *L'Esprit*, (January 1995): 105–18.

Rustow, Dankwart. "Transitions to Democracy: Toward a Dynamic Model." *Comparative Politics* (April 1970): 337–63.

Salamé, Ghassan. "Sur la causalité d'un manque: pourquoi le monde arabe n'est-il donc pas démocratique?" *Revue Française de Science Politique*, 41 (June 1991): 307–41.

Sadowski, Yahya. "The New Orientalism and the Democracy Debate." *Middle East Report* (July–August 1993): 14–40.

Sereni, Jean-Pierre. "L'Algérie, le FMI, et le FIS." *Les Cahiers de l'Orient*, 25–26 (1992): 225–35.

Stora, Benjamin. "Deuxième guerre Algérienne? Les habits anciens des combattants." *Les Temps Modernes*, 50, 580 (January–February 1995): 242–61.

Tahi, Mohand-Salah. "The Arduous Democratization Process in Algeria." *Journal of Modern African Studies*, 30 (1992): 397–419.

Tlemçani, Rachid. "Les conditions d'émergence d'un nouvel autoritarisme en Algérie," *Revue du monde musulman et de la Méditerranée*, 72 (1995): 108–18.

Vergès, Meriem. "I am Living in a Foreign Country Here: A Conversation with an Algerian Hittiste." *Middle East Report*, 25 (January–February 1995): 14–17.

Yefsah, Abdelkader. "Algeria: The Constitution." *Arab Law Quarterly*, a (1994): 107–29.

———. "Algérie." *Les Cahiers de L'Orient*, 23 (1991).

———. "Armée et politique depuis les événements d'octobre 1988: l'armée sans hidjab." *Les Temps Modernes*, 50, 580 (January–February 1995): 154–76.

Zahouane, Hocine. "Paradoxes algériens." *Confluences Méditerranée*, 3 (Spring 1992): 75–86.

Zoubir, Yahia H. "Algerian Islamists' Conception of Democracy." *Arab Studies Quarterly*, 18 (Summer 1996): 65–85.

———. "Islamist Political Parties in Algeria." *Conference Group: The Interface of State and Society in the Middle East and North Africa* (August–September 1996): 1–7.

———. "Stalled Democratization of an Authoritarian Regime: The Case of Algeria." *Democratization*, 2 (Summer 1995): 109–39.

Notes

Chapter One

1. I do not mean to imply that authoritarian and arbitrary rule suddenly is necessarily replaced. In fact, authoritarian structures may last a long time. But they no longer have "hegemony," in Gramsci's sense. The authoritarian regime cannot count on passivity or acquiescence. There is contestation. In this sense we can speak of post- or late-authoritarianism.

2. Francis Fukuyama, *The End of History and the Last Man* (Free Press, 1992).

3. Robert D. Kaplan, *The Ends of the Earth: A Journey at the Dawn of the 21st Century* (Random House, 1996); Samuel Huntington, *The Clash of Civilizations and The Remaking of World Order* (Simon and Schuster, 1996); and responses to Huntington's original article, "The Clash of Civilizations," in *Foreign Affairs* (Summer and Fall 1993) and *Foreign Policy* (Fall 1994).

4. Alistair Horne, *A Savage War of Peace: Algeria, 1954–1962* (Viking Press, 1978); Maurice Viollette, *L'Algérie vivra-t-elle?* (F. Alcan, 1931).

5. Gerard Chaliand and Juliette Minces, *L'Algérie independante; bilan d'une revolution nationale* (Maspero, 1972) and Robert Malley, *The Call from Algeria: Third Worldism, Revolution, and the Turn to Islam* (University of California Press, 1996).

6. William B. Quandt, *Revolution and Political Leadership: Algeria 1954–1968* (MIT Press, 1969), pp. 236–63.

7. Michael Hudson, *Arab Politics: The Search for Legitimacy* (Yale University Press, 1977), p. 364. "Despite serious obstacles, Algeria has emerged as one of the most stable and seemingly successful of the Arab revolutionary republics." But, Hudson warns, "Algeria's political legitimacy may be more fragile than it seems."

8. Lahouari Addi, *L'Algérie et la démocratie: pouvoir et crise du politique dans l'Algérie contemporaine* (Editions la Découverte, 1994) and Ghazi Hidouci, *Algérie: la libération inachevée* (Editions la Découverte 1995); Giacomo Luciani, "The Oil Rent, the Fiscal Crisis of the State and Democratization," in Ghassan Salamé, ed., *Democracy Without Democrats? The Renewal of Politics in the Muslim*

World (I. B. Tauris Publishers, 1994), p. 45, where he claims that Algeria is "in many ways a perfect candidate for democratization."

9. Graham Fuller, *Algeria: The Next Fundamentalist State?* (Rand, 1996).

10. Guillermo O'Donnell and Philippe C. Schmitter, *Transitions from Authoritarian Rule: Tentative Conclusions about Uncertain Democracies* (Johns Hopkins University Press, 1986), pp. 3–4, on the importance of choice in periods of transition because of the high degree of uncertainty and the weakness of institutions.

11. Augustus Richard Norton, ed., *Civil Society in the Middle East* (Brill, 1995) and Robert D. Putnam, *Making Democracy Work: Civic Traditions in Modern Italy* (Princeton University Press, 1993). See Joe Foweraker and Todd Landman, *Citizenship Rights and Social Movements: A Comparative and Statistical Analysis* (Oxford, 1997), pp. 239–43, for a sharp critique of Putnam. "[T]he democratic qualities of civil society do not have to do with 'civicness' but with the associationalism which supports social mobilization and political contestation; . . . democracy is not the comfortable result of righteous conduct but the result of prolonged struggle in often difficult and dangerous circumstances; and . . . this struggle is not ultimately motivated by goods but by the individual rights which compose the popular substance of democracy" (p. 243).

Chapter Two

1. For a compelling picture of French Algeria by one of France's greatest novelists of Algerian origin, see Albert Camus, *The First Man* (Knopf, 1995) and *L'Etranger* (Gallimard, 1970).

2. Bruno Etienne, *Abdelkader: isthme des isthmes* (Editions Hachette, 1994) and *La Magazine de Libération* (March 25–31 1995), p. 15, where Etienne gives the figure of 15,000 Algerians who were forced into exile along with Abd al-Qadir.

3. Jules Cambon, as quoted in Roger Murray and Tom Weingraf, "The Algerian Revolution," *New Left Review* no. 22 (December 1963), p. 23.

4. See Robert A. Dahl, *Polyarchy: Participation and Opposition* (Yale University Press, 1971), pp. 91–105 on the advantage of expanding contestation before expanding participation. But see the critique by Robert H. Dix, "History and Democracy Revisited," *Comparative Politics* (October 1994), pp. 91–105, who argues that pacts before opening of the system can serve as the functional equivalent of a prolonged period of habituation.

5. Kateb Yacine, *Nedjma* (University Press of Virginia, 1991), captures the atmosphere of incipient violence in Algeria as World War II comes to a close and the French repress by force a mass demonstration around the town of Sétif. This was a radicalizing event for a whole generation of Algerians. See Mohammed Harbi, *Le FLN, mirage et réalité: des origines à la prise du pouvoir (1945–1962)* (Editions J. A., 1980), pp. 28–30.

6. Lahouari Addi, *L'Algérie et la démocratie: pouvoir et crise du politique dans l'Algérie contemporaine* (Editions Découverte, 1994), pp. 15–33.

7. Redha Malek, *L'Algérie à Evian: histoire des négociations secrètes 1956–1962* (Editions du Seuil, 1995).

8. William B. Quandt, *Revolution and Political Leadership: Algeria, 1954–1968* (MIT Press, 1969), pp. 164–78.

9. Quandt, *Revolution and Political Leadership*, pp. 148–74. Also, Yves Courrière, *Les fils de la Toussaint* (Fayard, 1968); and Harbi, *Le FLN: mirage et réalité*, pp. 195–223.

10. Ben Bella was kept in prison until the early 1980s. It is worth noting, however, that Algeria, rare among Arab countries, does have living ex-presidents, and not just in exile. In the late 1990s, Ben Bella, Chadli Benjedid, and Ali Kafi are all ex-presidents still living in Algeria.

11. Addi, *L'Algérie et la démocratie*, pp. 41–46.

12. John Waterbury, *Exposed to Innumerable Delusions: Public Enterprise and State Power in Egypt, India, Mexico, and Turkey* (Cambridge University Press, 1993), pp. 24–25.

13. See Yahya M. Sadowski, *Political Vegetables? Businessman and Bureaucrat in the Development of Egyptian Agriculture* (Brookings Institution, 1991), pp. 67–80, for a nuanced discussion of "urban bias"; also see Iliya F. Harik, *Economic Policy Reform in Egypt* (University Press of Florida, 1997). For the Syrian case, see David Waldner, *State Building and Late Development* (Cornell University Press, forthcoming).

14. Giacomo Luciani, "The Oil Rent, Fiscal Crisis of the State and Democratization" in Ghassan Salamé, *Democracy without Democrats? The Renewal of Politics in the Muslim World* (I. B. Tauris Publishers, 1994), pp. 130–55. In fact, state salaries were taxed at the source, but overall Algerians did not have a heavy tax burden.

15. Ahmed Rouadjia, *Les frères et la mosquée: enquête sur le mouvement islamiste en Algérie* (Editions Karthala, 1990), pp. 77–109.

16. See Yahya Rahal, *Histoires de pouvoir: un général temoigne* (Casbah Editions, 1997), pp. 66–72, on the succession struggle within the party as seen by an insider.

Chapter Three

1. See Albert Hirschman, *Exit, Voice and Loyalty: Response to Decline in Firms, Organizations, and States* (Harvard University Press, 1970), for a theoretical discussion of political options available when loyalty fades—voice, meaning various forms of opposition; and exit—leaving the political arena altogether.

2. Max Weber, *The Theory of Social and Economic Organization* (Free Press, 1964), pp. 363–73.

3. In Algeria, the Islamic Salvation Front (FIS) criticized the National Liberation Front (FLN) in the late 1980s by evoking the original principles of the FLN itself.

4. Some of the need for coercion stems simply from the collective action problem—how can society get all its members to contribute their fair share

for the costs of collective goods like security, clean air, and roads? This problem is well analyzed by Mancur Olson, *The Logic of Collective Action: Public Goods and the Theory of Groups* (Harvard University Press, 1965). See Max Weber's famous definition of the modern state as claiming to monopolize the use of force in *The Theory of Social and Economic Organization*, p. 156.

5. Samir Khalil, *Republic of Fear* (University of California Press, 1990).

6. Hanafi Taguemout, *L'affaire Zeghar: déliquescence d'un état. L'Algérie sous Chadli* (Editions Publisud, 1994). This is a case study of Messaoud Zeghar, a Boumediene ally. This case also shows how quickly the powerful can fall. When Boumediene died, Zeghar soon became the target of a Military Security investigation that left him in prison for years before he was finally released.

7. Zemri Benheddi, "Algérie: origines et aspects géopolitiques de la crise actuelle," *Hérodote*, no. 65-66 (1992), p. 54, notes that Chadli was able to disperse more patronage after the restructuring of national enterprises that took place in the early 1980s.

8. Patrick Seale, *Asad of Syria: The Struggle for the Middle East* (University of California Press, 1988), pp. 421–40.

9. The French term for this is *usure du pouvoir.*

10. See Ghazi Hidouci, *Algérie: la libération inachevée* (Editions la Découverte, 1995), p. 83, on edging out Yahyaoui, Bouteflika, and Abdessalam. But Chadli was not able to impose himself; he was a "consensus" president.

11. Lahouari Addi, *L'Algérie et la démocratie: pouvoir et crise politique dans l'Algérie contemporaine* (La Découverte, 1994), pp. 61–62, calls attention to the crucial part played by the Chaouia region in shaping Algeria's political identity.

12. Mohammed Harbi, *Le FLN, mirage et réalité: des origines à la prise du pouvoir (1945–1962)* (Editions J. A., 1980), pp. 59–67.

13. Smail Aouli and Ramdane Redjala, "La kabylie face à la dérive intégriste," *Les Temps Modernes*, no. 580, (January–February 1995), pp. 202–04.

14. Ahmed Rouadjia, *Les frères et la mosquée: enquête sur le mouvement islamiste en Algérie* (Editions Karthala, 1990), pp. 183–208; and Séverine Labat, *Les islamistes algériens: entre les urnes et le maquis* (Editions du Seuil, 1995), pp. 199–220.

15. Labat, *Les islamistes algériens*, pp. 90–94.

16. The reformers consisted of Ghazi Hidouci, Smail Goumeziane, Hadj Nacer, and Mouloud Hamrouche. See *Monde Arabe Maghreb-Machrek* (July–September 1995) for more on the reformers, including an article by Hidouci.

17. Monique Gadant, "Femmes en alibi," *Les Temps Modernes*, no. 580 (January–March 1995), p. 229, on the divisions among women.

18. See Marnia Lazreg, *The Eloquence of Silence: Algerian Women in Question* (Routledge, 1994), pp. 118–41.

19. On the Family Code see Lakhdar Belaid, "Femmes algériennes: victimes de l'histoire," *Etudes* (January 1996), p. 13; and Lazreg, *The Eloquence of Silence*, pp. 150–57.

20. Jean-Pierre Sereni, "L'Algérie, le FMI, et le FIS," *Les Cahiers de l'Orient*, no. 25-26 (1992), notes that the combined effect of the oil price collapse and

the weakening of the dollar meant that Algeria's foreign exchange earnings declined by 80 percent from 1985 to 1991.

21. Aïssa Khelladi and Marie Virolle, "Les démocrates algériens ou l'indispensable clarification," *Les Temps Modernes*, no. 580 (January–February 1995), p. 185. They see October 1988 as the culmination of a whole series of smaller protests earlier in the decade.

22. Robert A. Mortimer, "Algeria after the Explosion," *Current History*, April 1990, vol. 89, no. 546, pp. 163–64, traces the crisis to industrial strikes in the Rouiba district. He notes that the slogan of "Chadli assassin" appeared after the army had been called in and demonstrators had been shot. Furthermore, party headquarters were attacked during the demonstrations.

23. See the article by General Rachid Benyelles, "Les événements d'octobre 1988," *La Tribune* (Algiers), May 28, 1996, pp. 11–13.

24. Benyelles, "Les événements d'octobre 1988," p. 12.

25. Michael Willis, *The Islamist Challenge in Algeria: A Political History* (Ithaca Press, 1996), p. 58, quotes from Chadli's prime minister from 1984 to 1988, Abdelhamid Brahimi, to the effect that Chadli himself instigated the crisis because he feared that otherwise he would not be selected to run again for the presidency by the FLN. If he could manufacture a crisis, however, he could present himself as a unifying candidate.

Chapter Four

1. On democratic discourse in Algeria see Aïssa Khelladi and Marie Virolle, "Les démocrates algériens ou l'indispensable clarification," *Les Temps Modernes*, no. 580 (January–February 1995), pp. 177–95. They note that failure of the liberals in the preindependence period weakened the appeal of democracy. Also see Michel Camau, *La notion de démocratie dans la pensée des dirigeants maghrébins* (Centre Nationale de la Recherche Scientifique, 1971).

2. Guillermo O'Donnell and Philippe C. Schmitter, *Transitions from Authoritarian Rule: Tentative Conclusions about Uncertain Democracies* (Johns Hopkins University Press, 1986), pp. 19–21, on intra-regime conflict as an impetus to liberalization; see also David Waldner, *State Building and Late Development* (Cornell University Press, forthcoming).

3. Frederick Frey, *The Turkish Political Elite* (MIT Press, 1965); and Feroz Ahmad, *The Making of Modern Turkey* (Routledge, 1993), pp. 102–20.

4. Ghassan Salamé, ed., *Democracy without Democrats? The Renewal of Politics in the Muslim World* (I. B. Taurus Publishers, 1994), pp. 16–20. Salamé, p. 3, states: "Democrats may not exist at all, or they may not exist in great numbers. Yet democracy can still be sought as an instrument of civil peace and hopefully, gradually, inadvertently, produce its own defenders."

5. See Mohamed Brahimi, "Les événements d'octobre 1988: la manifestation violente de la crise d'une idéologie en cessation de paiement," *Revue*

178   NOTES TO PAGES 44-48

Algérienne des Sciences Juridiques, Economiques et Politiques, vol. 28 (December 1990), pp. 681-703.

6. Ahmed Rouadjia, "Du nationalisme du FLN a l'islamisme du FIS," *Les Temps Modernes,* No. 580 (January–February 1995), pp. 136, sees the FIS as a product of the FLN, "an opposition made in its own image." Hence the frequent play on words coined in 1989 by Mohammed Harbi—"*le FIS est le fils du (son of) FLN."*

7. General Rachid Benyelles, "Les événements d'octobre 1988," *La Tribune,* May 28, 1996, p. 11, claims Chadli was on good terms with both, but had to remove them to satisfy public opinion.

8. Omar Bendourou, "La nouvelle constitution algérienne du 28 février 1989," *Revue du droit public et de la science politique en France et à l'étranger* (September-October 1989), pp. 1305-28.

9. *Annuaire de l'Afrique du Nord,* vol. 29, 1989 (Paris: CNRS, 1991), p. 543. The number of "no" votes was actually quite high, 2.6 million, as were the number of nonvoters among those registered (another 2.5 million). This could be seen as an early indicator of the unpopularity of the regime more than a reflection on the details of the constitution.

10. Séverine Labat speculates that the military was skeptical of the democratic experiment and did not want its reputation tarnished when things turned sour. See her *Les islamistes algériens: entre les urnes et le maquis* (Editions du Seuil, 1995), p. 101. See also the statement by Col. Yahya Rahal, "directeur central du commissariat politique" of the Algerian army, cited in "Chronique Algérie," *Annuaire de l'Afrique du Nord,* vol. 29, 1989 (Paris: CNRS, 1991), p. 551: "The ANP should not get involved in the complex game of factions, since it owes itself, as the force behind the only legal power, to preserve intact the unity of it ranks and the discipline of its engagement in the defense of the higher interests of the nation and the free choice of the people." See also the book by Rahal, *Histoires du pouvoir: un général temoigne* (Editions Casbah, 1997), pp. 75-80.

11. Jean-Jacques Lavenue, *Algérie: la démocratie interdite* (Editions L'Harmattan, 1992), p. 47.

12. Benyelles, "Les événements d'octobre 1988," p. 13, implies that recognition of Saadi was a payoff for keeping Kabylia calm during October 88. And once RCD was recognized, it was hard not to recognize FIS, which had a much wider following.

13. Abed Charef, *Algérie: le grand dérapage* (La Tour d'Aigues: Editions de l'Aube, 1994), p. 12, says that Mouloud Hamrouche, at the time secretary general at the presidency, claims there was no real discussion about the wisdom of recognizing the FIS. In an interview in June 1996, Hamrouche said that it was Merbah, not him, who legalized the FIS. General Mohammed Touati, in an interview with the author on June 16, 1996 in Algiers, said that Chadli himself, not Merbah, made the decision to legalize the FIS. Rémy Leveau, *Le sabre et le turban: l'avenir du Maghreb* (Editions François Bourin, 1993), p. 139, also says that Chadli, not Merbah, made the decision to legalize the FIS. His reason for doing so was to weaken the FLN in the upcoming

elections. Michael Willis, *The Islamist Challenge in Algeria: A Political History* (Ithaca Press, 1996), pp. 126–127, claims that the decision to recognize the FIS was related to splits within the FLN.

14. Robert Mortimer has raised the possibility that Merbah was removed because he opposed recognition of the FIS. This would be consistent with the information that Chadli himself made the decision (personal communication).

15. Adam Przeworski, *Democracy and the Market: Political and Economic Reforms in Eastern Europe and Latin America* (Cambridge University Press, 1991), pp. 136–46. He maintains that the initial phase of reform makes things worse.

16. Ghazi Hidouci, *Algérie: la libération inachevée* (Editions la Découverte, 1995), p. 178, and my interview with Mourad Benachenou, minister of the economy and privatization, June 11, 1996, in Algiers, where he referred to the FIS as an "objective ally of economic reform."

17. See Ignace Leverrier, "Le front islamique du salut entre la hâte et la patience," in Gilles Kepel ed., *Les Politiques de Dieu* (Editions du Seuil, 1993), pp. 28–51 for an excellent account of the origins of the FIS. See also Ahmed Rouadjia, "Discourse and Strategy of the Algerian Islamist Movement (1986–1992)" in Laura Guazzone, ed., *The Islamist Dilemma: The Political Role of Islamist Movements in the Contemporary Arab World* (Ithaca Press, 1995), pp. 69–104.

18. For diverse perspectives on political Islam, see Olivier Roy, *The Failure of Political Islam* (Harvard, 1994); John Esposito, *The Islamic Threat: Myth or Reality?* (Oxford, 1995); and Dale F. Eickelman and James Piscatori, *Muslim Politics* (Princeton, 1996).

19. Ahmed Rouadjia, "Du nationalisme du FLN à l'islamisme du FIS." *Les Temps Modernes*, No. 580 (January–February 1995), pp. 134–35 argues that FIS supporters were not particularly interested in Islam and Arabism, but were unified by "their hatred of the system, sentiments of injustices and revenge. . . ."

20. Labat, *Les islamistes algériens*, pp. 98–101. The "Algerianist" tendency, especially Mohammed Said, blamed Ben Hadj for the violence on October 10, 1988.

21. Charef, *Algérie*, p. 40. On the day that the party sought recognition from the government, Madani said that if the government did not recognize the party, the people would rise up in revolution. On this occasion, Ben Hadj was more restrained, merely saying that Islam would respect freedom of opinion. Charef, p. 41, notes that from this time onward, Madani and Ben Hadj tried to make Islam the centerpiece of Algerian politics and branding anyone who opposed them, even other Islamists, as anti-Islam.

22. Labat, *Les islamistes algériens*, p. 101, has a list of the founders.

23. Labat, *Les islamistes algériens*, pp. 22–23, profiles the typical FIS followers: middle-class city dwellers who were left out of clientalist networks, shopkeepers and artisans, and the alienated young.

24. Ahmed Rouadjia, *Les frères et la mosquée: enquête sur le mouvement islamiste en Algérie* (Editions Karthala, 1990), pp. 82–92. Ignace Leverrier, "Le front islamique du salut entre la hâte et la patience." in Gilles Kepel, ed., *Les politiques de Dieu* (Editions du Seuil, 1993), p. 51, notes that the FIS appealed to the subproletariat, the rejects of Algerian society, not the established urban

working class. He terms the FIS supporters "exclus et deçus," excluded and disappointed.

25. Rouadjia, *Les frères et la mosquée*, p. 48, notes that the FIS gained considerable credit in October 1989 for its quick response in providing aid to the victims of the Tipaza earthquake."

26. Rabia Bekkar, "Taking up Space in Tlemcen: The Islamic Occupation of Urban Algeria: An Interview with Rabia Bekkar" *Middle East Report*, vol. 22 (November–December 1992), pp. 11–15, on FIS social work in Tlemcen.

27. Willis, *The Islamist Challenge*, pp. 128–30, speculates that Chadli and the FIS had an understanding. The FIS would be tolerated as long as it supported the reform program and did not challenge Chadli directly.

28. Juan J. Linz and Alfred Stepan, *Problems of Democratic Transition and Consolidation: Southern Europe, South America, and Post-Communist Europe* (Johns Hopkins, 1996), p. 4, correctly warn against the "electoralist" fallacy. Elections alone do not a democracy make, as the Algerian case, and many others, demonstrate. But the Iranian presidential election in 1997 also showed that elections, even in very controlled circumstances, can sometimes produce surprising outcomes.

29. The best analysis is in Fawzi Rouzeik, *Annuaire de l'Afrique du Nord*, vol. 29, 1989 (Paris: CNRS, 1991), pp. 555–61. Also Charef, *Algérie*, p. 620.

30. See Rahal, *Histoires de pouvoir*, p. 90, where he reports on a conversation with Chadli and the head of the FLN before the communal elections where they express their confidence that the FLN would win 75 percent of the vote.

31. Arun Kapil, "Portrait statistique des élections du 12 juin 1990: chiffres clés pour une analyse," *Les Cahiers de l'Orient*, no. 23, 1991, p. 44. This is not to say that women did not support the FIS. See Laetitia Bacaille, "L'engagement Islamiste des femmes en Algérie." *Monde Arabe*, vol. 144, (April–June 1994), pp. 105–18.

32. Kapil, "Portrait statistique," *Les Cahiers de l'Orient*, no. 23, 1991. Also see Pradeep K. Chhibber, "State Policy, Rent Seeking, and the Electoral Success of a Religious Party in Algeria," *Journal of Politics*, vol. 58 (February 1996), pp. 126–48, who provides a political economic explanation for the vote. In essence he sees the economic reforms as alienating much of the middle class, especially small entrepreneurs who voted for the FIS. With the same data, however, one might conclude that those who left the ranks of the FLN ended up abstaining, which helped the FIS to win.

33. On the disarray in the FLN, see Mohand Salah Tahi, "The Arduous Democratization Process in Algeria," *Journal of Modern African Studies*, vol. 30, no. 3, 1992, pp. 402–05.

34. Fawzi Rouzeik, *Annuaire de l'Afrique du Nord*, vol. 30, 1990, (Paris: CNRS, 1992), pp. 640–41.

35. Leverrier, "Le front islamique du salut entre la hâte et la patience," pp. 56–59, unlike most observers maintains that the Syndicat Islamique du Travail (SIT) played an important role in some areas in the May–June 1991 strike.

36. See Rémy Leveau, *Le sabre et le turban*, pp. 144–45, on the impact of the Gulf crisis of 1990–91.

37. See Ramdane Babadji, "Le FIS et l'héritage du FLN: la gestion des communes." *Confluences Méditerranée*, no. 3 (Spring 1992), p. 106, on the many restrictions imposed by Islamic communes.

38. Amine Touati, *Algérie: les islamistes à l'assaut du pouvoir* (Editions L'Harmattan, 1995), p. 23.

39. A poll published in mid 1991 in the Algerian press showed that the FIS and FLN would run about evenly in urban areas, with the FLN dominating the rural areas. See Fawzi Rouzeik, *Annuaire de l'Afrique du Nord*, vol. 31, 1991 (Paris: CNRS, 1993), pp. 622–31.

40. Willis, *The Islamist Challenge*, pp. 173–82, maintains that Madani felt betrayed by the election law and therefore broke his understanding with Chadli. Henceforth the FIS would adopt a more radical posture, seeking the downfall of the president. Many within the FIS were opposed to the call for a general strike.

41. Touati, *Algérie*, pp. 21–22, and text of Mekhloufi pamphlet on civil disobedience, pp. 249–52.

42. Touati, *Algérie*, pp. 24–25.

43. Touati, *Algérie*, p. 25

44. See Abdelkader Yefsah, "Armée et politique depuis les événements d'octobre 88: l'armée sans hidjab," *Les Temps Modernes*, vol. 50, no. 580 (January-February 1995), pp. 163–65, on why the military intervened.

45. Touati, *Algérie*, pp. 61–62, for Madani's press conference on June 8.

46. Touati, *Algérie*, pp. 263–64, June 6, 1991, for the text of the FIS calling on followers to continue the fight and prepare to attack security forces and arrest regime personalities (but not to torture them), if FIS leaders were arrested. The text said only Madani and Ben Hadj could call off the strike.

47. Charef, *Algérie*, pp. 96–97, indicates that during the strike there were regular contacts between heads of the security services and FIS leaders. He implies that Military Security used the FIS to get rid of Hamrouche, who had stripped them of some of their power. In particular, he notes that Hamrouche abolished the "fiche bleue," the blue card, which was provided by military security before anyone was given a job in government (pp. 14–15).

48. Charef, *Algérie*, pp. 70–71. Algerianists were more urban and educated in comparison to the "salafiyyists," such as Ben Hadj. They were also strongly opposed to external links with other Islamic movements, unlike Nahnah's Hamas.

49. In an interview published in early 1992, Ghozali took his distance from the FLN, claiming that his government was independent of the party. At the same time he praised the army as the last bastion of "November values" and a rampart against violence. Finally he envisioned the possibility of an "atomized Assembly" coming out of the elections. See *Arabies*, no. 61 (January 1992), pp. 12–14.

50. An important FIS congress was held in Batna in July 1991 to select a new leadership after the arrest of Ben Hadj and Madani. See Leveau, *Le sabre et le turban*, p. 153, and Labat, *Les islamistes algériens*, pp. 119–24.

51. See Jacques Fontaine, "Les eléctions législatives algériennes: résultats

du premier tour." *Monde Arabe Maghreb-Machrek*, Vol. 135 (January–March 1992), pp. 155–64. See also his "Quartiers défavoris et vote islamiste à Alger," in Robert Baduel, ed., *L'Algérie incertaine* (Edisud, 1994), pp. 145–64.

52. The official results for the 1991 election were as follows: 13.3 million registered voters; 7.8 million votes cast; .9 million blank ballots; 59 percent of registered voters actually voted; 3.26 million voted for the FIS; 1.6 million voted for the FLN; .5 million voted for the FFS; 1.5 million voted for all other parties.

53. Hocine Zahouane, "Paradoxes algériens." *Confluences Méditerranée*, no. 3 (Spring 1992), p. 79, notes that it took 17,000 votes to elect a FIS deputy and 107,000 to elect a FLN deputy.

54. Some analysts of a conspiratorial mind argue that Ghozali wanted the FIS to win, so that the military would have no excuse but to intervene and ban the FIS and depose Chadli. There is no evidence to support this widely believed view.

55. See General Khaled Nezzar, "Devoir et vérités," *El Watan (Algiers)*, May 15, 1996, p. 3.

56. For more details on Chadli's ouster, see Nicole Chevillard, "Algérie: l'après guerre civile," *Nord Sud Export Conseil* (1995), p. 49.

57. See Rémy Leveau, "Algérie: des adversaires à la recherche du compromis incertains," Institut d'Etudes de Sécurité, Union de l'Europe occidentale, Paris, September 1992, pp. 27–28, on Chadli's strategy for survival, including trying to use the FIS against both the FLN and the army. Chadli supposedly met Hachani alone, giving rise to rumors of an impending deal. See also Willis, *The Islamist Challenge*, pp. 249–52, on the events of January 1992. Mouloud Hamrouche, in an interview March 8, 1998, in Algiers, strongly denied that Chadli had any intention of siding with the FIS in order to save his position.

58. Many Algerians who opposed the FIS nonetheless felt ambivalent about the army intervention. See, for example Mohamed Harbi, "Algérie: l'interruption du processus électoral: Respect ou déni de la constitution?" *Monde Arabe Maghreb-Machrek*, no. 35 (January–March 1992), pp. 145–54.

Chapter Five

1. Mahfoud Bennoune and Ali El Kenz, *Le hasard et l'histoire: entretiens avec Belaid Abdesslam*, two volumes (Algiers: ENAG, 1990).

2. Interview with Belaid Abdessalam, Algiers, September 1992.

3. Nicole Chevillard, "Algérie: l'après guerre civile," *Nord Sud Export Conseil* (1995), pp. 76–77, quotes from a poll reporting in Algiers in late 1992 that showed a great deal of skepticism about politics. Some 27 percent of those polled said that they would vote for Islamist candidates if new elections were held. Their main concerns were unemployment, housing and corruption.

4. Luis Martinez, "Les groupes Islamistes entre guérilla et négoce: vers une consolidation du régime algérien?" *Les Etudes du CERI*, no. 3 (August 1995), pp. 2–26. This unique analysis explains the GIA networks, in part, by examining how they manage to control sectors of the economy. The image

which emerges is of gangs involved in racketeering. He compares the FIS leaders with those of the GIA, seeing the latter as less educated, more likely to come from the slums around Algiers.

5. In 1997 the killing of whole families in remote rural areas became commonplace, especially in the so-called triangle of death in the Mitidja plain southwest of Algiers. Several explanations for this particularly ferocious form of violence were offered. Some attributed it to internecine fighting within the GIA; others maintained that the underlying issue was a fight over land ownership, prompted by new laws returning collectivized land to its original owners; others saw the government-armed militias as a contributing factor. See Luis Martinez, "Une guerre par procuration," L'Express, no. 2395 (May 29–June 4, 1997), p. 92. See also Roula Khalaf, "Spectre of FIS Hangs Over Bitter Algerian Elections," The Financial Times (London), May 31, 1997, p. 3, where villagers who had formerly supported the FIS blamed the GIA for attacks on them because they were unwilling to provided support for the GIA. Some former FIS supporters indicated that they had shifted their loyalty to the Hamas-MSP party of Nahnah. See also Scott Peterson, "Algeria's Village Vigilantes Unite Against Terror," The Christian Science Monitor, November 5, 1997, p. 8.

6. See "Algeria, Fear and Silence: A Hidden Human Rights Crisis," Amnesty International, November 1996; and "Algeria: Elections in the Shadow of Violence and Repression," Human Rights Watch/Middle East, vol. 9, no. 4(E), June 1997.

7. See Alan Richards and John Waterbury, A Political Economy of the Middle East: State, Class, and Economic Development (Westview Press, 1990), pp. 227–36 for a discussion of the standard reform package.

8. See Le Monde, May 29, 1997, Frances Ghilès, "Réformes économiques dans une Algérie à feu et à sang."

9. Jocelyne Cesari, "Chronique intérieure 1993," in Annuaire de l'Afrique du Nord, vol. 33, 1993 (Paris: CNRS, 1995), p. 400, notes that Zeroual had opposed Chadli in 1988–89 for his lenient treatment of the Islamists and was therefore sent abroad to a minor diplomatic post. Others see Zeroual's split with Chadli as involving issues of modernizing the armed forces.

10. Chevillard, "Algérie: l'après guerre civile." pp. 46–48, 62.

11. John Waterbury, "Democracy Without Democrats? The Potential for Political Liberalization in the Middle East," in Ghassan Salamé, ed., Democracy without Democrats? The Renewal of Politics in the Muslim World (I. B. Tauris Publishers, 1994), pp. 36–39; Adam Przeworski, Democracy and the Market: Political and Economic Reforms in Eastern Europe and Latin America (Cambridge University Press, 1991), p. 70.

12. This theme was particularly pronounced in letters written by Ben Hadj from prison dated October 2, 1994, November 8, 1994, and January 20, 1995, which I have read in translation.

13. See the profile of Hanoun in Libération (Paris), June 5, 1997, p 16. See also Belaid, "Femmes Algériennes: victimes de l'histoire," p. 23, quoting Hanoun on why it is necessary to speak to the FIS to bring an end to the violence.

14. See the text in Andrew J. Pierre and William B. Quandt, *The Algerian Crisis: Policy Options for the West* (Carnegie Endowment for International Peace, 1996), pp. 59–63.

15. For details of the FIS-Zeroual talks, see Ahmed Rouadjia, "L'armée et les islamistes: le compromis impossible," *L'Esprit*, January 1995, pp. 114–16. He argues that reconciliation between the two is precluded because they represent two competing legitimacy formulas. See also Hugh Roberts, "Algeria's Ruinous Impasse and the Honourable Way Out," *International Affairs*, vol. 71, no. 2 (1995), p. 258, and Chevillard, "Algérie: l'après guerre civile," p. 54.

16. Hachani was released shortly after the June 1997 elections; Madani was freed without explanation on July 15, 1997, but shortly thereafter was placed under house arrest.

17. Some observers professed to see signs of the collapse of the state. On the contrary, the state was omnipresent and very much in control when and where it chose to be.

18. The key documents are "Dialogue National: Memorandum," Presidence de la République, May 1996, and "Plate-forme de l'Entente Nationale," September 1996.

19. On Nahnah as a campaigner, see Sylvaine Pasquier, *L'Express* (Paris), no. 2396, June 5–11, 1997, pp. 96–98.

20. For a rather pessimistic assessment of the elections, see Jean-Paul Mari, *Le Nouvel Observateur* (Paris) no. 1700 (June 5–11, 1997), pp. 36–38; no. 1701 (June 12–18 1997), pp. 14–17.

21. Lahouari Addi, *L'Algérie et la démocratie: pouvoir et crise du politique dans l'Algérie contemporaine* (Editions Découverte, 1994), pp. 188–95.

Chapter Six

1. *Human Development Report 1997* (Oxford University Press, 1997), p. 188.

2. In the 1980s, Iran with a population of about 50 million, was able to produce about 3 million barrels per day (bpd) of oil; Algeria, with about half Iran's population, produced about 1 million bpd of oil and condensates.

3. Yahia H. Zoubir, "Stalled Democratization of an Authoritarian Regime: The Case of Algeria." *Democratization*, vol. 2 (Summer 1995), p. 126, argues that the May–June 1991 strike by the FIS was an attempt to overthrow the regime.

4. The militias have been accused of operating outside the law, thus inviting revenge attacks from the armed Islamists. A rare public account implicating a local government leader in the town of Relizane in massacres of civilians was reported in *El Watan* (Algiers), April 18, 1998.

Chapter Seven

1. Max Weber, *The Protestant Ethic and the Spirit of Capitalism* (Scribner, 1958).
2. Robert D. Putnam, *Making Democracy Work: Civic Traditions in Modern Italy*

(Princeton University Press, 1993); and Edward C. Banfield, *The Moral Basis of a Backward Society* (Free Press, 1958).

3. Fareed Zakariyya, "A Conversation with Lee Kuan Yew," *Foreign Affairs* vol. 73, no. 2 (March/April 1994) , pp. 109–26.

4. Samuel Huntington, *The Clash of Civilizations and the Remaking of World Order* (Simon and Schuster, 1996).

5. Lahouari Addi, *L'Algérie et la démocratie: pouvoir et crise du politique dans l'Algérie contemporaine* (Editions Découverte, 1994), p. 8.

6. Lisa Anderson, "Democracy in the Arab World: A Critique of the Political Culture Approach," in Rex Brynen, Baghat Korany, and Paul Noble, *Political Liberalization and Democratization in the Arab World* (Lynne Reinner Publishers Inc., 1995), pp. 77–92.

7. Barrington Moore Jr., *Social Origins of Dictatorship and Democracy: Lord and Peasant in the Making of the Modern World* (Beacon Press, 1966), pp. 414–32.

8. Germaine Tillion, *Le harem et les cousins* (Editions du Seuil, 1966).

9. Ben Hadj is something of an exception in the extent to which he quotes from writers such as Sayyid Qutb and Mawdudi.

10. *Salifiyya*, a word meaning "of the ancestors," but denoting the scripturalist/reformist tendency in Islam, particularly as it developed after Rashid Rida. See Albert H. Hourani, *Arabic Thought in the Liberal Age, 1798–1939* (Oxford University Press, 1962).

11. Bruno Etienne, "L'Algérie entre violence et fondamentalisme," *Revue des Deux Mondes* (January 1996), p. 50, speaks of violence in Algeria as part of the political culture, a result of a continual history of uprisings.

12. Benjamin Stora, "Deuxième guerre Algérienne? Les habits anciens des combattants." *Les Temps Modernes* vol. 50, no. 580 (January–February 1995), pp. 260–61. He speaks of a "culture of war" emerging from thirty years of glorifying the violence of the liberation struggle. In reality, he maintains, it was the strength of Algeria's society and culture that forced the French to leave Algeria, not defeat on the battlefield.

13. Frantz Fanon, *Les damnés de la terre* (Découverte, 1985).

14. M'Hammed Boukhobza, *Octobre 88: évolution ou rupture?* (Editions Bouchène, 1991), pp. 24–25 and especially pp. 50–51, where he argues that Algerians blame state for "social inversions." Boukhobza was later assassinated, reportedly by Islamist radicals, as were a number of other intellectuals and journalists.

15. Robert Malley, *The Call from Algeria: Third Worldism, Revolution, and the Turn to Islam* (University of California Press, 1996), pp. 17–33.

16. Algeria initially toyed with "self-management" models akin to those in Yugoslavia, but eventually reverted to management by state-appointed bureaucrats.

17. Boukhobza, *Octobre 88*, pp. 50–51.

18. Olivier Roy, *The Failure of Political Islam*, (Harvard University Press, 1994); and Gilles Kepel, *Muslim Extremism in Egypt: The Prophet and Pharaoh* (University of California Press, 1993).

19. Ben Hadj wrote at length on the topic of democracy in the FIS publi-

cation *Al-Munqid* (Algiers, 1989–91), especially numbers 14, 18, and 25. He shows considerable ambivalence about the FIS participation in the 1990 local elections. At one point he describes democracy as *kufr*, heresy, and later explains (in no. 25) that he opposes both dictatorship and democracy.

20. Michael Willis, *The Islamist Challenge in Algeria: A Political History* (Ithaca Press, 1996), p. 144, quotes Ali Ben Hadj to the effect that democracy has no place in Islam. *Shura* (consultation), not majority rule, is the guiding principle for Islamic leaders.

Chapter Eight

1. Yahya Sadowski, "The New Orientalism and the Democracy Debate" in Joel Beinin and Joe Stork, eds., *Political Islam: Essays from Middle East Report* (University of California Press, 1997), pp. 33–50.

2. Ernest Gellner, *Muslim Society* (Cambridge University Press, 1981); and Ghassan Salamé, " 'Strong' and 'Weak' States: A Qualified Return to the *Muqaddimah*," in Ghassan Salamé, ed., *The Foundations of the Arab State* (Croom Helm, 1987), pp. 205–40.

3. Rémy Leveau, *Le sabre et le turban: l'avenir du Maghreb* (Editions Franqis Bourin, 1993), p. 129, says, "The destruction of all bases of social autonomy outside the state system leaves no choice to individuals except submission, tempered by clientelism, or departure."

4. Mohammed Harbi, *Le FLN, mirage et réalité: des origines à la prise du pouvoir (1945–1962)* (Editions J. A., 1980), p. 381, says, "The role of the state was decisive in the formation of the society. It created, from whole cloth, a bourgeoisie and a new working class, and it turned the intellectuals into bureaucrats. All classes became subordinate to the state."

5. Abdellatif Benachenou, "Inflation et chômage en Algérie: les aléas de la démocratie et des réformes économiques," *Monde Arabe, Maghreb-Machrek*, No. 139 (January–March 1993), p. 34, notes that in 1988 there were 450,000 students graduating from secondary schools, but only 50,000 new jobs awaiting them. From the mid-1980s to the mid-1990s, there was a substantial decline in the standard of living (p. 35). See also Omar Carlier, "De l'islahisme à l'islamisme: la thérapie politico-religieuse du FIS," *Cahiers d'Etudes Africaines*, 126, XXXII-2 (1992), pp. 185–219. He notes that the census of 1987 showed that 54.8 percent of the population was below the age of twenty. See also his longer study, *Entre nation et jihad: histoire sociale des radicalismes algériens* (Paris: Presses de la fondation nationale des sciences politiques, 1995), especially pp. 340–65.

6. Luis Martinez, "Les groupes islamistes entre guérilla et négoce: vers une consolidation du régime algérien?" *Les Etudes du CERI*, no. 3 (August 1995), p. 7.

7. Clement Henry Moore, *Tunisia Since Independence: The Dynamics of One-Party Government* (Greenwood Press, 1965).

8. Frederick Frey, *The Turkish Political Elite* (MIT Press, 1965).

9. Iliya Harik, *Economic Policy Reform in Egypt* (University Press of Florida, 1997).

10. Ted Robert Gurr, *Why Men Rebel* (Princeton University Press, 1970).

11. Emad Eldin Shahin, *Political Ascent: Contemporary Islamic Movements in North Africa* (Westview Press, 1997), pp. 113–25, stresses the continuities from the Ulama of the 1930s, through the Qiyam Association of the early 1960s, to the eventual emergence of the FIS.

12. William B. Quandt, *Revolution and Political Leadership: Algeria, 1954–1968* (MIT Press, 1969), pp. 148–74.

13. *La Libération*, April 3, 1997. Jose Garọn notes that the Rabah Kebir faction condemned FIS radicals for "outbidding in violence." The key issues leading to the split were the attitude to adopt toward negotiating with the regime and toward the violence of the GIA.

14. Even in Khomeini's Iran there was a period of internecine violence following the revolution as first the moderates and then the leftists were purged from the victorious coalition. See Moshen Milani, *The Making of Iran's Islamic Revolution: From Monarchy to Islamic Republic* (Westview, 1994); Ervand Abrahamian, *Iran Between Two Revolutions* (Princeton University Press, 1982); and Shaul Bakhash, *The Reign of the Ayatollahs: Iran and the Iranian Revolution* (Basic Books, 1989).

15. The United Nations gives a figure of $5,442 per capita GDP in 1994 in the *Human Development Report* (Oxford University Press, 1997); the *CIA Worldbook* for 1995 says $3,800. Both figures are in $PPP.

16. The other part of the picture was the weakening of traditional tribal and family ties. Those who did not succeed in the new order, the rejects of modernization, flocked to the FIS in the late 1980s. See Ahmed Rouadjia, "Du nationalisme du FLN à l'islamisme du FIS." *Les Temps Modernes*, no. 580 (January–February 1995), pp. 133–34.

17. An International Monetary Fund official, in a private conversation in March 1994, stated that the Algerian government's wage bill was almost 10–11 percent of GDP, one of the highest percentages in the world. Comparable developing countries spent 6 percent on government salaries.

18. Adam Przeworski, *Democracy and the Market: Political and Economic Reforms in Eastern Europe and Latin America* (Cambridge University Press, 1991), p. 145, shows that the ratio of the top quintile's income to that of the bottom quintile in most Western European countries is about 5:1 to 7:1; In Latin America, that ratio is 11:1 to 30:1; Turkey is 16:1; the United State is 7.5:1. Only the communist countries were lower, with a ratio of 3:1 to 4:1.

19. *Human Development Report 1997*, p. 147.

20. See the data in *The Middle East Economic Digest (MEED)*, June 14, 1991, p. 51; April 24, 1992, p. 12.

21. Gurr, *Why Men Rebel*; Crane Brinton, *Anatomy of Revolution* (Vintage Books, 1965).

22. See the remarkable interview by Meriem Vergès, "A Conversation with an Algerian "Hittiste," *Middle East Report*, 192 (January–February 1995), pp. 14–17 for a sense of hopelessness felt by many young Algerians.

23. Philippe Fargues, "Demographic Explosion or Social Upheaval?" in Ghassan Salamé, ed., *Democracy Without Democrats?* pp. 156–57. In his words (p. 175), sometime around 2030, the Algerian schoolboys of today will become fathers and for the first time fathers and sons will both be equally literate in the same language.

24. Giacomo Luciani, "The Oil Rent, the Fiscal Crisis of the State and Democratization," in Salamé, ed., *Democracy Without Democrats?* pp. 130–55.

25. This can lead to a leadership quite cut off from society, a caste of sort. See Mohamed Harbi, "Violence, nationalisme, islamisme" *Les Temps Modernes*, vol. 50, no. 580 (January–February 1995), p. 25, where he states, "cut off from society, living like a caste, they manage the petroleum rent as they like without control from society. . . ."

26. See Ghassan Salamé, "Sur la causalité d'un manque: pourquoi le monde arabe n'est-il donc pas démocratique?" *Revue Française de Science Politique*, vol. 41 (June 1991), pp. 319, 337–39. He also notes that democracy cannot take root until differences and conflict within a society are accepted as legitimate. In his words, there is no democracy without *fitan* (plural of *fitna*, Arabic for disorder, upheaval), p. 339.

27. Yahya M. Sadowski, *Political Vegetables? Businessman and Bureaucrat in the Development of Egyptian Agriculture* (Brookings, 1991), pp. 138–40.

28. Lucile Provost, *La seconde guerre d'Algérie: le quidproquo Franco-Algérien*, (Editions Flammarion, 1996). Provost paints a picture of generals deeply engaged in control of parts of the market, making fortunes, unwilling to give up power because the profits are so great. Hers is the classical image of a predatory state.

29. Luciani, "The Oil Rent. . . ," p. 132. As Luciani points out, regimes could also try to borrow from the domestic market, but most citizens have so little confidence in government that they will not buy government bonds.

30. After the 1997 parliamentary elections, Hamas was given the portfolio for privatization; the FLN was put in charge of housing.

31. Ghazi Hidouci, *Algérie: la libération inachevée* (Editions la Découverte, 1995); and Smail Goumeziane, *Le mal algérien: économie politique d'une transition inachevée 1962–1994* (Editions Fayard, 1994).

32. Luciani, "The Oil Rent. . . ," p. 146.

33. Ibid., pp. 148–49.

34. Karl Marx, "The Eighteenth Brumaire of Louis Napoleon," in Lewis S. Feuer, ed., *Basic Writings on Politics and Philosophy by Karl Marx and Friedrich Engels* (Anchor Books, 1959), p. 320.

Chapter Nine

1. Adam Przeworski, *Democracy and the Market: Political and Economic Reforms in Eastern Europe and Latin America* (Cambridge University Press, 1991), pp. 10–14.

2. Adam Przeworski, *Sustainable Democracy* (Cambridge University Press, 1995).

3. Note the strong resemblance to features of the constitution of the French Fifth Republic.

4. "Opinion Poll Reveals 64 Percent to Vote," Algiers ENTV Television Network, Nov. 16, 1996, in Foreign Broadcast Information Service, Daily Report: Near East and South Asia, Nov. 16, 1996. It is not clear from the report if the 70 percent in favor of the reforms were drawn only from those planning to vote.

5. *Al-Khabar* (Algiers), March 10, 1997.

6. The Palestinian elections in January 1996 show how a different institutional choice can affect political outcomes. The Palestinians used lists by region, but voters could choose specific names from whichever parties they wanted. Some individuals with particularly large votes thereby gained more status within the new National Authority, but parties were not particularly strong.

7. Hamrouche explained his thinking in an interview with the author on June 15, 1996.

8. For the FIS party platform, see *La Tribune d'Octobre* (insert), no. 11, July 21, 1989. Ahmed Rouadjia, "Discourse and Strategy of the Algerian Islamist Movement (1986–1992)" in Laura Guazzone, ed., *The Islamist Dilemma: The Political Role of Islamist Movements in the Contemporary Arab World* (Ithaca Press, 1995), pp. 80–86. This provides a good analysis of the FIS platform.

9. Nicole Chevillard, "Algérie: l'après guerre civile," *Nord Sud Export Conseil*, (1995), pp. 59–63, provides a detailed account of the inner circle of military officers as of 1995–96.

10. Note the important role of military defeat in both the Argentine and Greek cases.

11. This was reportedly the issue over which discussions with Abdalaziz Bouteflika deadlocked in 1994. When the High State Council's mandate was about to expire, the military approached Bouteflika to see if he would become acting head of state. He insisted on control over military appointments, which was more than the military was ready to accept.

12. John Waterbury, "Democracy Without Democrats? The Potential for Political Liberalization in the Middle East," in Ghassan Salamé, ed., *Democracy Without Democrats? The Renewal of Politics in the Muslim World* (I. B. Tauris Publishers, 1994), pp. 39–42; and Guillermo O'Donnell and Philippe C. Schmitter, *Transitions from Authoritarian Rule: Tentative Conclusions about Uncertain Democracies* (Johns Hopkins University Press, 1986).

13. "Algeria's Sham Election," *New York Times*, June 7, 1997, p. 18.

14. Personal communication to author from several observers, June 1997. See also Roula Khalaf reporting from Algiers in "Observer Doubts Hit Algeria Poll Image," *The Financial Times*, June 10, 1997, p. 4. She notes that UN observers visited 1,307 polling stations and found 1,169 were run in a "satisfactory" manner. She estimates that the questionable voting practices for the security forces and in some remote rural areas could have affected at most

800,000 of the nearly 11 million votes cast. The detailed summary of the observers views can be found in "Summary of Form Results," International Observer Group. The summary shows that on the question of ballot secrecy, for example, 1,253 polling stations were judged to provide satisfactory conditions for a secret vote, while only 23 were not satisfactory. Typical problems are detailed for each district. For more details on the election monitoring, see the useful report "Algeria's June 5, 1997, Parliamentary Election," prepared by The National Democratic Institute for International Affairs, 1997.

15. See *El Watan* (Algiers), May 21, 1996, pp. 1–5, for public opinion data on attitudes toward democracy and level of confidence in government. Only 34.5 percent say that they are satisfied with the performance of the Zeroual government since its election; 25.8 percent say that the practice of democracy in the country is very good, 45.8 percent say it is good, and 19.4 percent say it is bad. All but 9.7 percent say the security situation has been improving. The main concerns reported by those polled were housing (32.4 percent), unemployment (21.1 percent), and injustice or *hogra* (14.8 percent).

16. Olivier Roy, *Le Monde*, April 29, 1997, p. 2, mentioned that the FIS was becoming more moderate; Bruno Etienne, "L'Algérie entre violence et fondamentalisme," *Revue des deux mondes* (January 1996), p. 55, claimed that the FIS and GIA have both ceased to exist as structured organizations and have been replaced by a "nébuleuse de groupuscules" (miasma of little groups) without any coordinated leadership.

Chapter Ten

1. Samuel P. Huntington, *The Third Wave: Democratization in the Late Twentieth Century* (University of Oklahoma Press, 1991), p. 9.

2. Robert A. Dahl, *Polyarchy: Participation and Opposition* (Yale University Press, 1971).

3. Adam Przeworski, *Democracy and the Market: Political and Economic Reforms in Eastern Europe and Latin America* (Cambridge University Press, 1991), p. 19.

4. Fareed Zakaria, "The Rise of Illiberal Democracy," *Foreign Affairs*, vol. 76, no. 6 (1997), pp. 22–43.

5. Guillermo O'Donnell and Philippe C. Schmitter, *Transitions from Authoritarian Rule: Tentative Conclusions About Uncertain Democracies* (Johns Hopkins University Press, 1993), p. 19.

6. Przeworski, *Democracy and the Market*, p. 57: "popular mobilization and splits in the regime feed on each other."

7. Dankwart Rustow, "Transitions to Democracy: Toward a Dynamic Model," *Comparative Politics* (April 1970), pp. 337–63.

8. Rustow, "Transitions to Democracy," p. 355.

9. John Waterbury summarizes and analyzes Rustow's article in "Democracy Without Democrats? The Potential for Political Liberalization in the Middle East," in Ghassan Salamé, ed., *Democracy without Democrats? The Renewal of Politics in the Muslim World* (I. B. Tauris Publishers, 1994), pp. 34–39. The quote

is from p. 35. He goes on to note: "In Rustow's view, the building of democracy is carried out by non-democrats who had hoped to win everything, but learned through painful experience and stalemate that the *possibility* of winning something was better than the possibility of winning nothing at all or, indeed, losing everything, including one's life."

10. Juan J. Linz and Alfred Stepan, *Problems of Democratic Transition and Consolidation: Southern Europe, South America, and Post-Communist Europe* (Johns Hopkins University Press, 1996), pp. 38–54.

11. Linz and Stepan, *Problems of Democratic Transition and Consolidation*, pp. 55–65.

12. An IMF-imposed austerity program can lead a regime to decide to open up the political system to spread responsibility for hard decisions, or to tighten control to prevent protests.

13. Przeworski, *Democracy and the Market*, p. 58.

14. Smail Goumeziane, *Le mal algérien: économie politique d'une transition inachevée 1962–1994* (Editions Fayard, 1994), pp. 276–277, locates the political groupings in Algeria along two axes: those who depend on the state (the rent seekers), and those who contest the state; and Islamists versus secularists/modernists.

15. See in particular a remarkable opinion piece by Y. Benmiloud in *El Watan*, October 29, 1997, p. 24, in which he bluntly attacks Zeroual, Betchine, and Tewfik Mediène by name and warns that the Algerian people "will eat them alive if they continue to spit in their faces (*vont vous manger en salade si vous continuez à vous foutre de leur gueule*)." The author was interrogated and warned not to go too far, but he continued to write. See also the courageous editorial by Omar Belhouchet, *El Watan*, October 25, 1997, p. 1. Censorship on security matters was lifted in early 1998.

16. See the works cited in the bibliography by Lahouari Addi, Abed Charef, Aïssa Khelladi (pseud. Amine Touati), Ali el-Kenz, Ahmed Rouadjia, Rachid Tlemçani, Boutheina Cheriet, Yahia Zoubir, Omar Carlier, as well as those by political figures such as Mohammed Harbi, Ghazi Hidouci, Smail Goumeziane, Benyoussef Ben Khedda, and Redha Malek.

17. Nicholas Wahl, in Samuel H. Beer and Adam B. Ulam, eds., *Patterns of Government: The Major Political Systems of Europe* (Random House, 1958), p. 307.

18. Adam Przeworski and Fernando Limongi, "Modernization: Theories and Facts," *World Politics*, vol. 49, January 1997, pp. 155–83, show that no democracy ever failed in a country with a per capita income above $4,335 in 1985 PPP terms. Algeria, according to the United Nations, had reached about $5,442 PPP in 1994; the CIA says $3,500 PPP. This suggests that if democracy were to ever take root in Algeria, it would have a reasonably good chance of surviving. But level of income does not account for when countries make the transition to democracy.

19. Associated Press, April 27, 1997, quoting Algerian official sources.

20. In December 1997, massacres much like those in Algeria took place in the Mexican state of Chiapas. The response of both the state and society were revealing. Ordinary Mexicans demonstrated and called for an accounting of

what had actually happened. The minister of interior was replaced. By contrast, with similar atrocities nearly a daily occurrence, Algerian officials engage in denial and ordinary Algerians seem stunned and unable to organize to demand actions to bring the violence to an end.

21. Here I find myself in agreement with Lahouari Addi, "Violence et système politique en Algérie," *Les Temps Modernes*, vol. 50, no. 580 (January–February 1995), p. 56, where he argues that the crisis of the Algerian regime is a crisis of leadership. "The high-ranking officers in the military refuse to allow anyone from their ranks to assert himself politically. They prefer to designate a president whom they can dominate rather than allow someone from their midst to dominate them. Without a charismatic leader who can incarnate the authority of the state, the regime has created a virtual institutional void that inspires violent competition for power. Instead of controlling the presidency through a strong man whom they would install, the military prefers to play the game of democratic opening, hoping thereby to manipulate political life in such a way that they will still be the source of power behind a formal democratic façade." President Zeroual suddenly fell ill in March 1998, and immediately Algerians began to ask themselves who the military would pick to replace him if he did not recover. Few expected that an independent civilian would have a chance.

Index

Yacine, Kateb, 91
Yahyaoui, Mohammed, 29
Yemen, 149

Zakaria, Fareed, 148
Zbiri, Tahar, 24
Zeroual, Liamine, 68, 134, 135
Zeroual regime, 145; appointment of

Zeroual, 68; coalition government, 77; constitutional changes, 73–74; elections of 1995, 72–73; elections of 1997 (June), 74–77; elections of 1997 (October), 77–78; FIS, negotiations with, 68–69, 72; inner circle, 68; pluralist policies, 77; Sant'Egidio platform, 71, 72